ISBN 978-1-332-90581-2
PIBN 10435939

For support please visit www.forgottenbooks.com

1 MONTH OF
FREE
READING

at

www.ForgottenBooks.com

---◆---

By purchasing this book you are eligible for one month membership to ForgottenBooks.com, giving you unlimited access to our entire collection of over 700,000 titles via our web site and mobile apps.

To claim your free month visit:

www.forgottenbooks.com/free435939

English
Français
Deutsche
Italiano
Español
Português

www.forgottenbooks.com

Mythology Photography **Fiction**
Fishing Christianity **Art** Cooking
Essays Buddhism Freemasonry
Medicine **Biology** Music **Ancient**
Egypt Evolution Carpentry Physics
Dance Geology **Mathematics** Fitness
Shakespeare **Folklore** Yoga Marketing
Confidence Immortality Biographies
Poetry **Psychology** Witchcraft
Electronics Chemistry History **Law**
Accounting **Philosophy** Anthropology
Alchemy Drama Quantum Mechanics
Atheism Sexual Health **Ancient History**
Entrepreneurship Languages Sport
Paleontology Needlework Islam
Metaphysics Investment Archaeology
Parenting Statistics Criminology
Motivational

·DOCUMENTARY HISTORY

OF THE

AMERICAN REVOLUTION:

CONSISTING OF

LETTERS AND PAPERS RELATING TO THE CONTEST FOR LIBERTY,
CHIEFLY IN SOUTH CAROLINA, FROM ORIGINALS IN THE
POSSESSION OF THE EDITOR, AND OTHER SOURCES.

1776-1782.

BY R. W. GIBBES, M. D.,

MEMBER OF THE AMERICAN ASSOCIATION FOR THE ADVANCEMENT OF SCIENCE; OF THE NEW YORK
HISTORICAL SOCIETY; OF THE GEORGIA HISTORICAL SOCIETY; OF THE HISTORICAL SOCIETY OF
SOUTH CAROLINA; OF THE PENNSYLVANIA HISTORICAL SOCIETY; OF THE NATIONAL INSTITUTE,
WASHINGTON; OF THE ROYAL SOCIETY OF NORTHERN ANTIQUARIES OF COPENHAGEN; OF THE
ACADEMY OF NATURAL SCIENCES, PHILADELPHIA; OF THE BOSTON SOCIETY OF NATURAL
HISTORY; OF THE LYCEUM OF NATURAL HISTORY OF NEW YORK; OF THE NATIONAL
ACADEMY OF DESIGN OF NEW YORK, &C., &C.

NEW-YORK:
D. APPLETON & CO.
1857.

PRINTED AT THE COLUMBIA BANNER OFFICE, COLUMBIA, S. C.

TO THE

HISTORICAL SOCIETY OF SOUTH CAROLINA

THIS VOLUME

IS RESPECTFULLY DEDICATED.

PREFACE.

It is proper that I should make a special acknowledgment for contributions to the present volume to the following friends who have kindly aided me: Mrs. Dr. Holbrook, Mrs. A. E. Gibbes, and Col. Jas. Ferguson, of Charleston, S. C., Rev. J. M. Pringle, of Columbia, S. C., Hon. J. Buchanan, of Winnsboro', S. C., Capt. John Irvin, Abbeville, S. C., and Frank M. Etting, Esq., of Philadelphia, Pa.

Many of the unpublished papers of the Hon. Wm. H. Drayton, for which, in a previous volume, I have expressed my indebtedness to his grandson, Alfred Rose Drayton, Esq., of Charleston, are now given; and some of the letters collected by Gen. Peter Horry, of which my first volume was chiefly composed, are continued in the order of dates. For the present, this volume will be the last, though at a future day I may add others.

The very favorable notice which those previously published have received, has been very gratifying to me, and, if I have contributed to preserve important memorials of the history of my native State, I am fully repaid for any labor of mine in arranging the papers which for twenty-five years I have enjoyed much interest in collecting.

R. W. GIBBES.

ERRATA.

On page 91, in the note, read " Thos. Shubrick," instead of " Ladson."
On page 152, for " Martin," read " Mark."

TABLE OF CONTENTS.

DOCUMENTARY HISTORY.

GEN. PINCKNEY TO HIS MOTHER.

[Original MS.]

FORT JOHNSTON, June 5, 1776.

Lest my honored mother should be alarmed by hearing exaggerated reports of the fleet off the bar, I snatch a few minutes from the duties of my station to acquaint her of the particulars of it.

There are not more than fifty-two vessels altogether, many of which are very small. I do not believe there are above six or seven men-of-war and a few tenders amongst them; the rest I take to be transports—some with soldiers and some with provisions. They can not get over the bar with this wind, so that we shall have no fighting to-day. We are preparing to receive them properly when they do come over. Our men are in fine spirits and I doubt not will behave as they ought to do on the occasion.

Mowatt arrived last night with an express from Gen. Lee, who is on his march from North Carolina to this colony with two thousand men. If the wind should prove unfavorable for a few days to the gentry on the other side the bar, he may be able to join us before an engagement. My brother is exceedingly well. Dr. Spence is with us. I hear the country militia are hurrying to town every hour.

Give my love to Harriott, Dan, Mrs. Doyly and her family; my compliments to Mrs. Elliott and all my friends, and believe me to be

Your dutiful son,

CHARLES COTESWORTH PINCKNEY.

EXTRACTS FROM MAJOR ELLIOTT'S ORDERLY BOOK.

[Original MS.]

June 6, 1776.

The following disposition is to be made of the Artillery Regiment:

Forty men from Capts. Beekman's and Drayton's companies are to take part at the battery on the south end of the bay, Grenville Bastion.

Fifty-six matrosses from Capt. White's company at the battery on Col. Laurens' wharf.

Ten men, one sergeant, and one corporal to attend at the battery on Gibbes' wharf.

Twelve privates, one sergeant and one corporal, barrack guard.

Ten privates, one sergeant and one corporal, town guard.

Two sentries at President's.

One sentry at Gen. Armstrong's.

Major Elliott, with Capt. White's officers, to command at Laurens' Battery; Lieut. Villepontoux at Gibbes'; and the remaining officers of Capt. Drayton's Company at the south end of the bay.

June 9, 1776.

The town guard to be augmented to sixteen privates; two sentinels at the President's, two at Gen. Lee's, one at Gen. Armstrong's; orderly sergeant to be sent daily to Gen. Lee.

June 10, 1776.

Barrack guard augmented to sixteen privates; two sentries to be placed over the *Fire Vessels.*

General Lee's Orders in case of Alarm.

June 12, 1776.

The Artillery Regiment and militia acting as artillery to their stations heretofore allotted them. The remainder of the town militia, to the State House. The country militia, in that part of Lynch's pasture nearest the town—the North Carolina troops, in a distinct line on the more remote part of it, at least two hundred yards in the rear of the country militia—the town militia to receive their orders from Brigadier General Armstrong—the country militia, from Brigadier General Howe—North Carolina forces to be considered a corps of *Reserve*, to be under the immediate command of Gen. Lee.

General Orders.

June 15, 1776.

One field officer, three captains, nine subalterns, and two hundred rank and file, to form main guard at State House.

One captain, three subalterns, four sergeants and seventy-two rank and file at the distillery.

One subaltern, two sergeants, two corporals and twenty-four privates at the magazine.

One subaltern, two sergeants, two corporals and twenty-four privates at the point behind Gibbes' wharf.

One captain with same number at Gadsden's wharf.

One subaltern, two sergeants, two corporals and twenty-four privates at the fleches, to the right of Grimball's battery.

One subaltern, two sergeants, two corporals and twenty-four privates rear of Grenville Bastion.

One subaltern, two sergeants, two corporals and twenty-four privates at the Exchange.

One subaltern, two sergeants, two corporals and twenty-four privates at Roper's wharf.

One captain, three subalterns, four sergeants and seventy-two men at St. Philip's church.

Every corps de guard, which is to mount the *quais*, is to throw up *Fleches, cannon proof, at their respective stations;* after the model of that to the right of Grimball's battery.

A field officer of the day to be warned—to be distinguished by carrying a *spontoon*, or half *pike* in his hand—the sentries and guards are to salute him, with *rested arms.*

The guards are to turn out and rest their arms to the *President* or *Major General;* but this only once a day.

The Brigadier to be received by them with *shoulder arms.*

The Major General wears a *Blue Ribbon.*

The Brigadiers, a *Pink Ribbon.*

Aides-de-Camp and Brigade Majors, *Green Ribbon.*

June 28, 1776.

Ten minutes before eleven o'clock this morning, the bomb ship threw a bomb of 13 inches diameter into Fort Sullivan, which fell upon the Magazine there; but did no considerable damage—at same time, the Bristol of 50 guns, &c., unites the engagement.

June 30, 1776.

General Lee visited Fort Sullivan and returned them thanks, &c.—Cannonade of 11 hours, and bombardment of 7 hours.

GEN. C. C. PINCKNEY TO HIS MOTHER.

[Original MS.]

FORT JOHNSTON, June 15, 1776.

HONORED MADAM:

No attack has been made upon us yet, and from the strange conduct of the gentry in Five-Fathom Hole, I don't know when to expect one. One man-of-war and seven transports went out of the harbor this morning; they sailed to the north-east, but I can now plainly see them lying at anchor on the other side of the bar. They are certainly much weaker than they are generally reputed to be, or their councils are much divided, or they would not have conducted their affairs in the dilatory manner they have done. If they postpone their attack 'till Monday, and I do not imagine it is in their power (such has been their conduct) to attack us before that time, we shall be in exceeding good order for them at every outpost and also in town. If they should however visit us to-morrow, I believe they will heartily repent it. You would scarcely know the environs of the town again, so many lines, bastions, redans, and military mince-pies have been made all around it, that the appearance of it is quite metamorphosed. All the houses on the wharves are pulled down, so that the town looks from the water much handsomer than it ever did. Every person there is obliged to work; and the tories (reluctantly I believe) now work with the rest. General Lee appears very clever, but is a strange animal; however, as Adams said, we must put up with ten thousand oddities in him on account of his abilities and his attachment to the rights of humanity. Do give my love to my sister and Dan, and my compliments to Mrs. Elliott, W. Gadsden and all at Sandy Hill. Col. Gadsden is well and desired me to acquaint you that he begs his compliments to you all and is much obliged to you for the care of his son. My brother is well and I remain

Your dutiful son,
CHARLES COTESWORTH PINCKNEY.

GEN. C. C. PINCKNEY TO HIS MOTHER.

[Original MS.]

FORT JOHNSTON, June 17, 1776.

HONORED MADAM:

The enemy has not thought fit to make any attack upon us yet. They employed themselves yesterday in landing some men on Long Island (a small creek parts it from Sullivan's Island), but whether it was meant as a feint, or whether they were to make a descent on Sullivan's Island in the rear, while the shipping batter it in front, I cannot determine. In either case they will be handsomely received. I have just heard that a battalion of Virginia Riflemen are arrived in town; so that we are now very strong. We were unlucky enough yesterday to have a small sloop, which was bringing us powder from Eustatia, run aground near Stone Inlet. She was pursued by several of the men-of-war's barges, and rather than that they should make prize of her, the captain blew her up. The explosion was great; perhaps you heard it at Sandy Hill. With my love to Harriet and Dan and my compliments to Mrs. Elliott and the company at Sandy Hill, I remain

Your dutiful son,

CHARLES COTESWORTH PINCKNEY.

A RETURN OF THE TROOPS IN PORT MOULTRIE, 28TH JUNE, 1776, UNDER THE COMMAND OF COL. WILLIAM MOULTRIE.

[Original MS. of W. H. Drayton.]

SECOND REGIMENT.

Commissioned Officers.—Colonels, 1; Lieut.-Colonels, 1; Majors, 1; Captains, 10; 1st Lieutenants, 7; 2d Lieutenants, 10; Total, 30.

Staff Officers.—Adjutants, 1; Quarter Masters, 1; Surgeons, 2; Surgeons' Mates, 2; Total, 6.

Non-Commissioned Officers.—Sergeants, 24; Drums and Fifes, 14; Total, 38.

Rank and File.—Fit for duty, 306; Sick present, 33; Absent, without leave, 5; Total, 344.

Total of all ranks, 413.

THE KILLED AND WOUNDED.

Wounded.—Subalterns, 1; Sergeants, 1; Fifers, 1; Privates, 20; Total, 23.

Killed.—Sergeants, 1; Corporals, 1; Privates, 8; Total, 10.

FOURTH REGIMENT ARTILLERY.

Commissioned Officers.—Captains, 1; 1st Lieutenants, 1; Total, 2.

Rank and File.—Fit for duty, 17; Sick present, 3; Total, 20.

Total of all ranks, 22.

Wounded.—Privates, 2; Total, 2.

Killed.—Privates, 1; Total, 1.

N. B.—The quantity of ammunition in the Fort was 26 rounds for the cannon, and 20 rounds of musketry per man.

MAJOR B. ELLIOTT TO MRS. ELLIOTT.

[Original MS.]

CHARLES TOWN, ½ after 7 o'clock, A. M., 29th June, 1776.
MY DEAR WIFE:

As soon as I got to my battery, after leaving you, we took up several pieces of the inside of the cabin, upon which were brass screws, all bespattered with blood, and other ornaments of the man-of-war. The firing continued till near 10 o'clock, and I have the pleasure to inform you that we have lost but ten men and twenty-two wounded. Dr. Faysseaux came up this morning with the latter. He tells me that Richard Baker, our nephew, behaved gallantly, as did all the officers and men. The expression of a Sergeant McDaniel, after a cannon ball had taken off his shoulder and scouped out his stomach, is worth recording in the annals of America: "Fight on, my brave boys; don't let liberty expire with me to-day!" Young, the barber, an old artillery man, who lately enlisted as Sergeant, has lost a leg. Several arms are shot away. Not an officer is wounded. My old grenadier, Serj. Jasper, upon the shot carrying away the flag-staff, called out to Col. Moultrie: "Col., don't let us fight without our flag." "What can you do?" replied the Col.; "the staff is broke." "Then, sir," said he, "I'll fix it to a halbert, and place it on the merlon of the bastion, next to the enemy;" which he did, through the thickest fire. General Lee crossed from Haddrell's to Sullivan's in the heat of the cannonade, and was at the Fort. His letter to the President says he never saw but one cannonade equal to this, though he has seen many; nor did he ever see officers and men behave better, nor could any in the world exceed them.

A fine sight from our cupola.* I wish you and Rinchey were here to look at it, viz. :—One of the finest of the enemy's frigates was all in a blaze, and has been burning two hours. She is one of the two that got on shore on the middle ground, which they not being able to get off, have burnt. A bowsprit was shot away yesterday afternoon; part of her rigging came up with the tide—also, several yards of the masts.

The Bristol, of 50 guns, the Roebuck, of 44 guns, and the Syren, of 28, were the three ships that lay nearest the Fort. The distance, though it appeared great from our cupola, did not exceed 400 yards. Six men-of-war engaged. Col. Moultrie has sent up for ammunition.

* Meeting street near Queen.

The President told me he had sent to Dorchester for 2000 lbs. The Fort was three-quarters of an hour yesterday without powder.

I think you and Rinchey may come down with safety to-day, and if they should renew the attack in the afternoon, you may stay till Johnston's Fort is engaged. Now, my dear wife, let us not forget to whom we are indebted for this success against our enemy. Let us return God thanks for it. It is He that does all for us—He inspires our officers and men with courage, and shields their heads in the day of battle— He is the wonderful God of victory.

The enemy made three attempts to land on the north of Sullivan's during the cannonade, but were each time repulsed without any loss on our side. Let Mr. Baker have this letter after you have read it, and when he has seen it, you can order the boy to bring it to you, or send it to Mr. Piercy, if an opportunity can be had.

The house looks melancholy without you, pray come down. You can retreat time enough. I long to see you, and am

Your very affectionate husband,

BARNARD ELLIOTT.

GEN. C. C. PINCKNEY TO HIS MOTHER.

THE BATTLE OF FORT MOULTRIE.

[Original MS.]

FORT JOHNSTON, June 29, 1776.

I am sure my honored Mother must be anxious to know the event of yesterday's cannonade. I therefore take the earliest opportunity of acquainting her with the particulars of it. As my station was at Fort Johnston, and the whole of the engagement was at Sullivan's Island, I was only a spectator, though I and every man here declared they longed earnestly to have been there, to have partaken the honor and danger with their fellow soldiers.

Yesterday, about eleven o'clock, the Bomb Ketch, and a ship-of-war, came up from Five-Fathom Hole, and a signal was fired from the Commodore for the other ships of war to weigh anchor. At about half after eleven, the Ketch began to favor Sullivan's Island with some bombs. I could distinctly see many of them burst in the air. Five fell in the Fort at Sullivan's Island, but did no other damage than slightly wounding one man. The Solebay, of 28 guns, who was ahead of the line, received a shot from the Island, and immediately returned it with her whole broadside. The enemy then formed in two lines to attack the Fort on Sullivan's Island. In the first line the Bristol, of 50 guns, the Solebay, of 28, the Active, of 28, and a 40 gun vessel, which I am told is called the Roebuck, (I am not sure of her name, but certain of her strength, for I could plainly see her guns.) In the second line was the Syren, of 28, and two other frigates, whose names I do not know; behind them were the Bomb Ketch, and a heavy hulk of a vessel something like our Prosper.

A brisk and heavy cannonading was kept up at first, both from the ships and the Fort. Some shot from the Fort put their second line into disorder, and carried away the bowsprit of one of the frigates; and as they were near that bank of sand which runs out from the Fort towards Sullivan's Island, and then turns towards Cummins' Point (called the Lower Middle), the two ships, whose names I do not know, ran aground there. The first line of the enemy appeared to us at this place to be about six or seven hundred yards from the Island, but from them I hear they were within 500 yards. All the 26 pounders were pointed at the Bristol, and about two hours after the cannonading began, she received so much damage that she was obliged to draw back, but still continued to fire, though not so briskly as before. At about three o'clock the Fort had expended all its ammunition, (it had thirty odd rounds to each gun, and thirty-two guns.) The shipping still kept up a heavy cannonade; the Fort could not return it. In about two hours they got a supply of 200 lbs. of gunpowder from Tufts', and 500 lbs. from Haddrell's Point. They fired again, but slowly, and with great judgment. Night came on, and the cannonading still continued on both sides, and the greatest number of our shot (if we may judge from the noise they made against the sides of the ships) took place, but the ships fired near fifty for one. A little after nine o'clock, the ships thought they were sufficiently battered, and ceased firing; and half after nine began to work down again to their old station in Five-Fathom Hole. One of the ships which ran aground got off again, the other (at least a twenty-gun ship) stuck fast there. Upon being fired at from the Island this morning, she returned the fire; the Island fired again. The men then that were on board her loaded all their guns, set her on fire, got into her boats, leaving all the colors flying aboard the ship, and rowed off to the rest of the fleet. When she burnt down to her cannon, she gave a noble discharge. A boat from the Island went on board of her, and brought away her Jack. She is now almost burnt down to the water's edge; in a little while we shall scarcely see the remains of her. The ships that warped off must have received considerable damage, as in general the shot from the Island was exceedingly well placed. The Bristol's mizen mast is this moment fallen down, doubtless in consequence of the shot she got yesterday. Several parts of the ships, and some parts of the cabin, have floated up to town, so that I believe they have met with a reception they little expected. The officers and men at the Island I am informed, behaved with the greatest bravery; and notwithstanding so heavy a cannonade for ten hours, we had but ten men killed and twenty-two wounded. There were only Moultrie's Regiment, consisting of about 350 men, and thirty of Roberts' Artillery, in the Fort. The officers behaved nobly, and pointed every gun themselves; and what is remarkable, though there was not a man killed but what was close to an officer, yet only Lieut. Gray was slightly wounded by a splinter from a carriage in his thigh, and a spent ball on his breast. Lieuts. Hall and Mazyck received two contusions in their faces. The first man that was killed was a Corporal of Grenadiers. The rest of the men who belonged to his gun immediately threw him off the platform with their handspikes, crying out, " Revenge, let us revenge our comrade's death!" and immediately returned to their gun with the greatest eagerness.

The enemy shot away the flag-staff, with our colors. A grenadier immediately ran through a shower of grape shot, and stuck up the colors on a pike. One McDonald, a sergeant in Capt. Frank Huger's Company, being mortally wounded, as they were carrying him away, cried out, " I am killed my brethren, but don't let liberty expire with me !" While this happened at the end of Sullivan's Island, where this Fort is, the enemy, whose troops are on Long Island, attempted to pass over to that end of Sullivan's Island which was nearest them, but received so warm a reception from Thompson's Rangers, the Virginia Riflemen, some of the North Carolina troops, a few of the Militia, and an eighteen pounder that we had there, that they were obliged to retreat, without wounding so much as one of our men. The enemy's loss in men must have been considerable, as our shots were chiefly levelled at the hull of the ships. The transports lay in Five-Fathom Hole during the whole engagement. I assure you I never saw men in higher spirits than ours were during the whole cannonade; and though from our station here we were unfortunate enough to be out of it, there was not a man but was wishing most earnestly to be there.

The Fort, though well peppered with shot, has received scarcely any damage, not a single breach being made in it, nor did the Palmetto logs, of which it is built, at all splinter. The powder room on board the burning frigate, has this instant blown up. You cannot conceive what a noble column of smoke it makes till it loses itself among the highest clouds.

My brother is well. Pray give my love to my sister and Dan, and compliments to Mrs. Elliott, and the ladies at Sandy Hill. I remain,

Your dutiful son,

CHARLES COTESWORTH PINCKNEY.

BATTLE OF FORT MOULTRIE.

[MS. of William Henry Drayton.]

JUNE 28, 1776.

Only 470 men to sustain the attack at the advance guard from Clinton. At five in the afternoon they were re-inforced by 700 Contineutals. At ten, bare of ammunition; only one cartridge in the 18 pounder, and one out, and only two or three charges for the two field pieces. After being reduced to this state, the enemy continued firing more than an hour. Lee had been so dissatisfied with Moultrie's conduct, that he had determined to supersede him in the command of the Fort; and leaving the President on the morning of the action, he told him he was determined to do it that day if he did not, on his going down, find certain things done that he had ordered.

4,600 lbs. at the beginning.

300 lbs. from Haddrell's and Tuffts' about five o'clock.

200 lbs. from town in the night—none of this fired.

When left off firing at night, had 13 cartridges—that is, 144—so that 4,766 lbs. were expended, and about 600 shot.

From three to five, had no powder, but a few cartridges for grape shot, in case the enemy attempted to land. Lee came about five o'clock, when the first of the supply of powder arrived, the General having some hours before sent word by an aide-de-camp that a supply would be sent. He stayed about a quarter of an hour. Ten killed and twenty-two wounded. Commodore and Experiment lay within 480 yards, the others about 550 yards. These five engaged instantly—the Bomb covered by the Friendship, and two on shore. Two hours after the engagement began, orders arrived from General Lee that when the powder was expended, to spike the guns and evacuate the Fort. The day he arrived there were 1,200 on the Island, but he soon reduced them to about 600, and averred in public, before the men and officers, that the Fort could not hold out half an hour, and that the platform was a slaughtering stage.

NARRATIVE BY THOMAS BENNET, OF COL. DONNELSON'S MASSA-
CHUSETTS REGIMENT, DANIEL HAWKINS, OF BOSTON, ROBERT
SCOTT AND EDMOND ALLSTON, OF NEW HAMPSHIRE, AND JAMES
SCOTT, OF VIRGINIA—AMERICANS TAKEN BY THE ENEMY AT SEA,
AND DESERTERS FROM THE FLEET, WHICH ATTACKED AND WAS
REPULSED FROM SULLIVAN'S ISLAND, JUNE 28, 1776.

[Original MS.]

Bristol, 50 guns, Sir Peter Parker, Commodore; Experiment, 50
guns, twelve-pounders, on two decks; Solebay, 28 guns; Active, 28
guns; Acteon, 28 guns; Syren, 28 guns; Sphinx, 20 guns; Thunder
Bomb; Friendship an hired vessel, 26 guns.

The Bristol, greatly damaged in her hull, large knees and timbers
shot through, and if the water had not been very smooth, it would
have been impossible to have saved her from sinking. Her mizen mast
was shot away—three shot in her main mast, which is badly wounded
—two shot in her fore mast—rigging, sails and yards much damaged.
The Captain of the Commodore lost his arm above the elbow. He was
sent yesterday, June 30, to England. The Commodore's breeches were
torn off, his backside laid bare, his thigh and knee wounded. Forty-
four men killed and thirty wounded, of which twenty are since dead.
When lightened as much as possible she draws 18 feet 7 inches.

Experiment exceedingly damaged in her hull. Killed fifty-seven,
including the captain, and thirty wounded. When lightest, draws 17
feet.

In coming up, the Sphinx and Actcon got on ground. The Sphinx
cut away her bowsprit and got off. The Acteon was burnt next day by
her own people; and while she was on fire, Lieut. Milligan boarded
her, and brought off her colors, bell, and as many sails as three boats
could hold.

The Thunder Bomb lay at a considerable distance, covered by the
Friendship and Syren, the first throwing shell, and the two others
firing briskly shot ricochet at the Fort. The Thunder, by overcharg-
ing, is so much damaged, as to require being docked before further
service.

The whole fleet badly manned and sickly, particularly the Syren; at
two-third short allowance; no fresh meat since their arrival, June 1.

Lord Wm. Campbell had been very anxious for the attack, and proposed to be sent with the Syren and Solebay to take all the Forts.

The Pilot Sampson much caressed by the Commodore. When the

fleet sailed, there were about 4,000 land forces, but eleven transports had been separated from the rest, and had not been heard of.

Between nine and ten at night, the squadron, slipping their anchors, dropt down from before the Fort.

About two o'clock, when the Fort was silent, and waiting for a supply of powder, some of the men-of-war's men, mistaking the silence for a surrender, cried out: "The Yankees have done fighting." Others replied, "By God, we are glad of it, for we never had such a drubbing in our lives. We had been told they would not stand two fires, but we never saw better fellows." All the common men in the fleet spoke loudly in praise of the garrison, and the seamen in general are desirous of getting on shore to join the Americans.

A deserter from Fort Johnston informed the Commodore that he had spiked up all the cannon, and that the place might be easily taken.

A report prevailed in the fleet that no quarter was to be given to the Americans, and that £5000 had been offered for Gen. Lee.

ACCOUNT OF THE ATTACK ON FORT MOULTRIE.

[The South Carolina and American General Gazette of August 2, 1776.]

CHARLES TOWN, August 2, 1776.

It having been deemed expedient that the printing presses should be removed out of town during the alarm, the publication of this Gazette has been necessarily discontinued for the last two months. As the transactions in this province during that period will probably make it a distinguished one in the American annals, we doubt not but a succinct account of them will be very acceptable to our readers.

On the 1st June, his Excellency, the President, received advices of a fleet of forty or fifty sail being at anchor about six leagues to the northward of Sullivan's Island. Accounts of the arrival of Sir Peter Parker's fleet in North Carolina, and that it was destined either for Virginia or this province, having been received about three weeks before, put it beyond a doubt that this was his fleet. Next morning the alarm was fired, expresses having been sent ordering the country militia to town; the fortifications were all visited by his Excellency and Gen. Armstrong, and preparations for the most vigorous defence ordered. In the evening a man-of-war, thought to a twenty-gun ship, beat up to windward and anchored off the bar; next day she was joined by a frigate, and, on the day following, June 4, by upwards of fifty sail of men-of-war, transports, tenders, &c. We have since learned that the men-of-war were the Bristol, of 50 guns, on board of which the Commodore had his flag; the Solebay, Capt. Symonds, 28; Syren, Capt. Furneaux, 28; Active, Capt. Williams, 28; Acteon, Capt. Atkins, 28; Sphinx, Capt. Hunt, 20; Ranger, sloop, of 8; Thunder Bomb, of 6 guns and 2 mortars—one of them thirteen inches, and the other eleven; an armed ship, called the Friendship, of 18 Guns, with some smaller armed vessels. The same day Capt. Mowat arrived from North Carolina, with an express from General Lee, informing that the fleet had left North Carolina, and that he would be here, as speedily as possible, with several Continental Regiments to our assistance.

A few days after the arrival of the fleet, several transports and small armed vessels went to Long Island, situated to the eastward of Sullivan's Island, from which it is separated by a small creek called the Breach, where they landed a large body of troops, who encamped there. The wind and tides being favorable for the four following days, about thirty-six vessels came over the bar, and anchored at about three miles distance from Sullivan's Island. Two of their transports got aground in coming over; one got off, but the other went to pieces. On the 10th the Bristol came over, her guns being previously taken out.

On the 7th, a boat, with a flag of truce from the enemy, came towards the Island, but was fired on by an ignorant sentinel. The boat thereupon immediately put about, and would not return, notwithstanding the officer who was sent to receive the flag waved his handkerchief, and desired them to come ashore. Next day Col. Moultrie sent an officer to the fleet to acquaint them of the sentinel's having fired without orders, and that he was ready to receive anything they had to send. Gen. Clinton was satisfied with the apology, and said the intention of the flag's being sent was only to deliver the following Proclamation, which the officer brought on shore:

A PROCLAMATION BY MAJOR GENERAL CLINTON, COMMANDER OF HIS MAJESTY'S FORCES IN THE SOUTHERN PROVINCES OF NORTH AMERICA, &C., &C.

Whereas, a most unprovoked and wicked rebellion hath for some time past prevailed, and doth now exist, within his Majesty's Province of South Carolina; and the inhabitants thereof, forgetting their allegiance to their sovereign, and denying the authority of the laws and statutes of the realm, have, in a succession of crimes, proceeded to the total subversion of all legal authority, usurping the powers of Government, and erecting a tyranny in the hands of Congresses and Committees of various denominations, utterly unknown and repugnant to the spirit of the British Constitution; and divers people, in avowed defiance to all legal authority, are now actually in arms, waging an unnatural war against the King. And whereas, all the attempts to reclaim the infatuated and misguided multitude to a sense of their error have hitherto unhappily proved ineffectual, I have it in command to proceed forthwith against all such men, or bodies of men in arms, and against all such Congresses and Committees thus unlawfully established, as against open enemies to the State. But, considering it as a duty inseparable from the principles of humanity, first of all to forewarn the deluded people of the miseries ever attendant upon civil war, I do most earnestly entreat and exhort them, as they tender their own happiness and that of their posterity, to return to their duty to our common sovereign, and to the blessings of a free Government, as established by law, hereby offering, in his Majesty's name, free pardon to all such as shall lay down their arms and submit to the laws: And I do hereby require that the Provincial Congress, and all Committees of Safety, and other unlawful associations, be dissolved, and the Judges allowed to hold their Courts according to the laws and Constitution of this Province, of which all persons are required to take notice, as they will answer the contrary at their peril.

Given on board the Sovereign transport, off Charles Town, this sixth day of June, 1776, and in the sixteenth year of his Majesty's reign.

H. CLINTON, *Major-General.*

By command of Gen. CLINTON,
RICHARD REEVE, *Sec.*

Major-General Lee, Brigadier-General Howe, Colonel Bullet, Col. Jenifer, Otway Byrd and Lewis Morris, Esquires, aides-de-camp to General Lee, with some other gentlemen, arrived at Haddrell's Point on the morning of the 9th. After having viewed the fortifications there, and on Sullivan's and James' Islands, they came to town. Orders being given on the 10th for a number of buildings on the wharfs to be pulled down, intrenchments to be thrown up all around the town, and barricades to be made in the principal streets—every person, without distinction, were employed on these works.

On the 12th, there blew a violent storm, in which an hospital ship and the Friendship, which were at anchor on the other side of the bar, were obliged to put out to sea, but returned in a few days after. A schooner, having on board some provisions and coals, drifted a little way from the fleet, was taken by one of our pilot-boats, and brought to town. Her crew took to their boat on observing the pilot-boat approach.

His Excellency, the President, on the 14th, proposed to the militia under arms an oath of fidelity, which was voluntarily and readily taken by every one excepting three. The next morning it was proposed to the country militia doing duty in town, and to the Artillery Companies, when it met with their unanimous assent.

A sloop from the West Indies for this port, with a cargo of gunpowder, arms, rum, &c., having, on the afternoon of the 16th, descried the fleet, attempted to make her escape; but, through the ignorance of her pilot, ran aground and bilged. Next day she was discovered by the men-of-war, and a tender, with several boats full of armed men, came towards her. The crew, being only twenty-two men, unable to cope with such a force in the situation the vessel was in, quitted her. She was soon after boarded, set on fire, and blew up with a great explosion.

By some sailors who deserted from the Ranger sloop, lying near Long Island, we were informed that the land forces were about 2,800 (some say 3,300) men, under the command of Major-General Clinton, who had under him Major-General Lord Cornwallis and Brigadier-General Vaughan.

On the 21st, our advanced party at the north-east end of Sullivan's Island fired several shot at the armed schooner, Lady William, an armed sloop, and a pilot-boat, lying in the creek between Long Island and the Main, several of which hulled them. For several mornings and evenings the enemy threw shells, and fired from some field pieces on our advanced post, but without any effect.

A large ship hove in sight on the 25th, in the morning. It was thought to be the Roebuck, but we have since learnt it was the Experiment, Capt. Scott, of 50 guns. Next day she came over, having her guns out. On the day following, the 27th, between nine and ten in the forenoon, as soon as the Experiment had her guns all in, the Commodore hoisted his topsails, fired a gun, and got under way. His example was followed by several others of the men-of-war; but a squall coming on, and the wind shifting from south-east to the opposite quarter, prevented their coming much nearer at that time. In the afternoon the Commodore again got under way, and came about a mile nearer Sullivan's Island.

Next morning, June 28, the following was the disposition of the ships-of-war :—The Friendship, at the distance of about a mile-and-a-half from Sullivan's Island, covering the Thunder Bomb, the Solebay, Sphinx, Bristol, Active, Experiment, Acteon and Syren.   About half-an-hour past ten o'clock in the forenoon, the Thunder began throwing shells on Fort Sullivan, and the Active, Bristol, Experiment and Sole-bay, came boldly up to the attack, in the order their names are put down.   A little before eleven o'clock, the garrison fired four or five shot at the Active, while under sail, some of which struck her.   These she did not seem to regard till within about 350 yards of the Fort, when she dropped anchor and poured in a broadside.   Her example was in a few minutes followed by the other three vessels, when there ensued one of the most heavy and incessant cannonades perhaps ever known.   The bomb vessel was at the same time throwing shells.   A firing was heard from the advanced post at the north-east end of the Island, and more vessels were seen coming up.   Our brave garrison (consisting of the 2d Regiment of Provincials, a Detachment of Artillery, and some Volunteers), under all these difficulties, which to the far greater part were entirely new, encouraged by the example of their gallant Com-mander, Col. William Moultrie, and the rest of the officers, behaved with the cool intrepidity of veterans.   Our cannon were well served, and did dreadful execution.   About twelve o'clock the Sphinx, Acteon and Syren, got entangled with a shoal, called the Middle Ground.   The two first ran foul of each other ; the Sphinx got off with the loss of her bowsprit, but the Acteon stuck fast.   The Syren also got off.   Much about the same time the bomb vessel ceased firing, after having thrown upwards of sixty shells.   We have since learnt, that her beds got damaged, and that it will require much repairing before she is fit for service again.   In the afternoon the enemy's fire was increased by that of the Syren and Friendship, which came within 500 hundred yards of the Fort.

Till near seven o'clock was the enemy's fire kept up, without inter-mission.   It slackened considerably after that, and they only returned the garrison's fire, but generally twenty fold.   At half after nine, the firing on both sides ceased, and, at eleven, the ships slipped their cables.

About the time the ships came up, an armed schooner and sloop came nearer our advanced post, in order to cover the landing of their troops, and every other preparation for that purpose was made—the soldiers even got into their boats, and a number of shell were thrown into our intrenchments, but did no other damage than wounding one soldier, notwithstanding which, they never once attempted to land.   At the ad-vanced post were stationed Col. Thomson with his Rangers, some com-panies of Militia and a detachment of Artillery.   They had one 18 pounder and two field pieces, from which they returned the enemy's fire. They were reinforced in the afternoon with Col. Muhlenburg's Virginia Battalion.

Next morning all the men-of-war, except the Acteon, were retired about two miles from the island, which they had quietly effected under cloud of night. The garrison fired several shot at the Acteon, which she returned; but soon after her crew set her on fire, and abandoned her, leaving her colors flying, guns loaded, with all her ammunition, provisions and stores on board. They had not been long gone before several boats from the Island went to her. Lieut. Jacob Milligan, with some others, went on board, and brought off her Jack, bell, some sails and stores, while the flames were bursting out on all sides. He fired three of her guns at the Commodore. In less than half-an-hour after they quitted her, she blew up.

The Bristol, against which the fire was chiefly directed, is very much damaged. It is said that not less than seventy balls went through her. Her mizen mast was so much hurt, that they have since replaced it with another. The main mast is cut away about fifteen feet below the hounds; and, instead of her broad pendant soaring on a lofty mast, it is now hardly to be seen on a jury main mast considerably lower than the fore mast. The Experiment had her mizen gaff shot away; the other vessels sustained little damage in their rigging. The loss in the fleet, according to the report of the deserters, is about 180 killed and wounded; among the former is Captain Morrison, of the Bristol. Sir Peter Parker had the hind part of his breeches shot away, which laid his posteriors bare, and his knee pan hurt by a splinter. There have been several funerals in the fleet since the engagement; and from the parade of some, it is conjectured they were of officers of ranks. Some of the deserters say that Capt. Scott, of the Experiment, is among the killed.

The loss of the garrison was as follows:

Artillery—Killed, 1 matross; wounded, 2 matrosses.

3d Regiment—Killed, 1 sergeant, 9 rank and file; wounded, Lieuts. Gray and Hall, the fife major, 1 sergeant, 19 rank and file.

An officer's mulatto waiting boy was killed.

Total—Killed, 12; wounded, 23. .

Both the officers were but slightly wounded, and are well—five of the wounded privates are since dead.

The works are very little damaged, but hardly a hut or tree on the island escaped the shot entirely. Many thousands of the enemy's shot have been picked up on the island.

2

General Lee was at Haddrell's Point at the beginning of the action, and went in a boat, through a thick fire, to the fort, where he stayed some time. He says, in the whole course of his military service he never knew men behave better, and cannot sufficiently praise both officers and soldiers for their coolness and intrepedity. The behavior of two sergeants deserves to be remembered. In the beginning of the action, the flag-staff was shot away, which, being observed by Sergeant Jasper, of the Grenadiers, he immediately jumped from one of the embrasures upon the beach, took up the flag, and fixed it on a sponge staff. With it in his hand he mounted the merlon, and notwithstanding the shot flew as thick as hail around him, he leisurely fixed it. Sergeant McDonald, of Capt. Huger's company, while exerting himself in a very distinguished manner, was cruelly shattered by a cannon ball. In a few minutes he expired, after having uttered these remarkable words :—" My friends, I am dying; but don't let the cause of liberty expire with me!" His comrades felt for him. The gallant Jasper immediately removed his mangled corpse from their sight, and cried aloud: " Let us revenge that brave man's death!" The day after the action, his Excellency, the President, presented Sergeant Jasper with a sword, as a mark of esteem for his distinguished valor.

We hear that the fort on Sullivan's Island will be in future called Fort Moultrie, in honor of the gallant officer who commanded there on the memorable 28th of June, 1776.

The men-of-war dropped down several miles further from the island a few days after. The carpenters in the fleet had sufficient employment in repairing the vessels. Several deserters came from both fleet and army, who all agreed we need not expect another visit at present—that it was talked that the two large ships would go to English harbor in Antigua to get refitted—the transports, with the troops, to proceed to New York, under convoy of some men-of-war, to join the grand army, and that two frigates would be left to cruise between North Carolina and Georgia.

On the 2d of July, Gen. Lee sent a flag to the enemy, with a proposal to exchange a prisoner for Col. Ethan Allen, who it was said was in the fleet. A present of some fresh meat and vegetables was sent at the same time. Gen. Clinton being at Long Island, an answer was not received till two days after, when he informed Gen. Lee that Col. Allen was not on board, and in return for his present, sent some porter, cheese, &c. Two engineers came in the boat, but as they were received at some distance from the fort, they were deprived of an opportunity of seeing what they were probably sent to observe.

A sloop from the West Indies, with gunpowder, &c., ran aground on the 5th, in coming into Stono Inlet. She, a few days afterwards, went to pieces, the cargo having been previously taken out.

A number of the enemy's transports went to Long Island about ten days after the repulse, and took on board all the troops on it and Goat Island. About the same time some of their frigates and armed vessels went over the bar; and, on the 14th, the Bristol made an attempt to go out, in which she failed, having struck on the bar. She succeeded in another attempt, four days after, and came to an anchor off the harbor.

The transports, with the Solebay, Thunder, Friendship, and some of the small armed vessels, sailed on the 20th, steering a southward course; they were afterwards seen standing to the eastward. On the same day a brigantine, having on board fifty soldiers and six sailors, got aground near Dewees' Inlet. She was left unobserved by the rest, and on the day afterwards was taken by an armed flat or floating battery, commanded by Lieut. Pickering. The brigantine could not be got off, and was, therefore, burnt. She was mounted with six 4 pounders. The soldiers threw their small arms overboard, on seeing the approach of the flat. Four of the crew escaped in their boat.

On the 25th, the Experiment went over the bar, her lower tier of guns being taken out. She came to an anchor near the Commodore, Syren, and three transports, lying off the harbor. A frigate, which had not been here before, came to the Commodore in the afternoon of the 25th. Next morning she sailed for the southward, and two days after the Syren followed her.

This forenoon the Active, Sphynx, and a large transport, being all of the enemy's vessels within the bar, went out, and with the Bristol, Experiment, three transports and a tender, stood out to sea, steering an E. N. E. course.

—

The following letter was found on Long Island, since it was evacuated by the British army:

CAMP, LONG ISLAND, 13th July, 1776.

DEAR BROTHER,

With great difficulty I have procured this small piece of paper, to inform you of my being very well, notwithstanding the miserable situation we are in. We have been encamped on this island for this month past, and have lived upon nothing but salt pork and peas; we sleep upon the sea-shore, nothing to shelter us from the rains but our coats, or a miserable paltry blanket—there is nothing that grows upon the island, it being a mere sand-bank, and a few bushes, which harbor millions of musketoes, a greater plague than there can be in hell itself. By this sloop-of-war you will have an account of the action which happened on the 28th June, between the ships and the fort on Sullivan's Island. The cannonade continued for about nine hours, and was, perhaps, one of the briskest known in the annals of war. We had two 50 gun ships, five frigates from 24 to 30 guns playing upon the fort—I may say without success, for they did the battery no manner of damage; they killed only about fifteen, and wounded between forty and fifty. Our ships are in the most miserable, mangled situation you can possible imagine. The Acteon, a 30 gun frigate, ran aground during the action, and, as it was impossible to get her off, we were obliged to burn and blow her up. Our killed and wounded amounts to betwixt 200 and 300. Numbers die daily of their wounds. The Commodore is wounded in two different places; his captain lost his arm and right hand, and was wounded in different parts of the body. He lived but two days after the action. Capt. Scott, of the Experiment, died of his wounds, and a number of officers. If the ships could have silenced the battery, the army was to have made an attack on the back of the island, where they had about 1000 men entrenched up to the eyes, besides a small battery of four guns, one 18 and three 4 pounders, all loaded with grape shot, so that they would have killed half of us before we could have made our landing good. We are now expecting to embark for New York, to join General Howe with the grand army.

My anxiety to inform you of bad news had well nigh made me forget to mention our passage to Cape Fear, where we arrived safely the 1st of May, after a passage of three months. Though it was long, yet it was not disagreeable, after we got out of the Bay of Biscay, where we met with the worst weather ever known at sea, and continued in that situation for sixteen days. After that time we had very fine weather all along, sometimes we were becalmed four or five days together, not going above ten knots a day. Upon our arrival at Cape Fear, we disembarked, and were encamped in the woods till the 27th May, when we went on board again, and sailed for this infernal place. The oldest of our officers do not remember of ever undergoing such hardships as we have done since our arrival here.

I hope you will be so good as watch every opportunity to let me hear from Mrs. Falconer and you, and at the same time to inform me how to do in case I shall be obliged to purchase my lieutenancy. I beg you will make my excuse to my dear sister for not writing to her at this time. It is not owing to want of affection, but to the want of proper materials. I am obliged to write upon the ground. You'll be so good as let Capt. Falconer know the same thing. I shall write again from New York. I am, dear sir,

Your most affect. brother,

WILL. FALCONER.

To the Hon. Anthony Faloner, at Montrose, Scotland.

—

Within these few days a cargo of seven tons of gunpowder, and a quantity of dry goods, have been safely landed in this colony.

In this Gazette of May 31, our advices respecting the Indians gave reasons to expect that they would remain quiet; since which we have certain accounts of the Cherokees having killed several white people, and taken some prisoners. The other nation seems averse to intermeddling in the present contest, and it is to be hoped the measures taken to fix them in their peaceable dispositions will be successful. There is the greatest reason to expect the Cherokees will soon repent of their rashness, as considerable bodies of men from Virginia, North Carolina, and this colony are actually on their march into their country.

We hear that about three weeks ago, two armed vessels from St. Augustine cut a sloop and schooner, loaded with rice, out of Ogeechee River in Georgia. A party from the same place have been employed in building a fort at St. Mary's. A boat belonging to them, with Capt. Peter Bachop and seven others on board, was taken about a fortnight since, after some shot being exchanged. Three of them were killed, and Capt. Bachop, with the other four, brought prisoners to Savannah.

We have just received accounts that the General Congress, on July 4th, declared these united colonies to be free and independent States; that one hundred and thirty sail of men-of-war and transports, with 10,000 men, under General Howe, had arrived at Sandy Hook, and forty-five sail had got above the Narrows, but that it was imagined nothing of consequence would be attempted by the enemy before the arrival of Admiral Lord Howe, with the fleet under his command, having on board 20,000 land forces. Reinforcements were pouring in from all quarters to New York, and there was but little doubt of Gen. Washington soon having an army of above 50,000 men under his command.

MAJOR WM.SON TO W. H. DRAYTON.

[Original MS.]

WHITEHALL, June 27, 1776.

DEAR SIR:

I have no later letters from Charlestown than those I showed to Mr. Salvador when here.

James Holmes left Charlestown a day later, and says no attempt was made against the town—that several of the small vessels had returned back over the bar, and several more getting under sail, apprehended to be bound the same way.

Your letter to the President I despatched to Charlestown with some of my men, on Friday last. The two Cherokee Indians returned to the nation on Wednesday week, seemingly well satisfied with their journey. I gave them a strong talk, the substance as follows: That I had, agreeable to the desire of the warrior of Sugar Town, acompanied them across the frontier settlements, and told them before I set out, that if they saw, and would show me any bad white warriors, who carried lies and bad talk amongst them from the settlements, that I would take them into custody, and punish; and in return demanded liberty to send some of our people into the nation to secure York, and other bad white people, who had carried lies and bad talk amongst them, and endeavored, by every method they could devise, to make them quarrel with us. If they complied with this proposal, I should then know they wanted to live at peace with us; but, if they denied us that liberty, I should believe they did not care to continue in friendship with us longer, and should either send, or come myself, and bring the bad people out of the nation by force. A string of white beads. I desired them to remember—talk well, and tell it to the warriors, and return an answer soon, which I received yesterday by one Price, a half breed. On receiving my talk, the warrior of Sugar Town summoned the other warriors of the lower towns, and returned an answer as follows:— Thanked me for the good talk in them, by Shurry Shurry, and believed every word therein was truth—that the warriors of the lower towns would not interfere between the white people in their quarrel, and in future would not prevent me sending men into the nation, to take into custody such white people as went into the nation with bad talk and lies. They remembered the good talk given them at Fort Charlotte, and were resolved to abide by them. . A string of white beads.

Mr. Hammond writes me on the 25th instant that Brown had met with an affront in the Creek nation, at a great ball play, where he and some white people, and Indians, by desire of Tate, the commissary, seized one Tapley, a trader, fitted out from Mobile; but the other Indians interfered, and rescued Tapley, and broke Brown's sword, and beat him and his party, and carried Tapley to Tate, and desired him to tell Tate what he had a mind to speak. Brown, it is thought, is gone to Florida, in great disgust for this treatment. The Creeks say they will suffer no ammunition to be carried through their nation for the Cherokees.

I received a kick from Major Downes' stallion the evening of the day I left you, which cut my leg, and my being careless of it, has brought on a fever for these two days past, which confined me to my chamber. I have sent Mr. Salvador a little powder and bullets. Mr. Williamson and Winter are well. They join me in best compliments to you and Mr. Salvador. I am, dear sir,

Your most humble servant,

A. WM.SON.

CHIEF JUSTICE DRAYTON TO PRESIDENT LAURENS.

[Original MS.]

July 7, 1776.

SIR:

As a magistrate I yesterday presented myself at your door to have the honor of paying my respects to your Excellency, and in the afternoon I attended there again, in order to beg to be honored with your commands in a military way; for I think that, at this time, while I have no occasion to wear my gown, I ought to wear a sword.

In a word, the favor I have to ask of your Excellency is, that you will be pleased to enable me, as a volunteer, to be active in the defence of my country.

I have the honor to be, sir, your Excellency's most obedient and

Most humble servant,

W. H. DRAYTON.

FRANCIS SALVADOR TO HON. CHIEF JUSTICE DRAYTON.

[Original MS.]

CAMP NEAR DEWIT'S CORNER, 18th July, 1776.

DEAR SIR:

Major Williamson has told me that you thought the present alarm a good opportunity to execute your commission. I have employed an unsuspected person, who has taken refuge in the same fort with Norwood, and am in hopes, by the time I return from the Cherokee Nation, it will be accomplished, though he is a most positive old blockhead.

You would have been surprised to have seen the change in this country two days after you left me.* On Monday morning one of Capt. Smith's sons came to my house, with two of his fingers shot off. I gave an account of the shocking catastrophe at his father's. I immediately galloped to Major Williamson's, to inform him, but found another of Smith's sons there, who had made his escape, and alarmed that settlement. The whole country was flying—some to make forts, others as low as Orangeburgh. Williamson was employed night and day sending expresses to raise the militia; but the panic was so great, that on Wednesday following the Major and myself marched to the late Capt. Smith's with only forty men. The next day we were joined by forty more, and have been gradually increasing ever since, though all the men in the country were loth to turn out, till they had procured some kind of fancied security for their families. However, we had last night 500 men, but have not been joined by any from the other side of the river. I rode there last Saturday, and found Col. Williams and Liles, and two companies from Col. Richardson's regiment, amounting to 430 men. They were attacked on Monday (July 15) morning, by Indians and Scopholites, but repulsed them, taking thirteen white men prisoners. The Indians fled the moment day appeared. I will not trouble you with more particulars, as Major Williamson will send a circumstantial account to his Excellency. I am afraid the burthen of the war will fall on this regiment, and that the people over the river will do nothing. They grumble at being commanded by a Major; and, I fear, if they join us at all (which I doubt), they will be very apt to prejudice the service by altercations about command. I cannot help saying, that if Williamson

---

* W. H. Drayton was at Mr. Salvador's plantation, called Cornacre, on the 28th of June, 1776, as appears by a letter to him directed there, and written by Major Williamson, on the 27th June, from White Hall, his plantation in the neighborhood.

is fit to conduct such an expedition, he certainly ought to have a much higher rank than any of these classes, who don't object to his person, but his rank. I likewise think it an omission that the colonels on the other side the river have no written orders to put themselves, or their men, under his command. On the last accounts from town, that Cunningham and his companions were set at liberty, we were very near having a mutiny in camp; and it is really a measure (which, though certainly intended for the best,) very alarming to all ranks of people. The ignorant look upon it as turning their enemies loose on their backs in the day of their distress; and the sensible part consider it as a dangerous exercise of a dispensing power, assumed contrary to the express determination of Congress, and a corroborating resolve of the succeeding House of Assembly. Pearis' house having been a rendezvous for the Indians and Scopholites, Col. Thomas intended to attack it on Monday. We are not yet informed if he did or not; but one of our spies was there on Tuesday, and saw many of our enemies about the place, and all the buildings in ashes. Whether they were burnt by friends or foes, is still uncertain; if by the first, I fear Pearis will injure us much. Our men seem spirited, and very much exasperated against our enemies. They one and all are displeased at the people over the river for granting quarter to their prisoners, and declare they will grant none either to Indians or white men who join them. We have just received an account that two of the Cherokees' head warriors were killed in the late skirmish at Lindley's Fort.

19th July, 1776.

Cunningham and Pearis came here last night, and by the former I imagine he was much caressed in town. Here he was treated politely, but with reserve, the Major and myself having advised him to go home, and mind his private business, at which he seemed chagrined. I am clear he had not yet given up the idea of being a man of consequence; but the friends of liberty in this part of the world are determined to have no connection with him, and to consider him for the future merely as an individual, and not as head of any party. We have just heard from over the river that the white people in general had quitted the Indians, after the repulse at Lindley's, and were delivering themselves up to Col. Liles. He has sent all those to Ninety-Six jail, against whom there is proof of having been in the action.

I hope you will pardon the freedom with which I express my sentiments; but I look upon it as an advantage to men in power to be truly informed of the people's situation and disposition. This must plead my excuse, and believe me to be, with great respect, dear sir,

Your obedient humble servant,

FRANCIS SALVADOR.

P. S.—We, this day, increased to 600, all from the same regiment.

Capt. McCall, with 20 men, was sent by Major Williamson to the Cherokees at Seneca, to make prisoners of some white men, by the encouragement of some Indians, who had been at the Major's. When the detachment got near, the Indians came out to meet them, spoke friendly to them, and invited the captain, lieutenant, and another man, to sup with them, leaving three of their own people in their room; and, in a few hours after, in the night, the Indians returned, and suddenly attacked the detachment, which fled as fast as possible. They are all returned but the captain and six men. This happened immediately before Smith's family was cut off, who lost five negro men, himself, wife, and five children. On this day Stringer and one child, three or four of Gillespy's family, in the same settlement. The ravage extended all along the frontier the same morning. At Lindley's Fort, Downes accidentally arrived with 150 men at night, on his way to Williamson's, when at one in the morning the fort was attacked by the Indians and white men—eighty-eight Indians and one hundred and two whites.

A. WM.SON TO ———.

[Original MS.]

CAMP AT BARKER'S CREEK, July 22, 1776.

DEAR SIR:

Your favor of the 12th instant is now before me, giving an account of the agreeable news of your having beat the British fleet. I shall try my utmost endeavors to follow your example, and beat the Cherokees, of whose treachery and faithless behavior you are well acquainted. I am now encamped here, with about 700 effective men from this regiment, which, with 136 who do duty in the different forts, you'll perceive have turned out pretty well. My numbers would soon increase if I had arms. If any can be spared from Charlestown, you can never do this part of the country a greater service than by using your endeavors to have them immediately sent here.

Capts. Tate and Prince's companies of Riflemen, have just now joined me. They consist of ninety-three effective men; and to-morrow Col. Williams, who has been at least fourteen days contriving a mode to cross Saluda River, will also join me, with about 200 men. Captain Hammond marched with a detachment of 100 picked men, on Friday morning, for Paris' House, where I am informed a party of the enemy have been skulking about there some days past. I expect hourly to hear from him, and some agreeable news. He has my orders if he can conveniently join Col. Thomas and Niel, to act in concert with them, and proceed directly into the nation by Estatoe, while I penetrate by way of Seneca and the Sugar Town. Thomas has acted in every respect agreeable to his declaration when at his house. I have wrote, and sent him express upon express, to no purpose. It is really disagreeable to have any connexion with such men. He has not wrote me a line since the Indians first commenced hostilities. Lieut.-Col. Polk, of Niel's regiment, with 300 men well armed, has joined Thomas; and I am told by Capt. Powes, who I sent on purpose to see his strength, and marked out a plan to act in conjunction with them, that Polk is eager to join me. It is agreeable to his sentiments, communicated by letter to me lately. Judge, then, what feelings such a man must be possessed of, who, in place of hastening to save or revenge his country, can content himself with doing nothing. Robert Cunningham and Paris came to my camp. The former, on his arrival, declared himself our fast friend, and that he came to stand and fall with us. I was sorry I could not show him the countenance I could have wished, owing to the people being so much exasperated at the behavior of Hugh Brown, and others, who have lately joined the Indians against us, thirteen of which were taken prisoners, a few days ago, and sent to Ninety-Six jail—four of which were found painted as Indians. I have no doubt of Cunningham proving true to his declaration, but at present it would be improper to confer any public trust on him. Mr. Salvador has been with me since my first taking the field. I showed him your postscript. He thinks of making the campaign to the nation. I understand last night, the Indians struck at North Carolina and Virginia the very day they commenced hostilities against our frontier. If these two colonies join heartily with us, I hope soon to have the pleasure of congratulating you of a happy issue being put to their expedition, and reduce the savages to such a state, as to wish they had never broke their faith with us. I am, with much regard, dear sir,

Your most humble servant,

A. WM.SON.

WM. H. DRAYTON TO FRANCIS SALVADOR.

[Original MS.]

CHARLES TOWN, July 24, 1776.

MY DEAR SIR:

I am much obliged by your favor of the 19th, which gave me not only a comprehensive view of affairs your way, from the beginning of the war; but, also, the ideas of people touching the discharge of Cunningham and his companions. We apprehended some dissatisfaction might arise; but the act was done, as you very justly thought, with the best intentions, and we hope good consequences will follow. I think I am pretty sure no bad ones can arise on that score, but from the mistaken warmth of our friends. I must applaud your resolution to consider Cunningham "in future merely as an individual, and not as head of any party." Such is the station he ought ever to hold.

As for the fate of the thirteen white prisoners taken upon the repulse of the Indians—speaking as W. H. D. in a private character, I think the public would have received an essential piece of service had they been all instantly hanged. I am not singular in this idea of justice and policy—inferior and superior public characters think so, too.

This day the Experiment, of 50 guns, and the Syren, of 28, got over the bar to join their shattered Commodore. Last Sunday the transports sailed with the troops and Clinton, leaving one brig with about forty Scots, of a regiment called Royal Highland Emigrants. This vessel got on ground. She has fallen into our hands. The men are prisoners—the vessel is burnt. I suppose some of the other men-of-war will go over the bar to-morrow. Perhaps all, perhaps not; for of this you know we cannot judge, as we are not of their counsels. The fleet stood off for the Gulf, and the deserters say they are bound for a Northern Long Island, as they are so much in love with the Southern Long Island they have just quitted.

Lee is very clever—and—very positive. The most positive of the Poetical Fates was, I scarce believe, more positive. Every idea of his must be right, and, of course, every contrary idea in every other person must be wrong; and, contrary to the saying of the wise man, we now find, that even in a multitude of counsellors there is no wisdom, when they entertain different ideas from him, even in cases as plain as my hand. However, the General has rather been unlucky in his ideas sometimes; for we have found salvation from a quarter whence he said none could come; and he has been served by Continental officers and troops in such sort, as to oblige him to preserve a mortifying silence on the expedition. From the zeal we have, and that only, for the welfare of the common cause, we are content to be silent to him on that point, also. We ought to have taken eighty British troops in the light-house, for we had 320 men to do it with; but the commanding officer kept 245 men and himself, to guard the boats, and sent the others on to look for the enemy—and after that sent them orders to retreat, when they were willing to have stormed the light-house. They returned to the boats and begged leave to return to the enemy; he ordered them to embark. Our friend, Capt. Richardson, of Huger's, commanded this little detachment.

No news yet from Philadelphia; every ear is turned that way, anxiously listening for the word, independence. I say, God speed the passage of it. Amen say you.

And now a word to the wise. It is expected you make smooth work as you go—that is, you cut up every Indian corn-field, and burn every Indian town—and that every Indian taken shall be the slave and property of the taker; that the nation be extirpated, and the lands become the property of the public. For my part, I shall never give my voice for a peace with the Cherokee Nation upon any other terms than their removal beyond the mountains.

As for town news, we have none but what is ridiculous, except that a quarrel has arisen between the Vice-President and Col. Pinckney. A challenge passed from the first; the last met him before the hour; there was no fight, but I have bound over the Colonel, and I have issued a warrant against his Honor, the Vice-President, because he hides himself at home. From what has passed, I begin to be of opinion that his Honor may be lodged in the common jail, because he is not inclined to be bound over. Is not this ridiculous? I will not say which is in the wrong. I saw the origin of the quarrel—it was a trifle; so much the worse say you. I should not have mentioned this affair; but that what I endeavored to have kept secret is, by a certain obstinacy, become public; and I say so much, that as much may be fairly represented.

I am much obliged to you for your having begun to feel Norwood's pulse. I hope you will succeed with him. He is another unreasonable man.

As for my friend, Major Williamson, I long to see him Colonel of the regiment now under his orders. In the station of Major, he does infinitely more honor to it than any Colonel it ever had; of this rank we must say something hereafter. At present the title of Commander-in-Chief of the expedition against the Cherokees, with which he is vested, will give him command of any colonel in his army. According to the military rule, any colonel in his army, though with part, or even the whole of their regiment, are to be considered as volunteers, and they cannot have any authority in the camp or army but what is derived from the Major. However, as in all probability the Major may authorize them to command their several detachments under him, I think they may expect to receive their usual pay while in actual service. But this may be depended upon, that any conduct that shall clash with Major Williamson's orders will be carefully examined into.

My paper puts me in mind that I ought to finish my letter, so I beg you will present my compliments to the Major, Capt. Hammond, and any of my acquaintances that you may know—to Mr. Rapley, who, perhaps, may be with you; and, that Victory will conduct your march, is the expectation of, dear sir,

Your most humble and obedient servant,
WM. H. DRAYTON.

REV. JAS. CRESWELL TO W. H. DRAYTON.

[Original MS.]

NINEY-SIX, 27th July, 1776.

HONORED SIR:

I make no doubt but you are anxious to hear how our affairs stand in this perplexed and unhappy district, since the heathen has broke in on our frontier. Some on such occasions speak variously; nor is it easy to report only real facts. You may rely on the following:

It is quite evident that the savages were made acquainted with the designs of the British fleet against Charlestown, and that there was a concerted scheme between them against our country. Nor is it less certain that the disaffected party among us knew the intention of the Indians, and were really elated with the prospect. They made no secret of their expectations of safety; and when the time drew near that was appointed for the savages to muster, they refused to muster, or obey any officer appointed by their country over them. This insolent behavior, at such a threatening time, very much alarmed us. At this time, it evidently appears that they were, by compact, to assist the savages to ruin the country; and had they been in possession of their arms, many of them would have actually engaged in the bloody scheme.

But, providentially for us, their arms were scarce, and the savages killed the disaffected in common, without distinction of party. That greatly alarmed them, changed their countenance and tone, and made them look out for safety for their families. Others of them justly supposed that any of their party that was killed must have suffered through mistake. This now appears plain to us, by the Indians giving up those of them which they had taken as prisoners.

The savages have spread great desolation all along the frontiers, and killed a great number. On the 14th they attacked a part of Colonel Williams' regiment at Lindlay's Fort, but were repulsed, by the loss of one lover of his country, who unfortunately suffered a cruel death by them. This attack was made by about ninety Indians, and 120 white men. Ten of the white Indians were made prisoners, nine of which were painted. They are now safe at Ninety-Six, where they will remain, unless released by their brethren. Major Williamson, and the officers under him, have exerted themselves in getting our forces together, and arming them as well as could be done among us. Our army is about 1,000, or 1,100 strong, and has advanced about fifteen miles over the line.

Ninety-Six is now a frontier. Plantations lie desolate, and hopeful crops are going to ruin. In short, dear sir, unless we get some relief, famine will overspread our beautiful country. As our army is now over the line, the dread of savages, and the disaffected, will deter the lovers of their country from looking after their affairs at home. Fences are thrown down, and many have already suffered great loss.

Such of us as are in forts have neither suitable guns nor ammunition, for the defence of our wives and little ones, as we were obliged to furnish our army with our best arms.

By every intelligence we have from Georgia, we learn that the new purchase is in great distress. Should the savages break through the new purchase, we will then be a frontier in that quarter. The release of the prisoners at Charlestown at this critical juncture very much alarmed us. We really dread that party. I cannot express our distress. Your friendship, on our behalf, with our Governor, to procure us the rangers, or part of them, to assist us, will be acknowledged by all with real gratitude, and by none more than by, honored sir,

Your very humble servant,

JAMES CRESWELL.

A. WM.SON TO W. H. DRAYTON.

[Original MS.]

CAMP AT SENECA, August 22, 1776.

DEAR SIR:

This is to acknowledge the receipt of your favor of the 10th instant, acquainting me of the independence of the United States of America being declared, which I agree with you is a glorious event. I asked Col. Thomas, who is now in camp, concerning the titles you mention. He says he sent them to Charleston by Capt. Ralph Smith, with directions to deliver them to Mr. Parsons or Ferguson, as you were at that time in the country; but, it being the day that General Lee had arrived, Capt. Smith had no opportunity to deliver them to any of these gentlemen, who, therefore, returned them again into his hands, and that he will forward them to you at the end of the campaign, or when he returns home.

I have now burnt down every town, and destroyed all the corn, from the Cherokee line to the middle settlements—*Little Choté excepted, which is said to stand on the Creek land,* concerning which, I wrote to Mr. Galphin, and recommended it to Col Rae (if Mr. Galphin approves of it) to march against Little Choté, at the same time I move into the middle settlement, which will attract the enemy's attention, and, of course, yield him an easy conquest. I have received letters from Gen. Rutherford, wherein he acquaints me that he will be in the middle settlements about the 4th or 5th of next month, with about 2,000 men. I have wrote him the day I am to move from home for the same place, where we are to endeavor to join, and act conjunctly, while Col. Lewis, from Virginia, attacks the Overhills, with about the same number. My last battle with the Cherokees has already produced some good effect, having in their confusion given an opportunity to James Holmes and family, and nine others, to make their escape. Mr. Galphin writes me the Creeks are fully determined not to assist the Cherokees in the present war, which is a great point gained; and I hope we shall soon put the Cherokees in such a condition as will deter any other nation, or tribes of Indians, disturbing the quiet of Virginia, North Carolina, Georgia, or this province, for some time to come.

Capt. Hammond is in camp, and well. He joins me in best compliments to you. I am, dear sir,

Your humble servant,

A. WM.SON.

FLORIAN CHARLES MEY TO WM. HENRY DRAYTON.

[Original MS.]

August 29th, 1776.

SIR:

I have had no letters from Mr. Gillon since the 15th July last, wherein Mr. Gillon mentions these particulars you have herein:

10,000 of the Jersey militia are at Amboy and Elizabeth Town, watching General Howe's motions, under command of General Mercer. All the town militia is gone to Trenton, and the Cambridge militia is coming down fast, so that this province will have about 24,000 men to march from Trenton to New Brunswick this week. 1,700 of the Maryland provincials are expected there this evening, so that by the end of this week there will be absolutely a camp of about 40,000 men, and well armed, at Brunswick, Elizabeth Town and Amboy. There is now, also, at least 35,000 men in and about the posts of New York, with 600 of the Connecticut light-horse, so that there is now 75,000 men watching the motions of Lord Howe's army, of about 20,000 men, when they all arrive, and Gen. Howe's sickly army of about 8,000 men, making in all 28,000 men. I am, sir,

Your most obedient servant,

FLORIAN CHARLES MEY.

———

MEMORANDUM OF MR. FARR FOR W. H. DRAYTON.

[Original MS.]

THURSDAY, Sept. 5, 1776.

By the several pay bills brought in of the country militia, who did duty in Charlestown, at Haddrell's Point, and Sullivan's Island, in the months of June and July last, there were paid, for those two months, 296 officers and 3,648 privates, making 3,944 men; and supposing one-half of those men to do duty in June, and the other half in July, makes 1,972 men, including officers. These country militia cost the public, for doing duty at the before-mentioned places, 16s. 9¼d. per day for each respective man, exclusive of provisions, fire-wood, &c., which 'tis supposed, the whole charges put together, comes to much more than 20s. per day per man.

3

If there were any more country militia in town either of those months, the bills have not been brought in to the paymaster; but he thinks the above account to be just.

Mr. Farr's compliments wait on Mr. Chief Justice Drayton, and has sent him the above calculation, which Mr. Farr has taken some pains to ascertain.

SPEECH OF HIS EXCELLENCY, J. RUTLEDGE.

[Original MS.]

Sept. 19, 1776.

Honorable Gentlemen of the Legislative Council,
     Mr. Speaker and Gentlemen of the General Assembly:

I think it my duty to pay this tribute of applause to those brave troops who, in repelling the formidable British armament which attacked them on Sullivan's Island, vainly flattering themselves with an assurance of easy conquest, displayed firmness and intrepidity that would have reflected honor on Roman veterans; and I must heartily congratulate you on their heroic behavior. It is an auspicious presage of what may be expected from the valor of our other troops, when theirs shall be the post of danger, as it demonstrates that men, animated by an ardent zeal for the sacred liberties of their country, and trusting in the Divine support, are capable of the most glorious achievements.

The Cherokee Indians having committed such barbarous acts of hostility as threatened desolation to the frontier settlements, at a time when the enemy lay in view of this town, and an attack on it was daily expected, a considerable force was immediately sent into that nation to obtain satisfaction for their cruel outrages, by acting with the greatest vigour. Our people have behaved with much spirit. It has pleased God to grant very signal success to their operations, and I hope, by His blessing on our arms, and those of North Carolina and Virginia, from whom I have promises of aid, an end may soon be put to the war.

Since your last meeting, the Continental Congress have declared the united colonies free and independent States, absolved from allegiance to the British crown, and the political connection between them and Great Britain totally dissolved—an event which necessity had rendered not only justifiable, but unavoidable. This declaration, and several resolves of that honorable body, received during your recess, shall be laid before you. I doubt not you will take such measures as may be requisite, in consequence of them. A well-regulated militia being essential to the preservation of our freedom, I am persuaded you will think, with me, that your time cannot be better employed than in framing a law for making such improvements in the militia as may produce the most beneficial consequences.

It is not improbable that, at the season appointed for the meeting of the next Assembly, the business of legislation must yield to that of a different nature, and it behoves us to employ the time of the enemy's absence in making the best preparations for defence, and enacting such laws as the present exigencies demand. I have, therefore, thought it for the public service to call you together now, that you may deliberate on these matters, which tend to the interest and security of the State.

I shall propose what, in the course of your session, appear to me, and be happy in receiving your advice on, and concurring with you, in any that may effect these important objects.

J. RUTLEDGE.

MESSAGE FROM THE PRESIDENT RELATIVE TO A FORT AT CHERAW HILL.

[Original MS.]

September 30, 1776.

Mr. Speaker and Gentlemen:

On the 7th of May I was informed, by a letter from the Committee of Secrecy, War and Intelligence, in North Carolina, of their having received advice that the enemy, who then lay in Cape Fear River, had planned a descent at the mouth of Little River, near the borders of this colony, in order to attempt a passage into the back country of that, by the Lake of Waccamaw. Having occasion to confer with the Hon. Colonel Powell on this subject, he urged very strongly to me the absolute necessity of building a stockade fort, and keeping a garrison, at the Cheraw Hill, as a security against incursions of the disaffected about Cross Creek, and for preventing or suppressing insurrections, which they might occasion amongst our own people, near the North Carolina line—events which, he feared, especially, if the intended junction between the British forces and the malcontents in that province;

had taken place. I thought so much attention and respect due to the representation of a gentleman in his station, who was well acquainted with that part of the country, and had the command of a large regiment there, as to lay it before the council for their advice, which I did. He attended them, and on considering what he offered on this head, they were unanimously of opinion that it was necessary to erect a fort, and keep only a garrison, in consequence of which I gave orders for that purpose.

J. RUTLEDGE.

GEN. HOWE'S LETTER TO GOVERNOR RUTLEDGE.

[From Original in State Department.]

CHARLES TOWN, October 6, 1776.

SIR :

The command of the Military Department in this State devolving upon me, I feel it my duty to lay before your Excellency, and by your means before the Honorable Council and Assembly, my sentiments respecting the situation of this country, and the measures which appear to me necessary to place it in a proper state of defence. I am happy to find that the works at Fort Moultrie, and those requisite for establishing, in case of accident, a secure retreat to the garrison, are progressing so rapidly. When the fort is finished, I have no doubt of its being able to repel any attack made upon it in front; but, without a considerable number of works to secure it from being assailed in reverse, it would not, in my opinion, be long maintained against any formidable attempt in that quarter. The methods best calculated to preserve it, would be to erect proper works on the point of Sullivan's Island, next to Long Island, where it is probable the enemy would attempt to land; and by a chain of redoubts, or other works, from thence to the fort, be prepared to dispute the ground with them, inch by inch, should they effect a landing. I at present imagine it may be necessary to throw up some defence where Colonel Moultrie kept his quarter guard; but the transient view I had of the island leaves me unprepared to speak with precision, either as to the number or form of the works, or the particular spots on which they ought to be erected. It is sufficient, however, that a variety of them are wanted, that a great many hands are requisite to carry them on; the number need not be ascertained, as the more there are employed the sooner we shall finish, and that the necessity for erecting such works is absolute and immediate. The post at Haddrel's ought directly to be put in a much more respectable state than it is in at present; that station would be important even if it had no connection with Sullivan's. How much more so must it appear when we consider that, should the enemy possess it, our soldiers on Sullivan's could neither retreat or be supported; indeed, circumstances that make it important multiply upon me as I write. I shall, however, suppress the expression of them, as I presume the consideration I have mentioned is alone sufficient to induce the attention of your Legislature.

The walls of Fort Johnston require to be well cased with palmetto logs, without which, I conceive a smart cannonade would so shock the foundation, that it would not support the superstructure. But, was there no danger of this, it ought not to remain as it is, as the fragments of brick, which would be shattered off by the shot, would inevitably destroy a great number of our men, and this both policy and humanity call upon us to prevent. I confess myself not pleased with the construction of the lower battery, and, if we have time after we get over those matters more immediately wanted, I should wish for an alteration.

I come next to an object very near my heart. I mean the preservation of this capital. The spirited conduct of its inhabitants, in opposition to the encroachments of tyranny, even at a time when their property was likely to fall a sacrifice to their laudable zeal, demonstrates that they nobly prefer public good to private considerations, however interesting, and gives them a just claim to assistance from their neighbors, though the common cause was not concerned in their safety. But, sir, when we contemplate the situation of this town, fixed at the confluence of several rivers, which open a passage into the very bosom of your country, commanding almost your whole inland navigation; and, if possessed by the enemy, all your exterior   , with houses sufficient to barrack comfortably a great body of troops, and an harbor extensive enough to admit almost any number of ships, surrounded almost by water, which the enemy would command, and approachable only by a narrow neck of land, which they would fortify—it would be, perhaps, the most secure and noble place of arms for them imaginable, from which they could, with the same body of troops, execute the purposes of despotism on three different States, and the possession give their arms an *eclat*, the influence of which might be dreadfully diffusive. It would bring upon our backs every tribe of Indians, and call to their banners a host of domestic insurgents. All these circumstances must make it a capital object to them, and combine to prove, that the loss of this town may be reckoned among the deepest wounds the cause of freedom could receive in this department. Public good, therefore, and private interest, unite to induce us immediately to put it into a proper state of defence. To hesitate one moment might possibly be to lose the opportunity which Providence has lent us; and all idea of expense, however great, should be lost in the importance of the object. One step towards obtaining this desirable end, would be to prevent, if possible, the approach of ships to the town; and this, I conceive, may probably be effected, by throwing obstructions across the channel opposite to Fort Moultrie, at those places which would expose them most to the fire of the fort. I am made happy at being informed this work is begun, and trust such hands are employed as will execute it properly. I must, however, take the liberty to say, that when I consider the amazing impetus with which ships, under full sail, come in contact with any body that obstructs their motion, that I doubt whether any single work can be made substantial enough to be effectual. The method I should recommend would be to have one work within another —the second so near the first, that it should take up the vessel, if she surmounted the first difficulty, before she had time to regain her way.

The next thing, sir, is to put the town in such a state of defence that the enemy, in case they get up with their ships, may meet with the most obstinate opposition. It gives me concern to think, that it is far from being in this state at present. Several of the batteries having capital errors, require to be pulled down and re-built; and it will, I am persuaded, be found necessary to erect others at different places. The extempore works thrown up about the town are by no means to be depended upon; they were executed in a hurry, and under the expectation of an immediate attack. They ought to be altered in many places, and at all to be made more effectual. As the interest of the inhabitants, and good of the common cause, will, I doubt not, dispose the people of this country to defend their capital to the last extremity; and, as the working of a number of traverses across the streets are not only necessary to the obstinate defence of it, but will prevent the great execution which might otherwise happen from an enfilade, the materials for building these works should directly be provided. They would at present, perhaps, incommode the passage of the inhabitants, so need not be immediately erected; but the necessary apparatus should be deposited at convenient places, to be ready occasionally. I have much to regret the exceeding weak state of the back part of your town. Assailable at many places, at none prepared to repel an attack, it requires our immediate attention. Nor am I less anxious about the Neck, that leads out of town. The officer we may have to deal with this winter is an officer of enterprise and resources, with judgment to discern, and a disposition to take all advantages he can not but observe, should the Neck remain as it is. How easy it would be for an inferior army to shut in a superior; and it admits not of a doubt but he will, if he can, avail himself of it. To prevent this, many works are requisite, and the sooner they are undertaken the better.

I shall now, sir, proceed to some circumstances of defence of a more general tendency. Among these, the building of some row-gallies appear to me as very consequential. I think it far from being improbable, that they may be so constructed as to be formidable to men-of-war in their progress over the bar; and, if it is certain they must be so, should the ships ever get up and lay before the town, they will prevent all tenders, or other small armed vessels, from marauding those inhabitants who live upon the river—make it difficult, if not impossible, for the enemy to transport their troops by water into the country—a circumstance essentially important to the very being of this State. They will convey your troops to Georgia with safety and expedition, should that State require your aid, and facilitate the arrival of theirs, should your exigencies make it necessary; in short, the advantages of them are so manifold, that I earnestly hope they may claim your attention.

As this State, and some neighboring ones are, unhappily, unequal in themselves to any formidable invasion, they must depend entirely upon that assistance they can mutually yield to each other. Every thing, therefore, which can retard the march of troops should be removed, and every measure fallen upon, which can contribute to bring them up with the utmost expedition. If North Carolina and Georgia would join your State in establishing magazines of provisions at proper places between your countries, it would certainly prevent a great delay; but this, I am afraid, will be a work of time.

I beg leave, sir, to urge the absolute necessity of keeping a great number of waggons always in the public service. Experience has taught me how difficult it is to procure them when suddenly wanted; and the time is probably at hand when the least delay may be attended with very fatal consequences.

The great delay I have met with in marching men at the ferries of every State, and at none more particularly than in this, induces me to wish that in future they may be better provided with boats. Few, if any of them, have more than one flat, and that generally not a good one, so that it will take a whole day to get over a battalion and its baggage. I leave you, sir, to judge what may be the event of this, when the fate of a country may depend upon a single hour.

The roads—at all times an object of public notice—become of peculiar importance at this crisis, as upon the goodness of them an expeditious march in a great measure depends.

I would urge as a circumstance exceedingly necessary, the collecting and keeping for public use, a great number of canoes, and other rowing boats; as in a country so cut to pieces with water courses, and penetrable at such a variety of places, it is very uncertain where you may have occasion to convey your troops, or from whence to bring them. A provision of this kind, therefore, seems to be an act of necessity. Certain I am, that in the late military operations of this country, the want of them was severely felt by the General, and the service greatly injured by it.

The short time I have been in this country renders it impossible for me to be so well acquainted with the geography of it as I wish, or as I hope soon to be. I, therefore, cannot undertake to point out every place where it may be necessary to erect works, or take other methods to prevent, or render difficult, the enemies' access. I am happy, however, in the consideration that you, sir, and many members of your Legislature, from your perfect knowledge of this country, are adequate to this, and in the firm persuasion that it will properly be attended to.

The building of barracks at those places where, in case of invasion, we should be obliged to station troops, particularly at Haddrell's, is a matter that ought, by no means, to be neglected. The inconveniences which the soldiers suffered for want of them, and the ill effect it had upon their health, even in the summer season, makes it evident that they cannot endure a winter campaign without them.

I am loth to mention a provision which I am fearful it will be difficult to make; I mean of clothes and blankets for the men. But I should be wanting in attention to them not to express a wish that every method may be fallen upon to procure them.

I know not whether the islands along your sea-board have any live stock upon them; but, if they have, and are suffered to remain there, I cannot but consider them as the absolute property of the enemy. I, therefore, think it my duty, in the most earnest manner to urge, that they be immediately removed; indeed, I think the proprietors of these islands ought not to be suffered to occupy them at all at present, that the enemy may have no temptation to make or receive benefit, by making a lodgment on them.

There are other matters which strike me as necessary to the defence of this country, and from further observation many may occur to me; but, as I presume Government, in the recess of Assembly, will be furnished with powers to provide for contingencies, I have no occasion to trouble you with them now. I enter into the next object of my consideration with exceeding diffidence and anxiety, lest I should be thought to have exceeded the bounds of propriety, by touching upon it at all. If, sir, unfortunately for me that should be the case, will your Legislature do me the justice to impute it to the zeal I have for the service of this State, and kindly admit the cause to excuse the effect? The number of regular troops allotted to this country is not enough for its defence, though all the battalions were full. This, sir, militates strongly in favor of a well-regulated militia, and I am happy to hear it is the subject of your present deliberation; but, as a military system, exclusive of militia, has been established in Virginia, which experience has shown to be a very good one, I presume just to hint it to you. I mean the establishment of minute battalions. In order to do this, their State was divided into districts, and each district furnished a battalion of minute men. Persons of the greatest consequence and influence were appointed as officers, who enlisted the men from the body of the militia. These men, beside attending a number of private musters, were at stated periods obliged to embody in battalion for a specified number of days, and go through all the discipline and manœuvres of a camp. During this time they were paid and provisioned by the public, and were at all times liable to be called into service. I had the honor to command a great number of them the last winter, and it is but justice to them to say, that they deserved to be ranked among the best of our troops. The men of these battalions being enlisted upon the express condition of turning out occasionally, are always in expectation of, and will be always prepared for it. They are, generally, better armed, and will probably be better disciplined, than militia; and may either make it unnecessary to call out the latter at all, or make a stand against the enemy while they are collecting. But whether such establishment may suit the policy of this country, the wisdom of your Legislature will determine.

Permit me, sir, again, in the most earnest manner, to urge the absolute necessity of immediately taking measures to place us in the best state of defence possible. Our private interest, and our fidelity to the common cause, exact it of us. To lose the opportunity we now have, is to neglect the first, and betray the latter. Happy should I have been, had not the necessity of service deprived you of the Commander-in-chief of the Southern department at this critical juncture, from whose indefatigable attention to his duty, and from whose spirit and abilities in the execution of it, you could not but have derived every possible benefit.

I, sir, have nothing to offer you but an assurance of the most un-wearied attention to the duties of my station—the utmost exertion of such abilities as I have; and that I shall, by my most strenuous efforts, in the service of your country, demonstrate the zeal and attachment I feel for the glorious cause of freedom, to which I have devoted myself.

I have the honor to be, with the greatest respect, sir,

Your Excellency's most obdt. and very humble servant,

ROBERT HOWE.

HIS EXCELLENCY JOHN RUTLEDGE TO HON. WM. HENRY DRAYTON.

[Original MS.]

CHARLES TOWN, Nov. 6, 1776.

SIR:

Enclosel you will receive an extract from the Journals of the Privy Council, in consequence of which, you will be pleased to repair to the Convention of North Carolina, and use your utmost endeavors to obtain such aid as the Council recommend should be applied for to that State. I am, sir

Your very humble servant,

JOHN RUTLEDGE.

IN THE PRIVY COUNCIL, Wednesday, October 30, 1776.

The Board, taking into consideration the danger this State would be in should the same be again invaded this winter, and the little proba-bility of our having assistance from the Northward, were of opinion, and advised, that a gentleman of character be sent to North Carolina to solicit the aid of 1,500 minute or militia men, to be immediately marched into this State, and to remain here for two months, from the time of their arrival, who should be allowed the same pay and rations as are allowed to our own militia, from the time of their setting out until their return to North Carolina.

Mr. Chief Justice being proposed, agreed to go on this business.

IN THE PRIVY COUNCIL, Saturday, November 2d, 1776.

The Board advised his Excellency to direct Mr. Drayton to solicit that, in case North Carolina shall agree to furnish us with 1,500 men, and the exigencies of this State shall, in the opinion of the President and Privy Council for the time being, require it, they may remain for two months longer than the time before proposed.

True extracts from the Journals.

J. N. COLCOCK, *Sec'y P. C.*

ROBERT HOWE TO THE PRESIDENT OF THE HONORABLE CONVENTION OF NORTH CAROLINA.

[Original MS.]

CHARLES TOWN, November 7, 1776.

SIR:

I have the honor to transmit you, by the Hon. Mr. Drayton, the copy of a resolution of the Council of this State, for obtaining the aid of 1,500 minute men, or militia men, from North Carolina, for a certain time; and, as I have been applied to by his Excellency, the President, to take every measure necessary to enforce this request, I take the liberty of troubling you upon this subject, fully persuaded that to induce your assistance to a sister State, nothing more is requisite than to show the necessity for it. My letter to you of yesterday in a great measure anticipates what I should otherwise have to say upon this occasion, because the same motives urged to obtain a permission for their officers to recruit, militate in favor of granting the request they now make. Suffice it, then, to say, that they are not in themselves equal to any very formidable invasion, and yet have every reason to expect one this winter; that they have innate foes, who wait but for an opportunity to rebel—who would fly to the banners of the enemy; several numerous tribes of Indians on their backs, whose present temper bears a very alarming construction; their militia but few, and those so divided and remote, as not to be collected in time for any sudden emergency, and not sufficient in number when they are got together; that, therefore, any aid which is to be sought for will, in all probability, arrive too late, the fatal consequence of which are too serious and melancholy to be dwelt upon. In this situation of danger and necessity, they apply to you for assistance, and the mode they have fallen upon seems calculated to obtain it without injury to you. The pay of their militia is more than equal to the labor of any common man—the rations more than sufficient for any appetite—the barracks they have built, comfortable and roomy. This, I presume, will induce your men to come willingly, especially at this idle season of the year, and the expense will be all their own. Upon these terms, I imagine, the aid they ask would be granted by any neighboring State, less zealous in the cause than yours. I should injure you, therefore, whose patriotic disposition and generous spirit I am so well acquainted with, were I to admit a doubt of your yielding them every assistance in your power. One benefit which may arise to you, particularly from this measure, is, that it may probably make it unnecessary to call away your regulars, who, by that means, will keep you in a state of security. The gentleman who visits you upon this occasion will fully explain to you every thing relative to this matter. His rank, character and capacity, can not but make him an object of your respect and attention.

I have the honor to be, with the greatest respect, sir,

Your most obedient humble servant,

ROBERT HOWE.

Resolved, That Mr. Drayton be sent to North Carolina to solicit 1,500 minute men or militia, to be immediately marched into this State, and remain here for two months from the time of their arrival, who should be allowed such pay and rations as are allowed to our own militia from the time of their setting out until their return; and that in case the exigencies of this State should, in the opinion of the President and Council, require it, they may retain them two months longer than the time above mentioned.

MAJOR F. MARION'S ORDERLY BOOK.

A COPY OF THE RESOLVES OF THE HONORABLE THE CONTINENTAL CONGRESS.

IN CONGRESS, July 22d, 1776.

Resolved, That the thanks of the United States of America be given to Major-General Lee, Col. Wm. Moultrie, Col. Wm. Thompson, and all officers and soldiers under their command, who, on the 28th of June last, repulsed, with so much valor, the attack which was that day made on the State of South Carolina, by fleet and army of his Britannic Majesty.

That the President transmit the same to General Lee, Cols. Moultrie and Thompson, by order of Congress.

A COPY OF A LETTER FROM THE HONOURABLE THE CONTINENTAL CONGRESS TO COL. WM. MOULTRIE.

PHILADELPHIA, July 22d, 1776.

SIR :

I am extremely happy to have it in my power to transmit to you, by order of Congress, the thanks of the United States of America, for your patriotic and spirited exertions in behalf of liberty and your country. This success of our arms, attended by every circumstance that can add lustre to the characters of those who conducted it, will forever render estimable your name with every friend of America; and posterity will be astonished when they read, that on the 28th June, an inexperienced handful of men, under your command, repulsed with loss and disgrace a powerful fleet and army of veteran troops, headed by officers of rank and reputation. May you go on thus to merit and receive the gratitude of your country; and, as a reward of your military service, may your name be enrolled in the list of American worthies, on whom posterity will bestow the most grateful and unceasing applause.

I have the honor to be, with respect,

JOHN HANCOCK, *President.*

GENERAL ORDERS BY GEN. HOWE.

NOVEMBER 23, 1776.

In consequence of the promotions of General Gadsden and General Moultrie, the following promotions take place in the 1st and 2d Regiment of the South Carolina Continental troops, viz.:

Lieut.-Col. Charles Cotesworth Pinckney, of the 1st Regiment, to be Colonel of the same.

Major Wm. Cattle to be Lieut.-Colonel, and Captain Adam McDonald to be Major.

Lieut.-Colonel Isaac Motte, of the 2d Regiment, to be Colonel of the same.

Major Francis Marion to be Lieut.-Colonel, and Capt. Peter Horry to be Major.

According to a resolution of the Honorable the General Assembly of this State, the following promotions take place in the 3d and 4th Regiments of Continental troops in this State, viz.:

Lieutenant-Colonel Wm. Thomson of the 3rd Regiment to be Colonel of the same. Major James Mayson to be Lieutenant-Colonel, and Captain Samuel Wise to be Major in the same.

Lieutenant-Colonel Owen Roberts of the 4th to be Colonel of the same. Major Bernard Elliott to be Lieutenant-Colonel, and Captain Bernard Beekman, Major of the same.

—

GENERAL ORDERS BY GEN. HOWE.

NOVEMBER 26, 1776.

The main guard to be re-inforced to-morrow with six men; two sentries to be fixed at his Excellency the President's door; the men to re-inforce the main guard to be taken by detachment from the 2nd and 5th Regiments in proportion to their strength. General Howe sets out for Georgia to-morrow. He strongly recommends to commanding officers of Battalions to have their men exercised frequently in the use of spears, and to the soldiers to be attentive in learning what in course of service may so essentially contribute to their honor and safety. He is obliged to the officers of every department for their attention, which he had with pleasure observed they pay to their duty, and takes this opportunity to express his approbation of the orderly behavior of the soldiers, of which he hopes a continuance. The important and beneficial public work General Gadsden has undertaken, and is so happily executing, on Sullivan's Island, requiring all his attention, he has desired to be confined in all his commands, at present, on this work and the Island. The command, therefore, of the town and outposts, in the absence of General Howe, will devolve on General Moultrie until General Gadsden chose to assume it.

Col. Motte, having represented to General Howe that James Kelly, now under arrest for desertion, has one circumstance in his favor which in some measure mitigates his crime, that is: that he had surrendered himself to one of his corporals, and, the Colonel having compassionately solicited his pardon, General Howe, in respect to Colonel Motte, will, for once, deviate from a resolution he had fixed, never to pardon a deserter, and consent to pardon James Kelly on this condition, namely: that of enlisting in his Battalion during the war, and by future good behavior he promises to atone for the heinous crime he has committed so contrary to all duty and to the solemn oath he had taken; he is to do duty in Colonel Motte's Regiment until the arrival of Colonel Thomson; and, lest this lenity should have a bad effect, the General warns all soldiers against desertion, which he now declares he never will again pardon on any condition.

This order to be read before the men on parade.

JOURNAL OF CAPTAIN CHARLES S. MIDDLETON.

[Original MS.]

DECEMBER 20, 1776.

The men all got over the river on our march southwardly. Colonel McIntosh, Major Malberry and Lieutenant Dogharty sat off from the river to join Captain Caldwell. Lieutanant West and myself with a small party stayed at the river that night.

SATURDAY, December 21, 1776.

Lieutenant West and myself, with the party, sat off early in the morning; returned one man that had lost the cock of his gun; joined the main body at Carnay's Old Cowpen.

SUNDAY, December 22, 1776.

Major Malberry took a detachment of thirty privates, three non-commissioned officers and one commissioned officer; crossed the river at the Bluff, where Lieutenant Jenkins was stationed, to join us at the old ferry; the main body sat off. Adjutant Fash waited on the Colonel to know whether the Carolinians were to take the front or rear; the Colonel did not chose to determine, as he did not know which was the oldest Regiment, but, in order to satisfy both parties, gave order that the officers and men were to fall in promiscuously and no distinctions made—which was agreeable to both parties until it was known which had the rank. On our march some one discovered, as he thought, a party of men running from us; a party pursued but could make no discovery of them. I was detached off with a party to stop the advance guard and join a small detachment that was sent round as a reconnoitering party. I met them at the place appointed, but never overtook the advance party until we got to Middleton's plantation, which was to have been our rendezvous that night, but the alarm altered our designs. We were to join and rendezvous that night at Mr. Williamson's cowpen, but the main party proceeded to pursue the tracks, following them some distance, found them to be cattle tracks. Judged the man who had thought he saw people made a mistake, and then proceeded on the old plan of going to Middleton's that night. On my return from Middleton's, met the main body and rendezvoused at Middleton's that night.

MONDAY, December 23, 1776.

Sat off; discovered some fresh tracks going down to Inglis'; Lieutenant Fitzpatrick was detached with ten men to find out whose tracks they were. We arrived at the old ferry; I was ordered with a party to reconnoiter the landing, but could make no discovery of the enemy. Ordered that every officer mounting a guard should sleep at the main guard, and visit the sentries at least three times a night. Placed a lance sergeant and four men as a guard at the river. Sergeant Warren, who was ordered from head-quarters to bring provisions round to us, arrived in the night; hailed the sentry, but was made no answer, came past them, landed and came up to the Colonel's camp; the Colonel immediately ordered the sentry under the main guard.

TUESDAY, December 24, 1776.

Major Malberry arrived with his detachment at the other side; a boat was sent for him immediately; he had seen no signs of the enemy. Lieutenant Dogharty came over the river; says he saw very fresh signs of four or five men crossing the river. Ordered that a Court Martial be held upon Abner Islands for being caught sleeping on his post. Lieutenant Fitzpatrick returned; says he followed the tracks up to Mr. Inglis' plantation; they appeared to have run off from there; they followed the tracks until they got intermixed with ours in such a manner that they could follow them no longer. The Court Martial were opinion that the prisoner should receive twenty lashes on the bare back, but my writing a note to the Colonel, informing him of the character of the soldier, of its being his first offence committed in the service, the Colonel thought proper to forgive the prisoner. The Regiment was drawn up and some of the articles of war I read to them. Ordered that every man hobble and bell his horse and have him ready to cross the river early in the morning.

WEDNESDAY, December 25, 1776.

The whole detachment crossed the river, all to a small guard at the river of a subaltern and twenty men. The detachment proceeded as far as Lee's hill. I was detatched to McGirth's as a reconnoitering party; could make no discovery of any sign fresher than three or four days; joined the party.

THURSDAY, December 26, 1776.

I was ordered to take a subaltern and twenty-three privates, volunteers, to cross the river St. Mary's in search of the Florida scouts; the men turned out, and we crossed the river that night and went as far as Taylor's.

FRIDAY, December 27, 1776.

We proceeded, and in about an hour afterwards came upon fresh signs of cattle, imagined to have been drove along late last night. I gave the necessary orders, as in all probability we might expect to come upon them every minute. However we did not come up with them until we got to Cornelious Rains', where they had just gone from, but discovering a house we made three different parties to surround the houses. Unluckily, Joseph Rains was going over to his brother's and discovered us creeping up; he immediately ran and gave the alarm at the house; then proceeded after the men who were driving the cattle and alarmed them also. We surrounded the houses and came in; the men were all gone; though I could not learn there were more than Cornelious Rains there at that time; the cattle drivers had been gone about half an hour before; Mrs. Rains and her daughter informed me that one Captain York, with a party, was with the cattle, and that James Moore and Sampson Williams were each to have been there the night before with each of them a company. We had several times information that there was a strong party of whites and another of indians coming out, though I did not put much faith in the report. I thought if it was true, and any strong party came against us and we should be defeated, I should be much blamed, my order being very particular to be as careful as possible what number I was to engage. Again our retreat was very bad no conveniency for crossing the river St. Mary's, we thought proper to retreat as fast as possible over St. Mary's and there ambuscade on the river bank, on the Georgia side, as there we might give them battle, be their number what they would. We took two negroes and three horses from Rains', and retreated. About two miles from there we met a party that was detached to join me on coming up with the sign where the cattle had crossed the river. Lieutenant Gooden commanded the party, fifteen strong, which made the command forty, officers included. We then thought we were strong enough for anything on this side St. John's, and returned and surrounded Rains' houses a second time, but

4

there were no appearances of the enemy. We then began to collect what intelligence we could. We were informed that one Capt. Jeffres had been there that morning, and went off with a party to William Mills'; that Colonel William McIntosh's fellow, Osker, was with them. Lieut. Gooden and Lieut. Daughty, and a number of the men, knew this Jeffres to be a noted tory, and had been among the Cherokee Indians endeavoring to, and did, bring them against us. I was very anxious to catch him. We were also informed of one McGuire, belonging to the Florida scout, about ten miles off, at one Loughton's, and that in all probability Jeffres was there, as it was on the way to Mills'. I took the men off immediately to Loughton's, and surrounded the house. McGuire, who was in the yard, spied us, and ran for the bush, which was not above twenty yards from the house—very thick. In his flight two of my men fired at him, but I believe with no success. We made a strict search in the bushes, but could not find him. Our horses were much jaded. Jeffres had not been that way. I was at a loss to think what was become of them. Our horses were not able to proceed any further, as some of the men then were obliged to walk on foot. We remained there that night; put all the men on guard. About break of day one of the sentry fired twice. We all ran out, thought the Indians and scouts were come up. I ordered the men to possess themselves of the houses, and detached a party to know the reason of the guns firing. The sentry says he shot at a man that was walking up within ten steps of him; he fired first with his pistol, then with his rifle On his firing his rifle, the man stumbled very much; he believes he hit him. I then thought it could be no one but McGuire, who was endeavoring to steal our horses. I sent parties all round the plantation, but they could discover no signs of any body there. We were very clever in turning out, and to all appearance would have fought bravely.

SATURDAY, December 28, 1776.

We got from McGuire a negro boy, who he had taken from Captain Anderson, and a mare, saddle and saddle-bags, and his rifle, and some of his cloth, and returned. Crossed the river that night.

SUNDAY, December 29, 1776.

Proceeded on and joined the main body at Sattillie, and informed the colonel of our proceedings.

MONDAY, December 30, 1776.

Sergeant Warren informed me that one of my men, George Hall, had a fall from his horse, and was dangerously hurt. I went to see him immediately, and believe he will die. A court-martial was summoned to hold and try Levi Coleman and John Bilbo, two soldiers, for sleeping on their posts. The court-martial were of opinion that Levi Coleman should sit down, and have one gun under his hams, and another over his neck, and brought as close together as possible, and tied fast, there to remain for the space of ten minutes, and at the expiration of the time the upper gun to be fired off—the whole detachment to be drawn up at the same time. John Bilbo, who had some favorable circumstances on his side, was to stand up alongide of Levi Coleman, with a gun across his head, and to remain ten minutes. Some of the plunder was sold. Ordered that every man be ready to march. We marched about six miles that night.

TUESDAY, December 31, 1776.

Several horses missing. We were obliged to wait until late in the afternoon. There were two sergeants and twenty men left to hunt the horses, and to follow. We proceeded as far as Red Cap that night.

WEDNESDAY, January 1, 1777.

We got to the Bluff, where we were to build the fort that night.

THURSDAY, January 2, 1777.

Nothing particular.

FRIDAY, January 3, 1777.

Ordered, that a court-martial be summoned to try Josiah Clark for sleeping on his post. The court-martial ordered him to ride the wooden horse ten minutes. The colonel thought proper to take off five minutes. The major and myself viewed the Bluff, in order to point out a proper plan for a stockade. The tools were got in order to begin.

Ordered, that thirty men be set aside as a guard in the day. The whole are to be on duty to guard the workmen and horses—that is, twenty-two as a guard round the workmen, and eight as a grass guard, to go out by turns, and at night fifteen men on duty, who will be relieved the next night by other fifteen.

That fifteen men, with an officer, be kept as a scouting party continually.

That the remainder be kept at work on the stockade, except a sergeant and six men, to be sent out occasionally to bring in cattle, or any other necessaries that should be wanting, as there is no commissary to supply them.

In case the scout or any other party discover any of the enemy, the commanding officer will act as he thinks best for the good of the service.

That John Bilbo act as sergeant to the first company.

That William Goold and   act as sergeants to Capt. Cade's company.

John Gray, one of my troop, arrived express to the colonel, the purport of which was, that there were four men of the third troop killed, and the rest had evacuated the fort on Beard's Bluff, saving two men, which were all that Lieut. Bug could get to stay with him. These two men and himself went to Fort Howe.

SATURDAY, January 4, 1777.

Lieut.-Colonel McIntosh, Major Marbury, Capt. Caldwell and Lieut. Daughty, left us. Lieut. West, with fifteen men, went as a scouting party as far as the Altamaha, and on their return to bring provisions. The command now fell upon me, the Colonel and Major being absent. We had a great deal of difficulty to get the men to work on the stockade; however, promising them that they and their horses should be exempt from guard duty, they went to work.

SUNDAY, January 5, 1777.

Desired the Adjutant to give James Murphy and John Nepper a severe reprimand, for leaving their posts before they were regularly relieved. Some favorable circumstances being on their side, was the reason of their not being regularly tried.

MONDAY, January 6, 1777.

The men continued on the stockade. The grass guard reported that there were many horses missing. Sent men in search of them all day, but could not find any. One of Capt. Cade's men, who had his leg much hurt, applied for leave to go to Fort Howe for the benefit of his leg. Sergeant Bryson applied for leave to go with him. I granted it.

TUESDAY, January 7, 1777.

Copy of a letter sent to the commanding officer at Fort Howe:

"Sergeant Bryson has liberty to go to the Altamaha with the man who has his leg hurt; he returns to-morrow. I shall be much obliged to you to procure a few tools for the stockade, as they are much hindered for the want of them; also, two or three sets of wedges are very much wanted, and a cross-cut saw, file, one or two chisels, and some nails.

Pray send by Sergeant Bryson what he can bring, and send the rest by the next opportunity. We get on very well with the stockade, considering the want of tools. Some axes are also wanted.

"There are a good many horses missing. I have had men out all day yesterday looking for them, but they could not be found. I have ordered men out again to-day.

"Our provisions are out. I hope though before this reaches you, the supply will arrive.

"C. S. M."

Sent men out in search of the lost horses, but they returned without them.

WEDNESDAY, January 8, 1777.

Sent Lieut. Fitzpatrick and fifteen men to scout up Sattillie as far as the Old Ferry, and round by Middleton's, as a reconnoitering party. Sent out again for the lost horses, but they were as unfortunate as the rest.   *   *   *   *   *

THURSDAY, January 9, 1777.

Capt. Donaldson, Lieut. Goodin and seventeen men, set off for Fort Howe.

Copy of a letter wrote to the commanding officer at Fort Howe:

"Lieut. Beams and his attachment arrived here 7th inst. I was a good deal alarmed that they brought no provisions, at least not enough to last two meals round to each man. We have here, including Lieut. Beams' party, near one hundred souls. I sent out Lieut. Fitzpatrick and fifteen men yesterday, with orders to scout as far as the Old Ferry, on Sattillie, round by Middleton's plantation, to answer two purposes—first, as a scouting party; second, in hopes they might meet with the lost horses. The horses mentioned in my last are not yet found. I hope there will be some method fallen upon to supply this place with provisions. The men seem eager to have an opportunity of complaining; they are coming to me every moment enquiring what they should eat. I have had hunters out since yesterday morning; they have not come in yet, so that we are out of beef as well as rice.

"The hunters are just come, and brought beef, which is some satisfaction. Pray, don't omit sending as much salt as possible, as we shall be obliged to keep a good deal of beef salted up, the cattle being very hard to get here unless it is breeding cattle. Some chisels are very much wanted to finish the fort gate. The horses are very troublesome, as they incline much to ramble."

FRIDAY, January 10, 1777.

Sergeant Crayton set off without liberty to the Altamaha, and was carrying one of the scout men's horses. I stopped him and ordered him to stay until I gave him orders, and that if he or any man attempted to leave the fort without my permission, should be sent after, and taken as a deserter. Several men leaving the place before, without my knowledge. In consequence of that I issued these orders. Lieut. Fitzpatrick and his party arrived; had discovered signs of Moccosins, very fresh, supposed to have crossed Sattillie about three or four hours, and signs of four horses, supposed to be the four that was lost on our march from the Old Ferry to the Bluff. There appeared by the signs of the tracks to have been about fifteen men. They crossed at Lemmons' ferry.

SATURDAY, January 11, 1777.

Early in the morning I wakened, and was told that Sergeant Crayton was gone off with the horse, notwithstanding the particular orders I gave him yesterday to remain here. I thought it such an insult upon orders, that I got immediately ready, took Sergeant Bilbo along with me, and hurried after him, and overtook him about one mile-and-a-half from the fort, brought him back, and had a strong guard put over him, for he could be looked upon as no other than a deserter, and in a particular manner guilty of breach of orders.

*   *   *   *   *

F. MARION'S ORDERLY BOOK.

GENERAL ORDERS BY GENERAL HOWE.

February 14, 1777.

Gen. Howe, with concern and surprise, has observed the frequent applications made by gentlemen of the army for leave to resign their commissions at this important crisis, when it is difficult to find any reason sufficient to excuse men for not endeavoring to get into the service. What can possibly exculpate those who desire to forsake it? The freedom of America, and all its essential privileges, are at present the objects of contest. Compared with these all private interests, however important, and every darling inclination, attachment and sympathy, however endearing and heartfelt, are but futile considerations. The present generation, and all the generations of succeeding ages, have the strongest claim upon a soldier for every strenuous endeavor and utmost effort to preserve and maintain such invaluable rights, and to hand them down to posterity unimpaired. Difficulty and distress and danger are the mediums through which this purpose is to be effected, which every officer must have been sensible of at the time he solicited a commission. Local advantages, therefore, and temporary inconvenience, are but contemptible pleas for retirement; an opinion of an officer's spirit and abilities—a belief that he would, by attention to duty and by every other means in his power, gain a proper knowledge of his profession, with a firm persuasion that he would not forsake the service at the very moment he has qualified himself to be useful, must have been what induced his country to honor him with a commission, which otherwise would undoubtedly have been granted to those who, emulous to serve, were probably possessed of equal abilities, and who, by greater perseverance, would have continued in the common cause. The benefit of that experience they must have obtained, had not the interference of those very officers who now wish to resign, deprived them of the opportunity. Let, therefore, those officers now solicitous of leaving the army, but for one moment consider that by the superior confidence placed in them by the country, they were preferred to those who would have served it to the last; and let them ask their own hearts, if withdrawing from their duty at this critical juncture, is not a poor return for the very honorary preference given them? Let them then add to this the noble and animating consideration that they are actors upon that glorious stage where every incident is to become an historical fact, and the General persuades himself that they will not, by future application for leave to resign, reduce him to the painful necessity of refusing the requests of gentlemen he respects, or by complying with them deprive the army of officers so capable of doing honor to themselves, and rendering service to the common cause. This order to be transmitted to the commanding officer at Haddrell's Point, Sullivan's Island and Fort Johnson, who are to take care that it is made known to the officers of their corps. Adjutant Dellient will inform Gen. Gadsden (if in town), Gen. Moultrie, and all the field-officers in town, that Gen. Howe would be glad to speak with them at his quarters, at 5 o'clock this afternoon.

PAROLE BEAUFORT.

May, 4, 1777.

For the day, to-morrow, Captain Potts, Town Guard from the 5th Regiment; Magazine, Fort Perrineau; Brick-house, Lieut. Read; Barracks, a sergeant. *

Gen. Howe approves of the proceedings of the General Court Martial lately held at Fort Moultrie, which he ratifies accordingly, with this only exception that the punishment to which Robt. Cunningham was sentenced is remitted, in respect to the court, as they recommended him to mercy; the judgment of the court to the other prisoners may be carried into execution at such time and in such a manner as the commanding officer for the time being shall direct; or is impowered if he thinks proper to pardon the criminals, provided they agree to enlist for the war. Adjutant Delliant is to transmit this order to Fort Moultrie.

PAROLE PUTNAM.

May 15, 1777.

For the day, to-morrow, Capt. Cogdell, Town Guard, Lieut. Mazyck; for the Magazine, Lieut. P. Gray; Brick-house, from the 5th Regiment; Barracks, a sergeant.

Gen. Moultrie is requested to appoint some officer of his Brigade to take an exact list of the prisoners of war in town and to make a report thereof at Head-Quarters.

The four following French vessels having come to this State under particular circumstances, viz: the Union, Capt. Laroach; the Marquis de la Chaletac, Capt. Poligny; the Thunder, Capt. Aldirron; the Andrea, Capt. Corronant; the men of these vessels are not upon any account whatever to be enlisted in the Continental Battalions, and if any of their men have been enlisted, the commanding officers of those Battalions into which they have entered are immediately to discharge them from the service, and have them safely conveyed to the officer of the main guard in Charleston, who is to have them taken care of and delivered, when demanded, to the master of the vessel to which they belong; the Adjutant is to transmit this order immediately to the outposts.

The honorable the Continental Congress, having entered into the following resolutions relative to some of the articles of war, Commanding Officers of Brigade and of Battalions not formed into Brigades are immediately to have them published to the army that none may plead ignorance thereof; this order is also to be transmitted to the outposts.

IN CONGRESS, April 14th, 1777.

Resolved, That from and after the publication hereof the 2nd Article of the 8th Section, the 1st Article of the 11th Section, the 8th Article of the 14th Section and the 2nd Article of the 18th Section of the

"Rules and Articles for the better Government of the Troops, raised or to be raised and kept in pay by and at the expense of the United States of America," passed in Congress the 28th September, 1776, shall be, and they are hereby repealed, and that the four following articles be substituted in the place and stead thereof:

ARTICLE 1ST.—All officers and soldiers shall have full liberty to bring into the forts or garrisons of the United American States any quantity of eatable provisions, except where any contracts shall be entered into by Congress, or by their orders, for furnishing such provisions so contracted for.

ARTICLE 2D.—If any officer shall find himself to be wronged by his colonel or commanding-officer of the regiment, and shall, upon due application made to him, be refused to be redressed, he may complain to the Continental General commanding in the State where such regiments shall be stationed, in order to obtain justice, who is hereby required to examine into the said complaint, and take proper measures for redressing the wrongs complained of, and transmit as soon as possible to Congress a true statement of such complaint, with the proceeding had thereon.

ARTICLE 3D.—No sentence of a general court-martial shall be put in execution till after a report shall be made of the whole proceeding to Congress, the Commander-in-chief, or the Continental General commanding in the State where such general court-martial shall be held, and there on his order being issued for carrying such sentence into execution.

ARTICLE 4TH.—The Continental General commanding in either of the American States for the time being, shall have full power of appointing general court-martial to be held, and of pardoning or mitigating any of the punishment ordered to be inflicted for any of the offences mentioned in the aforementioned rules and articles, for the better government of the troops, except the punishment of offenders under the sentence of death by a general court-martial, which he may order to be suspended until the pleasure of Congress can be known, which suspension, with the proceedings of the court-martial, the said General will immediately transmit to Congress for their determination, and every offender convicted by any regimental court-martial may be pardoned, or have his punishment mitigated by the colonel or officer commanding the regiment.

May 24, 1777.

Lieut. Thomas Shubrick is appointed Brigade-Major to Gen. Howe till the pleasure of the honorable the Continental Congress be known; he is to be respected and obeyed as such.

PAROLE BURKE.

June 10, 1777.

For the day, to-morrow, Capt. Conyers; town-guard, subaltern from 5th regiment; magazine, Lieut. Hort; brick-house, Lieut. Henry Grey.

The General having considered the proceedings of the general court-martial, lately held for the trial of Lieut. Raphel of the artillery, charged by Capt. De Treville for having ungenteelly and falsely aspersed his character in a manner unbecoming a gentleman and an officer, and for the trial of a number of prisoners of different corps for desertion, and other crimes, find that the sentence against Lieut. Raphel thus: That he was no wise criminal, but rather indelicate; the court, there-fore, find him not guilty. Lieut. Raphel, in consequence of his acquit-tal, will do duty as usual. The General, however, thinks it incumbent on him, for the sake of service, to observe that indelicacy in the con-duct of one officer to another in a profession so pure as that of a sol-dier, ought upon every occasion to be avoided as inconsistent with that nicety of honor which gives dignity to the character. The General thinks proper to suspend his determination till a further day upon those sentences which inflict capital punishment. All those inflicting corporal punishments he approves of and ratifies. The sentence respecting those criminals belonging to the corps in town will be carried into execution at such times and in such manner as the commanding officer of those corps shall think proper. Those under sentence belonging to outposts are to receive their punishment at those posts in the manner and at the time the commanding officer there shall direct, who are to order proper persons to receive the criminals of their several corps from the officer of the main-guard, and convey them safely to the place of punishment.

The commanding officers of the main-guard for the time being are in the most particular manner enjoined to be careful of Robert Potts, of the second regiment, and John Cooker, of the first—an escape of either of those prisoners will be considered as an unpardonable neglect of duty. The Adjutant-General will transmit a copy of these orders to the outposts, with a copy of the sentence of the general court-mar-tial relative to the criminals of each corps.

PAROLE DISCIPLINE.

June 19, 1777.

For the day, to-morrow, Capt. Lesesne; town-guard, from the 5th regiment; magazine, Lieut. Shubrick; brick-house, Dr. Burke.

The General, with surprise and displeasure, has observed the slovenly, indecent and dirty state in which the soldiers have of late, upon almost every occasion appeared, inconsistent to their health, disgraceful to the army, censurable at all times, and, when upon duty, absolutely unpardonable. He laments the inattention of officers of companies to their men, to which this degeneracy must in a great measure have been owing, and which it was their absolute duty, as much as possible, to have prevented. They cannot surely suppose that their whole duty consists in appearing at, and that it ends in, parade, or that their reputation is not concerned in the appearance of their men. If, however, they do, it behoves them to adopt ideas more consistent with their own credit, and the good of the service. The uncombed, unshaved and dirty condition of many soldiers, even upon duty—the rusty, improper condition of their arms, and degeneracy in other particulars of late, too discernible, denote past inattention, and will, if not corrected in future, be deemed and treated as disobedience of orders. The relief of sentries sent from guard, even to the President's door, and head-quarters, come up with flapped hats, bare legs, long beards and uncombed hair; in short, in a manner so shamefully dirty and indecent, that officers of guard permitting it may, with too much appearance of justice, be accused of inattention and neglect. The General hopes that reformation will follow reprehension in all persons, and every department, where requisite; the soldiers will, therefore, take care to appear at all times, but particularly for duty, in a manner as decent as the situation of things will permit; and all adjutants are warned against receiving them, and all officers of relief against marching them off, till that is the case. It is painful to the General to have occasion to remonstrate against any impropriety in the conduct of officers and men he has the honor of commanding. He wishes them to be assured that he never has, or never shall do it, but where duty exacts it of him, and that he has never served with any officers or men in his   more respectable than those he is now with.

REGIMENTAL ORDERS, COL. MARION.

June 23, 1777.

On Saturday, 10 o'clock in the morning, divine service will be performed by the chaplain in St. Michael's Church. All officers and men are desired to parade with their side-arms at the new barracks at nine o'clock in morning, from which the regiment will be marched to the church. It is expected the men will be clean and neat as possible, with their hair powdered—the men to receive their coats from the quarter-master that day, for which commanding officers of companies to give a receipt.

ORDERS BY GENERAL HOWE.

PAROLE MOULTRIE.

June 27, 1777.

For the day, to-morrow, Capt. Lesesne; town-guard, Lieutenant from 5th regiment; magazine, Lieut. Proveaux; brick-house, Lieut. Perrincan.

In commemoration of the 28th June last, on which day the good conduct and spirited behavior of the officers and men of this State deservedly obtained honor for themselves, and rendered essential service to their country and common cause of America, the following firing are to take place :—At Fort Moultrie, 13 pieces of cannon; at Fort Johnson, 11; at Broughton's Battery, 7; at Littleton's, 7; at Elliot's, at Gadsden's Wharf, 7. The firing to begin at Fort Moultrie, and when finished there, to commence at Fort Johnson, then at Broughton's, then at Littleton's, and to finish at Elliott's. Col. Huger (as General Moultrie is sick), will order an officer, with a proper number of men, from the 2d and 5th regiments, to get the guns in order at Elliot's, and to direct the firings at that place.

Captains Grimball and Darrell will be so obliging to order, at the batteries where they command, the signal for beginning the firing, which will be one piece of cannon from Broughton's battery, which will probably be about 10 o'clock. The 2d and 5th regiments will parade at some convenient place to-morrow morning, precisely at ten o'clock, when a *feu-de-joie* is to be fired. The commanding officer at Fort Moultrie will turn out the men of that fort at such time as the tide will permit, and he thinks proper, and fire either a *feu-de-joie*, or in platoons, though as the former will not probably be heard in town, the latter will be most eligible. This firing is to be answered by the corps at Fort Johnson, who are to take it up in the manner observed at Fort Moultrie. Some signal should be agreed upon between the two forts. The General thinks proper to add, that he hopes the common soldiers will not disgrace the festivity of the day by any improper behavior. The Adjutant-General will immediately transmit this order to the commanding officer at Fort Moultrie, and acquaint Col. Roberts, Captains Grimball and Darrel therewith.

REGIMENTAL ORDERS BY LIEUT.-COL. MARION.

Commanding officers of companies to apply to the quarter-master for their men's coats this afternoon, in proportion to the number of men in each company, and to-morrow to supply their men with leggings; all who have had a pair for last year to give Col. Marion their names. The quarter-master to take a receipt from an officer of a company for what clothing he delivers.

A number of ladies in this town have been so kind as to order a genteel dinner to be given the soldiers to-morrow, in memory of their good behavior the 28th June last past, at Fort Moultrie, and the officers of the regiment present them with a hogshead of claret and three barrels of beer.

Col. Marion hopes the men will behave with sobriety and decency to those ladies who have been so kind as to give them so genteel a treat; for soldiers being seen in the street drunk or riotous, will be scandal to the regiment, and prevent any farther notice being taken of them. He hopes they will keep in the barracks, and not a man go in town that day; and should any man be overtaken in liquor, the sergeants and corporals will have them put quietly in their barracks, for which reason the Colonel insists that every sergeant and corporal will stay in the barrack-yard, that they may take care of the men of their company. The sergeant-major in particular is to stay in the barrack-yard, and keep good order amongst the men.

Gen. Moultrie will be on the parade to-morrow morning, and it is expected the men will take care to be very clean in respect to him.

ORDERS BY GENERAL HOWE.

PAROLE MOULTRIE.

June 28, 1777.

For the day, to-morrow, Capt. Moultrie; town-guard, Lieut. Mazyck; magazine, from 5th regiment; brick-house, a sergeant.

Gen. Howe thinks proper to suggest to the army the necessity there is for propriety and conduct upon this memorable day, and hopes the soldiers will not suffer festivity and rejoicing to degenerate into riot and disorder. He wishes the men to confine themselves as much as possible to their barracks, that their excess (should any happen) may not exceed the limits of their own quarters. He enjoins them not to meet with any mobs, nor to have the least hand in any riotous proceedings whatsoever; and forbids, upon pains of his highest displeasure, the least offer of insult or injury to the persons or property of the inhabitants of this capital. A soldier should at all times consider himself as ordained to protect and defend the persons, and support and maintain the rights and privileges of his fellow-citizens; and, constituted for this noble purpose, disdain everything which counteracts it. The

General hopes the conduct of the soldiers on this occasion will demonstrate they act under the influence of such considerations.

BRIGADE ORDERS BY COL. HUGER.

One sergeant and fifteen privates from the 2d and 5th regiments to take charge of Elliot's battery, at half-past ten o'clock. This party to be commanded by a subaltern of the 2d regiment.

ORDERS BY GENERAL HOWE.

PAROLE LEE.

July 3, 1777.

For the day, to-morrow, Capt. Oliphant; town-guard, Lieut. Hall; magazine, Lieut. P. Grey; brick-house, from 5th regiment.

Gen. Moultrie will order an officer, with a proper detachment, to Laurence battery, near Gen. Gadsden's wharf, to conduct the firing which is to be to-morrow at that place. Particular firing will be directed at Fort Moultrie and Fort Johnson, and the garrison of each is to turn out in honor to that day, when the Declaration of Independence was published in this State, by which America was delivered from the thraldom of Great Britain, who, by reiterated insults and injuries, and by the most cruel and tyrannical invasion of every darling right and privilege, had rendered all further union with her absolutely impossible to minds not absolutely lost to every sense of freedom.

The firing is to begin at Fort Moultrie, is to be taken up by Fort Johnson, and will be carried on by Broughton's, Littleton's, Craven's, Granvile's and Laurence's batteries, in succession. Fort Moultrie fires 21 guns; Fort Johnson, 17; Broughton's, 14; Littleton's, 9; Craven's, Granvile's and Laurence's, 5 each; in all, 76. The notice for beginning the fire will be a signal hoisted from the steeple of St. Michael's Church, which will probably happen about twelve o'clock. The strictest attention is to be paid that no mistake may happen.

The regiments in town are to parade precisely at eight o'clock in the morning, and to go through the common firings, finishing by a general volley. The garrison at Fort Moultrie is to turn out at such time, and in such a manner as the commanding officer there shall direct, and it is to be followed by similar firings by the garrison at Fort Johnson; it may be, therefore, proper that the commanding officer there should be acquainted with the manner and time of firing at Fort Moultrie.

PAROLE WASHINGTON.

December 3, 1777.

For the day, to-morrow, Captain from 5th regiment; town-guard,

Lieut. H. Grey; magazine, Lieutenant from 5th regiment; brick-house, Lieut. Capers.

The following order of his Excellency Gen. Washington has not till lately been officially received. Gen. Howe expects, and is determined to exact the strictest obedience to it from persons of every rank in that division of the army he has the honor to command, and he hopes the salutary end it is intended to answer will induce all persons to obey it without reluctance:

"GENERAL ORDER BY GENERAL WASHINGTON.

"HEAD-QUARTERS, Morristown, May 8.

"As few vices are attended with more pernicious consequence in civil life, so there are none more fatal in a military one than that of gaming, which often brings disgrace and ruin upon officers, and injury and punishment upon soldiers; and reports prevailing, which it is to be feared are too well founded, that this destructive vice has spread its baneful influence in the army, and in a peculiar manner to the prejudice of the recruiting service. The Commander-in-chief, in the most pointed and explicit terms, forbids all officers and soldiers playing at cards, dice, or at any game except those of exercise for diversion, it being impossible, if the practice be allowed at all, to discriminate between innocent play for amusement and criminal gaming for pecuniary and sordid purposes. Officers alive to their duty will find abundant employment in training and disciplining their men, providing for them, and seeing that they appear clean, neat and soldier-like; nor will anything redound more to their honor, afford them more solid amusement, or better answer the end of their appointment, than to devote the vacant moments they may have to the study of military authors. The commanding officer of every corps is strictly enjoined to have their orders frequently read, and strongly impressed upon the mind of those under his command. Any officer or soldier, or other persons belonging to or following the army, either in camp or quarters, or the recruiting service, or elsewhere presuming, under any pretence, to disobey this order, shall be tried by a general court-martial. The general officers in each division of the army to pay the strictest attention to the execution thereof. The Adjutant-General is to transmit copies of this order to the different departments of the army; also, to cause the same to be immediately published in the Gazette of each State, for the information of officers dispersed in the recruiting service.

"By his Excellency's command,

"MORGAN CONNERS, A. G.

REGIMENTAL ORDERS, LIEUT.-COL. MARION.

All the officers off duty to be on the parade to-morrow afternoon, at usual time of exercise, to ballot for a   , to fill up one of the vacancies of the regiment.

ORDERS, LIEUT.-COL. MARION.

PAROLE DISCIPLINE.

January 8, 1778.

For the fort-guard, to-morrow, Capt. Ashby and Lieuts. Galvan and Capers; rear-guard, a sergeant.

No person whatever to do their occasion within the fort, or within twenty yards of the walls on the outside; no bones or other filth or litter whatever to be thrown in the fort; all persons who disobey this order may expect to be severely punished. Commanding officers of companies to order two men and a sergeant or corporal, as fatigue men to their companies, who are to clean daily all filth which may be about their barracks, and to do other company duties. It is expected that officers will visit their men's quarters daily, and see that orders are complied with.

The officer who reads roll-call morning and evening is not only to call the men's names over, but to see they have their arms and accoutrements, and in what order. Whenever they find a man without any part of his arms and accoutrements, they are immediately to confine him and bring him to a court-martial; otherwise, they will be liable for losses, and will certainly be called upon for payment.

That every officer may have it in turn to go to town, or be absent from garrison, the Lieut.-Colonel desires the   to observe that no more than three captains—to begin from the eldest in rank, if he should not choose to go the next may have the right—and two men of a company to have leave of absence at one time. This is not meant to include those men who obtain furloughs, but those only who may go to town.

As the regiment, by being in town too long, have lost a great part of their discipline, and it is necessary to reform all abuses and neglect of discipline, the Lieut.-Colonel calls upon every gentlemen in the regiment to aid and assist him to bring the regiment to true and exact discipline, that they may regain their former credit, and be an honor to themselves and their country. He promises on his part that he will exert his utmost to so good a purpose, and will think no pains or trouble too great to effect it, but must sink under the burthen without the

assistance of the rest of the officers. A little perseverance, with attention to all parts of duty, will soon bring them to what we could wish,
and make them equal to the best troops in the State, or in any of the
United States of America. He begs leave to observe a few regulations
necessary for each company; that besides the orderly-book for each
officer, one ought to be provided for the company, in which the orderly-
sergeant for the day should enter the orders as soon as they come out,
and carry the book to all the officers of his company (and not to
have it on a scrap of paper, which through negligence or laziness may
be lost), by which means the sergeant will know all orders, as they may
have full access to it. All the men for duty or parade to draw up
before their own barracks, there to be examined by the sergeants, and,
when ready, to be examined by their officer. Though men may not be
completed with clothes, yet such as they have should be put on to the
best advantage; their hair combed, their face and hands made clean.
The orderly-sergeant may be the one who is ordered for fatigue, and
should see the men receive their provisions, and properly distributed to
each mess; all the men to be in messes of six, and not less than five;
to visit the men at meal time, and see if their victuals are well-cooked;
to visit the sick and report everything which may happen during the
day, to the commanding officer of the company. Whenever any part
of duty is neglected, or done in a slovenly manner, though ever so
minute, it tends to destroy discipline entirely; that it is necessary never
to overlook any part whatever; many small crimes may be committed,
which would be best punished in the company by various ways' much
better, and with greater effect, than bringing them to a court-martial.
One corporal and six men, with twelve rounds per man, for the advance-
guard to-morrow, who will receive orders as soon as they are ready to
march; this guard to be relieved weekly. An officer of the guard in
garrison to visit the sentries at night, once between each relief, and to
send a subaltern to visit the rear-guard, and a sergeant to patrol within
the fort every half hour during the night. The sergeant of the rear-
guard to visit his sentries between each relief during the night; when
he goes his rounds to leave the corporal the charge of his guard till he
returns.

"ORDERS TO THE SERGEANT OF THE REAR-GUARD.

"SIR,—You are to stop and bring to all vessels, boats or canoes,
which may attempt passing the bridge, either up or down, and send the
principal person with your corporal to the captain of the fort-guard;
and you are to examine all such vessel or boat, and give an account of

5

what she may have have on board, particularly all such who may come from town, and detain them until you have orders to the contrary. You are not to let any boats land near your guard, without examining them, without there should be an officer belonging to the Continental forces of the United States of America, or the President of this State, or any of his council. You are to make a report of anything which may happen, to the captain of the fort-guard; you are to give orders to the sentry on the bridge not to let any soldier go over it in the day time without a permit from some officer, nor suffer any person to pass after retreat beating, without such a pass. This order to be given to the relieving sergeant, and to be continued till further orders."

PAROLE—EGYPT.

January 23, 1778.

For the fort-guard, to-morrow, Capt. Dunbar, Lieuts. Burke and Guerry; rear-guard, Sergeant Keels.

As long hair gathers much filth, and takes a great deal of time and trouble to comb and keep clean and in good order, the Lieut-Colonel recommends to every soldier to have their hair cut short, to reach no further down than the top of the shirt-collar, and thinned upwards to the crown of the head, the fore-top short, without toupee, and short at the side. Those who do not have their hair in this mode, must have it plaited and tied up, as they will not be allowed to appear with their hair down their backs and over their foreheads, and down their chins at the sides, which make them appear more like wild savages than soldiers. The major will please pick out three men to be regimental barbers, who are to be excused from mounting guard, or doing fatigue duty. They are daily to dress the men's heads, and shave them, before they mount guard—the men to pay them half-a-crown a week each man. Any soldier who comes on the parade with beards, or hair uncombed, shall be dry-shaved immediately, and have his hair dressed on the parade. The orderly-sergeant, or corporal of companies, are to call on and see the barber dress and shave their men that are for duty, and see that they are clean, and their clothes put on decently, or must expect to answer for the neglect.

The commissioned officers are desired to pay attention to their men's dress at all times, particularly when for duty.

No officer to take charge or march off a guard without the men have complied with the above orders, and are as clean and decent as circumstances of clothing will permit.

No person to sell any spirituous liquors or beer without leave from the commanding officer of the regiment; but may sell candles, soap, or all kinds of eatables.

The sutler, Mr. Young, has leave to sell one gill rum and one quart beer per man a day, and no more, without a written permit from an officer of the company the man belongs to. He is not to let, have or sell, any liquors before the guard is relieved, or after retreat beating.

Any persons who cut, lop, or bark any trees on this island, must expect to suffer agreeably to a former order.

It is expected the guards will pay the usual compliments to all field officers of the regiment, as well as to the commanding officer.

No officer to go to Haddrell's Point, or off this island, without leave from the commanding officer; and all officers to see the orders of the day before they go any distance from the fort. Sergeant Newton, of Capt. Harleston's company, to do duty in Capt. Motte's till Sergeant Laurence returns from command.

A court-martial to sit this morning at 11 o'clock, to try all prisoners brought before them; all evidences to attend—Capt. Moultrie, President; Capt. Dunbar, Lieuts. Guerry, Burke and Hart, members.

OFFICIAL ORDERS.

One sergeant and three privates to be added to the advance-guard immediately, and to follow such orders as he will receive from the corporal he will relieve. He is to post one sentry by day, and three at night. James Campbell, of Capt. Ashby's company, Timothy Green, of Capt. Chamock's, and David Stewart, of Ashby, are appointed barbers to the regiments.

ORDERS, MAJOR HORRY.

PAROLE—SOUTH CAROLINA—WM. AFFLUENT.

March 13, 1778.

For the fort-guard, to-morrow, Capt. Motte, Lieuts. Grey and Roux; rear-guard, Sergeant Coleman.

GENERAL ORDERS BY BRIG.-GEN. MOULTRIE.

12th instant.

The General orders the following resolution to be read at the head of every corps in this State, that every member may be acquainted with the same. A. DELLIANT, *B. Major.*

"IN THE GENERAL ASSEMBLY, March 2, 1778.

"*Resolved,* That instead of the clothing hitherto allowed to the regiment of this State on the Continental establishment, each non-commissioned officer, drummer, fifer and private, shall in future be annually found with one coat, waistcoat and breeches of woollen cloth, one cap or hat, one blanket, four shirts, four pair stockings, and four pair shoes, two pair breeches of Osnaburgs or coarse linen, two waistcoats of the same, two leathern stocks, and two leathern gaiters; and that five watch-coats be allowed to a company of fifty men, and so in proportion—but that this allowance of watch-coats be not annually, but to last till they are worn out.   That each officer and soldier be allowed their full Continental rations, besides the half-pound of beef allowed by this State; and that if any person do not choose to receive his rations in   , he may receive the same in money at 5s. currency per ration.

" *Resolved*, That the future daily pay of non-commissioned officers of the several regiments of infantry of this State be as follows, viz. :— That of sergeant-majors, 20s. ; quarter-master sergeants, 17s. 6d.; drum-majors, 17s. 6d.; fife-majors and other sergeants, 15s. ; armorer's mate, 15s. each per diem.

" *Resolved*, That the daily pay of the subaltern officers in the troops of this State, be increased as follows, viz. :—First lieutenants, 45s.; second lieutenants, 40s.; ensigns, 37s. 6d., and of the quarter-master, 40s.; and that, agreeable to the spirit of the resolution of the Continental Congress, the adjutants be allowed full captain's pay from the date of the resolutions of the Continental Congress respecting adjutants; that the corporals, drummers and fifers in the regiment of artillery, be allowed 12s. 6d. per diem, and the subaltern officers, adjutant and sergeants, the same pay respectively as those of the like rank in the regiments above mentioned; and that in future there shall be only one captain and a first and second lieutenant to each company in the regiment of artillery; and the colonel in the regiment of rangers be allowed per diem, to commence from the date of his commission as colonel; the first lieutenants, 50s.; the second, 50s.; the adjutant, 60s., agreeable to the resolve of Congress; and all non-commissioned officers in the same regiment, in proportion to the pay of   regiments allowed the officers respectively, in the regiment of infantry.

" And whereas, the Continental Congress, by the seventh resolve of the 22d day of November last—*Resolved*, That it be earnestly recommended to the several States from time to time, to exert their utmost endeavors to procure to the addition of clothing made heretofore by Congress, of blankets, shoes, stockings, shirts, and other clothing for the comfortable subsistence of the officers and soldiers of their respective battalions, and to appoint one or more persons to dispose of such articles to the officers and soldiers, in such proportion as the general officer from the respective States, commanding in such army shall direct, and at such reasonable prices as the clothier-general or his deputy shall deem right, and being in just proportion unto the wages of the officers and soldiers; and all clothing hereafter to be supplied to the officers and soldiers of the Continental Army out of the public stores of the United States, beyond the bounty already granted, shall be charged all at the like price, the surplus to be paid by the United States, provided that effective measures be adopted by each State for preventing any competition between their purchasing agent and the clothier-general, or his agents, who are severally directed to observe the instructions of the respective States relative to the price of clothing purchased within such State; therefore,

" *Resolved*, That the above resolution of the Continental Congress be adopted by the States, and carried into effect. Assented to.

(Signed) JNO. RUTLEDGE."

REGIMENTAL ORDERS, MAJOR HORRY.

March 5, 1778.

That at the turning out of the battalion this afternoon, the above resolution be read to the men at the head of the battalion by the adjutant. The above commanding officer cannot but observe the liberal manner in which the late General Assembly has provided for better and more comfortable sustenance of the troops of this State, that truly merits their acknowledgment; that he cannot doubt the same ideas being diffused through all ranks in the regiment—that by their perseverance in, and strict attention to, every part of duty, they only can render service adequate to such generous bounty; that the consideration of the trust reposed in them by their country should stimulate to actions becoming their profession and the noble cause they are engaged in, and that at length they may be the means of restoring to their country peace, and plenty abounding in, and smiling on, the countenance of every individual therein.

ESTABLISHMENT OF THE AMERICAN ARMY—1ST INFANTRY.

IN CONGRESS, May 27, 1778.

Resolved, That each battalion of infantry shall consist of nine companies, one of which shall be of light infantry, the light infantry to be kept completed by drafts from the battalion, and organized during the campaign into corps of light infantry. That the battalion of infantry consist of

	Pay per Month.
One colonel and captain,	$75
One lieut.-colonel and captain,	60
One major,	50
Six captains, each,	40
One captain, lieutenant,	26, 2–3d.
Eight lieutenants, each,	26, 2–3d.
Nine ensigns, each,	20
Paymaster (to be taken from the line),	20*
Adjutant " " " "	13*
Two Masters, " " " "	13*
One surgeon,	60
One surgeon mate,	40
One sergeant-major,	10
One quarter-master sergeant,	10
Twenty-seven sergeants, each,	10
One drum-major,	9
One fife-major,	9
Eighteen drums and fifes, each,	7, 1–3d.
Twenty-seven corporals, each,	7, 1–3d.
447 Privates, each,	6, 2–3d.

Each of the field-officers to command a company. The lieutenant of the colonel's company to have the rank of capt.-lieutenant.

Resolved, That the adjutant and quarter-master of a regiment be nominated by the field-officers out of the subalterns, and presented to the commander-in-chief, or the commander of a separate department, for approbation, and that being approved of, they shall receive from him a warrant agreeable to such nomination.

That the pay-master of a regiment be chosen by the officers of the regiment out of the captains or subalterns, and appointed by warrant as above. The officers are to risk their pay in his hands. The pay-master to have the charge of the clothing, and to distribute the same.

Resolved, That the brigade-majors be appointed as heretofore by the commander-in-chief, or commander in a separate department, out of the captains in the brigade to which he shall be appointed.

That the brigade quarter-master be appointed by the quarter-master general out of the captains or subalterns in the brigade to which he shall be appointed.

* In addition to their pay as officers of the line.

Resolved, That two aide-de-camps be allowed to each major-general, who shall, for the future, appoint them out of the captains or subalterns.

Resolved, That in addition to their pay as officers of the line, there be allowed to an aid-de-camp, $24; brigade-major, $24 per month; brigade quarter-master, $15 per month.

Resolved, That when any of the staff-officers appointed from the line are promoted above the ranks in the line, out of which they are respectively appointable, their staff appointment shall be vacated. The present aid-de-camp and brigade-majors to receive their present pay and rations.

Resolved, That aid-de-camps, brigade-majors and brigade quartermasters, heretofore appointed from the line, shall hold their present ranks, and be admissible into the line again in the same rank they held when taken from the line; provided, that no aides-de-camp, brigademajors, or brigade quarter-master, shall have the command of any officer who commanded him while in the line.

Resolved, That whenever the adjutant-general shall be appointed from the line, he may continue to hold his rank and commission in the line.

Resolved, That when supernumerary lieutenants are continued under this arrangement of the battalions, who are to do the duty of ensigns, they shall hold their rank, and receive the pay such rank entitles them to receive.

Resolved, That no more colonels be appointed in the infantry; but where any such commission is, or shall become vacant, the battalion shall be commanded by a lieut.-colonel, who shall be allowed the same pay as is now granted to a colonel of infantry, and shall rise in promotion from that to the rank of brigadier, and such battalion shall have only two field-officers, viz.: a lieut.-colonel and major, but it shall have an additional captain.

May 2,. 1778.

Resolved, That no persons hereafter appointed upon the civil staff of the army shall hold, or be entitled to, any rank in the army, by virtue of such staff appointment.

June 2d, 1778.

Resolved, That the officers hereinafter mentioned be entitled to draw one ration a day, and no more; that where they shall not draw such rations they shall not be allowed any compensation in lieu thereof; and to the end that they may be enabled to live in a manner becoming their stations.

Resolved, That the following sums be paid to them monthly, for their subsistence, viz. :—To every colonel, $50; to every lieut.-colonel, $40; to every major, $30; to every captain, $20; to every lieutenant and ensign, $10; to every regimental surgeon, $30; to every regimental surgeon's mate, $10; to every chaplain of brigade, $50.

Resolved, That subsistence money be allowed to officers and others on the staff, in lieu of extra rations, and that henceforward none of them be allowed to draw more than one ration a day.

Ordered, That the committee of arrangement be directed to report to Congress, as soon as possible, such an allowance as they shall think adequate to the station of the respective offices, and persons employed in the staff.

Extract of the minutes.

CHAS. THOMPSON, *Sec.*

EAST FLORIDA.

The following intelligence and letter were brought from St. Augustine by a Georgia gentleman who had been detained at St. Augustine for some time. The President laid them before the Council March 11, 1777, and also the Proclamation of Tonyn's, dated Feb. 10, 1777:

ST. AUGUSTINE, February 20, 1777.

SIR :—A sense of duty and humanity for the people at large, induces me to transmit to you the enclosed Proclamation and intelligence for their information. and I doubt not in justice to them, you will make as public as possible.

I am, sir, your most obedient and humble servant,

PAT. TONYN.

JOHN RUTLEDGE, ESQ.

His excellency the Governor having received the following intelligence desires the same may be made public.

NEW YORK, December 19, 1776.

Since the success of his Majesty's forces on Long Island, Gen. Howe has made very considerable progress, and has never yet met with a check, the rebels make no stand; their strong posts at and near King's

Bridge were relinquished the moment they were attacked. Fort Washington, which they deemed impregnable, surrendered with all its stores, cannon, &c., and above 2,500 prisoners, among whom were some of their best troops, if any of them with propriety can be called good.

A detachment of the army under Lord Cornwallis after the surrender of Fort Washington crossed the Hudson River and easily took possession of Forts Lee and Constitution, which are situated directly opposite to Fort Washington, the garrison retreating with usual precipitation, and Gen. Washington, collecting as well as he could such of his scattered forces as were in the Jerseys, took post at Brunswick, from whence, however, he retreated on the approach of Lord Cornwallis, and was soon after forced through that Province, and over the Delaware. Philadelphia had not any security left, but the passage of this river, which, from the want of boats, was found impracticable, and the season too far advanced to construct other means of crossing it.

It is computed that the rebels have lost about 25,000 men in the course of this campaign. The success of his Majesty's arms induced their Excellencies the Commissioners, in order to spare the effusion of more blood, to publish their proclamation of the 30th of November, of which a considerable number in the provinces of New York, Pennsylvania, Connecticut, Rhode Island and the Jerseys, have already availed themselves, and many others of real property, are making this submission.

NEW YORK, Jan. 14, 1777.

The king's troops were lodged in cantonment about the middle of December. The enemy getting once more in force, took advantage of this situation, and met with some success against three Hessian battalions at Trenton, who withdrew from that post with the loss of between 400 and 500 men.

A very considerable number of prisoners have fallen into our hands during the campaign—among others, Gen. Lee. Col. Harcourt, with a small party of light dragoons, surprised him and his party, and brought him off.

Lieut.-Gen. Clinton was detached with a corps the beginning of December to Rhode Island, and took possession of that important place on the 8th of the said month, without the least resistance. Every thing is quiet here, and the harbor well blocked up, to prevent any of the rebel vessels escaping.

Sir Guy Castleton has driven the rebels entirely out of Canada, constructed a naval force on Lake Champlain, with which he totally destroyed that of the enemy, and proceeded with his army to Crown Point; but the season being too far advanced, he retired to winter quarters in Canada.

By command of his Excellency,
(Signed)   DAVID YEATS, Sec.

LETTER TO THE CONVENTION OF GEORGIA.

[Original MS.]

SAVANNAH, January 22, 1777.

SIR:

By the Legislature of South Carolina, we are appointed Commissioners to make to the Convention of this State a proposition relative to the common welfare of the two States. Through you, sir, we beg to have this notified to the Convention, and that we request to be honored with an audience to-morrow, at any time they shall be pleased to appoint.

We are, sir, your most humble servants,

W. H. DRAYTON.
JOHN SMITH.

To NOBLE WIMBERLY JONES, Speaker.

REPLY.

[Original MS.]

SAVANNAH, January 22, 1777.

GENTLEMEN:

I laid your letter this afternoon before our Convention, who, after considering the same, directed me to inform you, that they will be ready to receive you on to-morrow morning, 10 o'clock.

I am, gentlemen, your obedient and very humble servant,

W. JONES, Speaker.

The Hon. WM. HENRY DRAYTON and JOHN SMITH, Esq.

W. H. DRAYTON TO COL. BULL.

[Original MS.]

February 8, 1777.

DEAR COUSIN:

I am sorry to find that you have not yet heard any thing from our uncle, respecting his ideas upon his situation at the present crisis, and this induces me to trouble you with this letter.

You will know to what a low ebb our affairs were reduced at the Northward; and that it is the received opinion that they were so reduced by the underhand management of persons on the other side of the question, from principle, or hopes of regaining their offices. In short, our moderation to such persons almost ruined our cause. You know, also, the inclination of our public, to expel such persons from among us, and the difficulty of any discrimination of persons, lest while every man endeavored to save his friend, the measure itself be defeated.

At length, driven thereto by recent danger, we have brought in an ordinance for the banishment of crown officers and suspected persons, upon a contingency therein expressed. Only five persons in the General Assembly appeared against it. You were not present in the debate, and I will, therefore, tell you what I said introductory to my support of the ordinance. My situation was truly disagreeable. I spoke but once, the last in the debate; and, considering the lead I have taken hitherto, it would have been justly and injuriously remarked, if on such a question I had been absent or silent. The conclusion of my last charge to the grand jury must have condemned me. I arose deeply impressed with a feeling I had never before experienced, and having observed that I was more tenderly interested in the debate than any man in the room, I lamented that the time was come when the public welfare called upon us to adopt measures that might effect the tranquility of our nearest relations; that I was sensible the present measure might effect, in its operation, a gentlemen to whom I was nearly related by blood—to whom I owe the greatest obligations, and to whom I bore the most respectful affection; that I was fully aware my appearing in support of such a measure would open the mouth of calumny to reproach me as an ingrate—a man void of natural affection. That it was out of my power to avoid reproach; but that as it was my inclination and duty, so it was in my power to avoid giving just occasion for censure. That there were various duties, public and private, each rising in gradation; that it was a first principle in society, that our duty to our country was the first of the social duties; that America had engaged in the present war upon this principle, and that our independence was to be supported only by carrying that principle into practice. In short, that in this particular case, as in all others, I firmly trusted that my conduct was, and would be, a sufficient refutation of every calumny. I then proceeded to support the ordinance, which I held to be absolutely necessary.

Having in this manner supported the uniform vigor of my public conduct, to find a flaw in which my private enemies have always sought, and having thus discharged my duty to the public, I lost no time, you know, to discharge my duty to our respected relation. I sought you through the town, told you what had happened, and laid down the only means by which, in my opinion, our uncle could with credit. preserve his tranquility. Many weeks ago I informed him such an event was to be expected, and I have never mentioned this conversation to any person but yourself. Let us consider what our uncle may do.

We know his situation. His good sense and integrity stand confessed. I will not determine upon his opinion respecting the present controversy. But, without any imputation, he may resign to the King of Great Britain, by a letter containing some such representation as the following. We will send the letter to Congress, and they, by a flag of truce, will send it to Lord Howe to be forwarded.

His infirmities of body, his advanced age, and the calamities of his country, which he can neither remedy nor alleviate by a continuance in office, impel him to resign a commission which he had accepted and hitherto held, only because it enabled him to serve his country. That his laborious services under the crown, from his early youth, entitled him to a retirement from public business in his advanced age; and that his infirmity of body, distress of mind and age, demanded a release from labor.

Is there an idea in that representation inconsistent with fact, or injurious to his character? Can such sentiments and corresponding conduct endanger him under the crown, or give offence to posterity? No! But even such sentiments will satisfy his countrymen and cotemporaries. How really fortunate, therefore, is his situation, who at such a time as the present can procure not only safety but tranquility, on both sides, by a conduct satisfactory to his countrymen, without incurring blame in the eyes of posterity!

I am persuaded no man has our uncle's tranquility, welfare and honor, more at heart than you have; and I am satisfied you do not, on these points, think amiss of me. I am also convinced that upon the subject of this letter no person can discourse to him so freely as your self. His situation is perilous with respect to his tranquility, and no time ought to be lost, or importunity omitted, in representing such a conduct, and pressing him to adopt it, as may ensure his tranquility.

If he resigns, let his letter be by you delivered open to the President, who will seal and forward it to Congress. The letter ought to be dated before Wednesday next. These things done, he will not be interrupted in his retirement. If there shall be occasion for your producing the letter, I shall ask you for it on Wednesday. If I do not then ask you for it, you may return it back, observing a profound silence to me and to every other person upon the subject, whether you ever received such a letter or not. For while by *importunity* I am inclined to do a violence to his judgment *to preserve* his tranquility, I am unwilling that he should *unnecessarily* do any thing against his free inclination. Adieu.

WM. H. DRAYTON.

PROPOSED UNION BETWEEN SOUTH CAROLINA AND GEORGIA.

[Original MS.]

SNOW HILL, S. C., June 8, 1777.

SIR: In compliance with your request, I do myself the pleasure of committing to paper some of the principal circumstances and arguments relative to the late proposition of an union between South Carolina and Georgia.

By our General Assembly, which is a pretty numerous body, it was unanimously resolved, that an union between the two States would tend effectually to promote their strength, wealth and dignity, and to secure their liberty, independence and safety. Commissioners were sent to Savannah to treat of an union, and I was honored by being sent upon this business.

Immediately after I arrived in Savannah, I found that every gentleman in public office, with whom I conversed, was strongly against an union. However, I had the pleasure to find some gentlemen of fortune, though not in office or convention, who heartily approved the measure.

The convention was adjourned when I arrived, the beginning of January last, but upon their meeting, I notified that I had important matters to lay before them, as commissioner from South Carolina. I then was assured and I gave full credit to it, that I should fail in my application, but I proceeded in the discharge of my duty.

Being admitted to an audience in convention, after a short introduction of what I had to say, I stated that chance had originally placed the present districts of South Carolina and Georgia under one government at Charles Town; and although these districts, then forming but one, had been separated and placed under two governments, yet nature pointed out that the two should again form but one; for their climate, soil, productions and interests were the same. That if they continued two States, we had only to recollect the history of mankind, and the nature of things to foresee that from such causes their counsels and conduct would clash; and, of course, jealousies, and rivalship would daily increase between them, to the natural prejudice of their internal improvement, common production and foreign commerce. That there might be dangerous disputes about boundaries and the property of the Savannah River; since on these subjects many people in Carolina and Georgia thought very differently; a natural and great obstruction to the rise of the value of property. But that on the other hand, by an union, all such jealousies, rivalship, prejudice, danger and obstruction would be removed. Improvements of every kind, especially in agriculture, inland navigation and foreign commerce would be studied and advanced with rapidity. The expenses of Government would be lessened, to the great ease of the people, because only one establishment of civil officers would be paid in the room of two. The public defence would be more powerful, and at a less expense under one Government than under two, which might be jealous of, and therefore often desirous to thwart each other, and at any rate certainly liable undesignedly to defeat each others plans, to the ruin of the people concerned. And thus, sir, you see many important advantages that would be common to the two States by an union. But there are others which would be peculiar to Georgia.

By an union, the land in Georgia would rise in value, because the Carolina planters would be encouraged to extend their improvements into Georgia, and the merchants carry that trade immediately to Georgia, which otherwise must continue to be carried on as it always has been, and especially of late, through Carolina. The Georgia currency, always hitherto of inferior value to that of Carolina, (some more than

20 per cent.,) would be put upon an equal footing with that of South Carolina. The town of Savannah, in particular, and the adjacent lands, would be of much more importance and value, because Savannah river would be immediately cleared, a measure that would encourage and occasion an immense increase of agriculture upon all the land within reach of its navigation, and hence an amazing increase of produce and river navigation, all of which would centre in Savannah. Thus, in a state of separation from South Carolina, Savannah could reasonably expect, and that but by slow degrees, and at a distant day, only the one-half of the produce of a well-improved cultivation of the lands on that river, but by an union, she would in a very short time receive the whole of that improved cultivation and trade; and her own commerce would be increased almost beyond imagination, although she would lose the seat of Government. Finally, I may add, that in a state of separation in all probability Savannah will be ruined, because it will be our interest to preserve our trade to our own people. A town will rise on the Carolina side of Savannah river, which will be sure to preserve our half of the trade of that river, and by being wisely supported, it may draw to it the other half, also; and let it not be said, we cannot find a situation for a town, because it ought to be remembered, that history is full of instances of towns having been built and made to flourish, in situations that had been deemed impracticable for such purposes. Rivers and lands make wealthy towns, for these are natural causes; the presence and expenses of a few officers of Government are but as drops of water in the ocean; these go but a little way towards filling a Government post with loaded ships. The principal material for the building of such towns are policy and opulence. I thank God Carolina is known not to be in want of either.

In short, sir, it was in vain I declared that Georgia should not be liable to pay a shilling of the public debts of South Carolina; that we would not be unwilling even to aid Georgia in the discharge of her own; that we would condition against the taking up of great tracts of land south of Savannah river; and that we were desirous of granting in the treaty of union, whatever they could reasonably ask for in case of an union. It would be the duty and interest of the inhabitants north of Savannah river, to promote the prosperity of those south of it equally the same, as it was the duty and interest of the people of Georgia north of Ogeechee, to aid those south of that river. Upon the whole, that we sought to promote the general welfare, and that we knew such an end would not be obtained but by an union having justice and equity for its basis.

Having discoursed upon such topics about an hour, I delivered a written proposition as a ground-work to proceed upon, and then departed. The Convention then determined (as it was said) to consider the subject the next day; and in the meantime, in the evening, I repaired to Dr. Jones, their speaker, and informed him, that as the public body of Georgia had heard at large the Carolina reasonings upon the expediency of the union, I thought it equitable that the representatives of Carolina should also hear at large the Georgia reasonings upon the same subject, in order that if objections were made, they might, by knowing, have an opportunity of endeavoring to obviate them—and I desired he would in the morning take the sense of the Convention on this subject. He did so, and informed me that I was not to be admitted as a public person to hear their reasonings. Thus, while I found they had shut my mouth, I was made sensible that they thought their objections would appear to be more weighty by being secured against the possibility of a reply. And so Mr. Button Gwinnett appeared as the champion against me, when he had taken care to deprive me of an opportunity of exposing the fallacy of his arguments.

However, I took notes of his principal answers to what I had said; and in an hour after, in presence of an officer of high military rank, and of three or four members of the Convention, I produced those notes, and asked if they were just; and they agreed with me that what he had said, was either gross misrepresentations of what I had advanced, or no answer to my arguments. In the afternoon the Convention delivered to me a paper containing their rejection of the proffered union, founded, as I apprehend, upon a reason which does not exist in nature. For, they declared, they could not treat of an union, *because* of such a particular article (which they specified) in as they said, the Confederation of the United States, to which they had acceded. A Confederation, sir, which I do assure you never existed as a public Act of the General Congress, binding upon the States; but which, nevertheless, the Convention were taught to receive as a public Act of Congress, and to consider as such. The Convention were certainly innocent, but some individual is culpable. I received the paper, and in silence quitted the room.

I am, sir, your most humble servant,

W. H. DRAYTON.

Humphrey Wells, Esq., near Augusta, Ga.

FORM OF THE REMONSTRANCE AND PETITION OF THE INHAB-
ITANTS OF IN THE STATE OF GEORGIA.

[Original MS.]

To the Honorable the   of Georgia:

HUMBLY SHEWETH : That, whereas it is the undoubted right of the
people to remonstrate to their representatives against such public measures done or pursued, as may be thought by the people to be prejudicial to the public interest; and to petition for such measures as may be
thought likely to promote their welfare, so, at this juncture, we respectfully desire your attention to this our remonstrance and petition.

It is with the deepest concern that we have beheld the progress of
public measures in this State; because those measures have progressed
without placing the government upon a respectable footing, or the con-
ducting of it into hands in which we can confide; for, while South Carolina, long since has enjoyed the blessings of regular government lodged
in the most respectable hands in the State; her ports, by the wisdom of
her administration, filled with shipping; her manufactures encouraged
and increased; her people supplied with foreign goods even directly from
Europe, and vent provided for almost the whole of her produce; Georgia
having had as much time as South Carolina, and better opportunity,
seeing our attention has never been called off to defend our government
against civil insurrections, to have procured, yet possesses no such advantages; ever has been and is distracted by dissentions among those
in authority; and is in a manner destitute of trade and commerce.

We have seen Continental money sent hither for Continental purposes, particularly for the payment of the troops, diverted from such
services and withheld after repeated applications from General McIntosh
for payment of the troops, even while the enemy attacked our Southern
frontier in January last; whereby the troops, having great arrears due,
were wantonly made dissatisfied and driven to a disobedience of orders,
and to desertion, to the great prejudice of the service and the danger of
the State.

We have seen the public treasure squandered by the passing by a
bare majority, in a thin convention, extravagant and unjust accounts for
public services and pretended services; to the great encouragement of
even bare-faced frauds and impositions upon the public.

We are alarmed with well-authenticated informations, that no less a
sum than about £7,000 sterling of public money, has been misapplied;

for which, no account can be given; and about which, as far as we can learn, no proper inquiry has even been made.

We have lately, to our astonishment seen a resolution of the last Convention to raise 15 battalions of 500 men each, as minute-men; although by a report to the Convention in June last, it appeared that all the effective male inhabitants in Georgia, did not amount to 2,000 men.

Finally, it is with the deepest concern, set from the strongest conviction we add, that inasmuch as the public affairs have been for so long a time as we have experienced, so destructively conducted; we are of opinion that, that which has been the cause thereof, is but too likely to continue the same effects, unless the most effectual remedy be applied.

To which end, at this, the first meeting of this honorable   , we have thought it our duty to lay these things before you, our representatives, chosen for the sole purpose of promoting the real happiness of the people; and, at the same time, respectfully to point out that public conduct, which we think will tend most effectually to remove our fears; relieve our distresses; advance our prosperity; increase our strength; secure our liberties; and insure our safety. Inestimable objects, and which we are confident may be procured by an union with South Carolina, whose just overtures upon that subject, were hastily and unadvisedly rejected by the late convention.

Wherefore, as we do most ardently desire such an union, we do humbly and most earnestly petition that you will be pleased to take such measures as may be best calculated to accomplish, as speedily as may be, an union of South Carolina and Georgia under one government.

And your petitioners, as in duty bound, will ever pray, &c.

Done this   day of   1777.

FORM OF THE ADDRESS AND PETITION OF THE INHABITANTS OF
IN THE STATE OF GEORGIA.

[Original MS.]

To the honorable the General Assembly of South Carolina:

HUMBLY SHEWETH : That being impressed with a just sense of the good consequences, that would result from an union between South Carolina and Georgia, under one government, we beg leave to present to you our thanks for your invitation to the Legislature of this State to treat of an union, and to lament that it was by them rejected, and that in such a manner, as to deprive your commissioners even of an opportunity to answer those matters that were objected.

Convinced that nature and good policy dictate, that South Carolina and Georgia ought to be united so as to form but one State, we have presented a remonstrance and petition to our new house of Legislature respecting this subject, a copy whereof is hereunto annexed, and we do humbly petition, that you will be pleased to resume your deliberations upon the subject of such an union, that by God's blessing, South Carolina and Georgia may be united into one State and ruled under one common government, and, as in duty bound, we shall ever pray, &c.

Done this   day of   .   1777.

PROCLAMATION BY HIS HONOR JOHN ADAM TREUTLEN, ESQ., CAPTAIN-GENERAL, GOVERNOR AND COMMANDER-IN-CHIEF, IN AND OVER THE STATE OF GEORGIA.

[Original Circular.]

Whereas, it hath been represented unto me, that William Henry Drayton, Esq., of the State of South Carolina, and divers other persons, whose names are yet unknown, are unlawfully endeavoring to poison the minds of the good people of this State against the Government thereof, and for that purpose are by letters, petitions and otherwise, daily exciting animosities among the inhabitants, under the pretence of redressing imaginary grievances, which by the said William Henry Drayton it is said this State labors under, the better to effect, under such specious pretences, an union between the States of Georgia and South Carolina; all which are contrary to the Articles of Confederation entered into, ratified and confirmed by this State as a cement of union between the same and the other United and Independent States of America, and also against the resolution of the Convention of this State, in that case made and entered into: Therefore, that such pernicious practices may be put an end to, and which, if not in due time prevented, may be of the most dangerous consequences, I have, by and with the advice and consent of the Executive Council of this State, thought fit to issue this proclamation, hereby offering a reward of one hundred pounds, lawful money of the said State, to be paid to any person or persons who shall apprehend the said William Henry Drayton, or any other person or persons aiding and abetting him in such unlawful practices, upon his or their conviction; and I do hereby strictly charge and require all magistrates, and other persons, to be vigilant and active in suppressing the same, and to take all lawful ways and means for the discovering and apprehending of such offender or offenders, so that he or they may be brought to condign punishment.

Given under my hand and seal, in the Council-Chamber, at Savannah, this fifteenth day of July, one thousand seven hundred and seventy-seven.

JOHN ADAM TREUTLEN.

By his Honor's command,
  JAMES WHITEFIELD, *Secretary.*

GOD SAVE THE CONGRESS.

TO HIS HONOR, JOHN ADAM TREUTLEN, ESQ., CAPTAIN-GENERAL, GOVERNOR AND COMMANDER-IN-CHIEF OF THE STATE OF GEORGIA, AND TO THOSE MEMBERS OF HIS EXECUTIVE COUNCIL WHO ADVISED THE ABOVE PROCLAMATION.

That terrible performance which, by-the-by, most wise and respected rulers, was torn down, as it were, from under your noses, almost as soon as it was stuck up in Savannah, reached this place only last night; and with all imaginable tenderness, I beg leave to assure you, that it is only to your own handy work you are indebted for this public reprehension.

In plain terms I tell you, your proclamation is a compound of nonsense and falsehoods. It is illegal and void in itself, for your law does not consider that an offence which you proclaim to be so. The King of Great Britain's late proclamation, even although by the advice of the House of Commons, to apprehend Wheble, the printer, is a case in point. The party was apprehended; but a magistrate of London, knowing that an apprehension under such a proclamation was illegal, discharged him. But, to satisfy you how I regard your proclamation, and the people of Georgia what an empty thing it is, I do hereby promise to furnish the necessary sums of money to institute and prosecute an action of damages for false imprisonment, against the party who shall apprehend any one in consequence of it; and I hint to you, that the famous cases of the journeymen printers against the king's messengers, are *in terrorem.*

The Confederation you speak of is an imposition upon the people of Georgia—no other of the States of America but yours having ratified or even considered of any such thing, or have had it to consider of.

Pray, how did you blunder upon it? The Congress never sent it to you. Why, they have not even concluded upon such a thing themselves, nor does the resolution you mention warrant your assertion relative to "letters, petitions, animosities, imaginary grievances," about "all which," to use your own words, it is absolutely silent. Why, you really bring yourselves into utter contempt, proclaiming, as you do to the people, *things that are not*. Let me whisper in your ears, that this proclamation of yours is not the first instance of your doing so.

You say I was "daily exciting animosities amongst the inhabitants, under the pretence of redressing imaginary grievances;" but you can not prove that I, even for an hour, endeavored to excite animosities. I was not among your inhabitants eight and forty hours. Twelve of these I spent in bed, the others at private entertainments by invitation, or while I travelled an unavoidable route; during the whole time of which, even the subject of an union, or your mal-administration, was scarcely mentioned. To some gentlemen of Georgia, who applied to me in my own State, I spoke in plain terms of the real grievances under which they labored. Upon their desire, I threw the matter into the form of a petition for a redress of them; and do you dare to threaten petitioners, or the promoters of petitions, for redress of grievances, with imprisonment? You would deserve to be hanged for doing so, but that you know not what you do.

In the year 1679, Charles II. issued a proclamation against petitions "for specious purposes relating to the public," "for that they tended to promote discontents among the people, and to raise sedition and rebellion." But, when the Parliament met, they voted that the subject had a right to petition, and "that to traduce petitioning as tumultuous, is betraying the liberty of the subject, and tends to the introducing of arbitrary power." Lord Chief Justice North drew the proclamation, and the Parliament ordered him to be impeached for it. He escaped condign punishment only because of his great caution in the draft of the proclamation, in which he only commanded all "magistrates, and other officers to whom it shall appertain, to take effectual care that all such offenders against the laws be prosecuted and punished according to their demerits." These magistrates and other officers saw no demerit in petitioning for redress of grievances; they, therefore, issued no process against persons promoting such petitions. But you (as traitors or simpletons only would do) traduce petitioning, and order petitioners to be apprehended—a step that Lord Chief Justice North did not even dare to advise.

As things are situated in Georgia, and as that Government is conducted, I think I am bound to proclaim to your people—and turn about, you know, is but fair play—that in my opinion, which, I believe, will go farther with them than yours to the contrary, their property is not secure under your Government—a disgrace and detriment to the American cause—that the life and liberty of the subject are in the greatest danger under your management, or we should not, among many other enormities, have seen George M'Intosh, Esq., who I consider as an abused gentleman, arbitrarily ordered into a distant State, to be tried by those who have no such jurisdiction in such a case, and far out of the reach of a jury of his vicinage; circumstances of tyranny, and total disregard to the most valuable rights of the people, that not only ought to alarm every honest and sensible man in Georgia, but fill such with indignation against you; that I highly approve the proposed union, and will promote it to the utmost of my power, notwithstanding (as you think) your formidable proclamations. That now, having the very great honor of addressing you, I snatch the opportunity to make even yourselves co-operate in advancing my plan of an union; and to make you instruments to convey to the inhabitants of Georgia my most friendly and pressing recommendations, that while their Assembly shall be sitting, they will redouble their efforts to procure a redress of their grievances, and an union with this State; and this my declaration, that I am inclined to think you are concealed Tories, or their tools, who have clambered up, or have been put into office, in order to burlesque Government—and I never saw a more extravagant burlesque upon the subject than you exhibit—that the people might be sick of an American administration, and strive to return under the British domination, merely for the sake of endeavoring to procure something like law and order. I respect the people of Georgia; but, most wise rulers, kissing your hands, I cannot but laugh at some folks. Can you guess who they are?

And so, you would fain use me ill? It is well for you that I am in a most excellent humor. See how handsomely I will treat you. A good book says, "Bless them that curse you." Let me assure you I obey the precept most devoutly. Could you have expected such a return?

I have now answered your proclamation, with what, as great folks should use great titles, I call a declaration. If you are content, I am satisfied, and we may possibly be good friends yet. However, if you have a mind to amuse the public with any other productions of your masterly pens, and wish to draw me in, to contribute to the entertainment, I have no objection to be of the party; but I warn you beforehand, that whatever I contribute shall be entirely at your expense. This is but equitable; so if you are for such a frolic, I am, with all due respect to your dignities, and compassion to your follies,

Tout à vous,

WILLIAM HENRY DRAYTON.

CHARLESTOWN, S. C., August 1, 1777.

A. WM.SON TO HON. W. H. DRAYTON, ESQ.

[Original MS.]

WHITE HALL, April 13, 1777.

SIR :

As the multiplicity of public business absolutely prevents my being able to attend at Ninety-Six as a juror, I enclose for your Honor's perusal, a letter received from Geo. Galphin, Esq., on Friday; as, also, copies of the talks he last received from the Creeks. He mentions in case the Congress he intends holding with the Creeks takes place about the time appointed for the Cherokees to come to Dewitt's Corner, that he and Col. Hammond must attend as Commissioners from this State at the Congress with the Creeks, by which means we shall fall short two out of the number appointed from this State to treat with the Cherokees, which may prove a disadvantage, in case the others do not attend.

Col. Mason informs me that he came up with an intention to recruit for the 3d regiment, and that many of the prisoners have promised to enlist with Capt. Hopkins, of the 3d regiment, who I have now ordered on a part of duty which he cannot have effected before Wednesday next. In this case he may be disappointed, if the prisoners are tried and discharged before his return. I promised Col. Mason that I would mention this matter to your Honor, and request you will postpone such persons' trial till near the last of the sitting of the court, by which period Hopkins will be at Ninety-Six.

I last night received a letter from Capt. Tutt, wherein he informs me that some Indians had carried off six horses belonging to the volunteer companies, who were arrived a few days before to reinforce Fort Rutledge, and that he had dispatched Capt. Rainey, with thirty men, to take their track, and endeavor to come up with them, which he thought he would be able to effect, and take satisfaction of them. I apprehend this robbery is done by some of the disaffected Indians who lately lived at Seneca; and if Capt. Rainey comes up with them, it may be a lucky circumstance, and prevent them attempting carrying off the horses in future. When court is over I expect to have the pleasure of your company at Whitehall.

It is his Excellency the President's express orders that Conner, who enlisted and afterwards run away to the Cherokee Nation, as also P. Hawkins, Robertson or any other prisoners who are committed to Ninety-Six gaol for seditious practices against the State, should be sent to Charlestown, together with those now under sentence of death in Ninety-Six goal. When you have perused the papers you will please return them.

I am, sir, your most humble servant,

A. WM.SON.

A. WM.SON TO HON. W. H. DRAYTON, ESQ.

[Original MS.]

WHITE HALL, April 25, 1777.

DEAR SIR:

I am ordered by his Excellency, the President, to send down to Charlestown immediately, under a strong guard, all the prisoners in Ninety-Six gaol, who are convicted on the Sedition Act, and are under sentence of death, together with the seditious persons lately committed, and the charges against them on oath. As I apprehend before the removal of these last it is necessary to obtain a writ of *habeas corpus*, I inform your Honor thereof, in order that the needful may be immediately done, as I intend Capt. Hopkins, who escorts them to Charlestown, shall set off on Saturday morning next.

I am, with great respect, dear sir, your most humble servant,

A. WM.SON.

EXTRACT OF A LETTER TO THE PRESIDENT FROM H. LAURENS.

[Original MS.]

September 10, 1777.

A QUESTION IN CONGRESS TO BORROW MONEY OF FRANCE.

First question to draw bills on the Commissioners for ten millions of dollars, passed in the negative, as did a second for five millions; but on the 9th September a question was put and carried, for drawing bills on our Commissioners at the rate of five livres of France for a Spanish dollar, for payment of interest at six per cent. per annum, of all money already brought into the loan-office, or that shall be brought in before the 1st of March.

It is expected that upon this encouragement money-holders will bring supplies into the loan-office, and that we may, without another emission of paper, raise before the 1st of March twenty millions of dollars, the annual interest of which will be about £270,000 sterling, besides the risks of loss and delay by remittances.

It is true the Commissioners have given Congress assurances of money received and promised, sufficient to pay the interest of five millions of dollars annually, and added, "we hope" to find sufficient by subsidies to pay the interest of twenty millions, if we should be obliged to borrow that sum. At the same time they inform us, that upon application to the Court of France to borrow two millions sterling, they were told it was "impossible" to spare such a sum; that they had been strongly pressed, and that the minister was "anxious" to contract for the delivery of 20,000 hhds. of tobacco, as a ground for raising money by taxes; that they had actually engaged to deliver 4,000, and had received a very considerable advance on the stipulation, and earnestly "entreat" Congress to enable them to comply with their part of the agreement, which, while our ports are stopped, will be impossible.

It appears to me that the foundation of drawing bills is not substantial, the practice dangerous, and the measure, except for articles absolutely necessary for carrying on our defensive war, not necessary.

The Commissioners speak positively of money advanced, and expected by periodical payment only, for payment of the interest of five millions—which sum, and a much larger, I apprehend, will be consumed by a variety of other demands on them, which it is impossible for our mode of transacting business, and our total ignorance of the public debt contracted and increasing, to form an estimate of. This forbids, in the strongest terms, the act of borrowing more money abroad. They say in a subsequent dispatch, that we may rely on punctual payment of Congress bills, drawn for the discharge of the interest of sums borrowed, but refer, I apprehend, only to the five millions per annum; and then they recommend that the interest should be reduced to five and four per cent.—but Congress, upon a question, confirmed six per cent. against five, and have put former loans upon a level with such as may be hereafter made.

The Court of France, on failure of our part of the contract for tobacco, our continued demands on them for money, for ship-building, cloths, arms, and many other articles, will have ground for complaint, and may make a pretext of failure on our side for withholding further payments to the Commissioners.

The drawing bills of exchange is to all intents and purposes emissions of paper money upon the very worst terms, aggravated by six per cent. per annum. It is putting our debt out of sight for a little time, but it will infallibly return upon us with accumulated force.

Although France has peremptorily told us it is impossible to lend us two millions sterling, we are hastening to make a demand for that, and for aught we know, a much larger sum.

We should pay proper regard to the conduct of the Court of Versailles, in refusing to receive our Commissioners openly in their ambassadorial characters—in "avoiding every act which should seem to acknowledge our independence"—in "refusing, positively," the naval aid which we had applied for—in neglecting to consider or give any answer to our plan for a treaty, and in betraying part of our proposals, and possibly the whole of them, to the British Ambassador—in a taunting, sarcastical remark to one of our Commissioners, that we had not bid high enough—in imprisoning one of our captains, seizing his vessel, ordering a restitution of his prizes, and, in a word, in carefully avoiding to give "umbrage" to the English.

To borrow money from a foreign power, is to mortgage our soil; that the boasted generosity of the King of France, in feeding us lightly, and demanding no security, is, when compared with the conduct abovementioned, liable to suspicion of being insidious. It will be the interest of the French minister to ensnare us by degrees into a considerable debt, and the knowledge of the negociation will be a strong incentive to the British for protracting the war.

That by altering the tenor of our loan certificates, making the payment of capital at one instead of three years, and of interest quarterly or half-yearly, money-holders would be induced to bring supplies into the office; that the expectation which the public have been held in, of an emission of bills of exchange for five or ten millions of dollars, had been no small impediment to the loan.

When the loan-office certificates are put on a beneficial plan, if money shall not be brought in sums equal to the public exigency, it will be a proof that past emissions are not excessive. The demand for money at this time is not confined to the capital towns and cities within a small circle of trading merchants, but spread over a surface of 1,600 miles in length, and 300 broad; nor is it now the practice to give credit for one and more years for seven-eighths of the whole traffic. Every man is now a money-holder, and every article is paid for in cash—it is hence obvious, that an immense sum is necessary for a complete circulation. No man would be so void of understanding as to keep Continental bills idle, and at a risk of loss in his desk, when he might, upon the same security, improve them at six per cent. per annum.

The sudden rise of price for domestic necessaries of life, is not wholly owing to great emissions of paper, but, in fact, principally to the total stoppage of imports, and the consequent scarceness and dearness of such articles as our real wants cannot, and too many which our luxury will not, forego.

Borrowing of a foreign power will not increase the value of our paper money; it may, and probably will, be the source of extending the depreciation to several years beyond the term when we might, if we were in debt at home only, have redeemed it.

Such and many other arguments I used upon this occasion, particularly recommending taxation, and the most vigorous exertions for opening our ports, and promoting exportation. The question being put, and the yeas and nays demanded, there appeared 21 yeas, and 5—Col. Harrison, Mr. Jno. Adams, W. Duane, W. Middleton and Mr. Laurens —nays. "The enemies very near each other, and within thirty miles of this city" (Philadelphia).

[Original MS.]

SAVANNAH, January 4, 1778.

*DEAR SIR:

You request in your letter that I would candidly give my opinion of your conduct, while you acted under me in a military capacity; what I think of your ability in discharging the duties of your department; and, also, that I would recollect, if possible, all that passed between us relative to the acceptance and resignation of your appointment to it.

When I was ordered to your State, several respectable characters requested to attend me as Brigade-Major, but, as I had made it a rule to appoint to office, whenever in my power, the inhabitants of that particular State where I was immediately acting, in preference to all others,

* Direction lost, but believed to be Major Ladson.

I declined accepting transfers; and never, as I recollect, deviated from this rule, but in the instance of Major Connor, whom I found established in that rank, and who, after your resignation, and Gen. Armstrong's departure, I therefore adopted. Gen. Lee, when he appointed me to command in your State, desired me to nominate some person as my Major of Brigade; at that time, you were personally unacquainted with me, but I had observed you very active in, and attentive to, duty, always attending parades, relief of guards, and, in short, so assiduous and useful, that I was induced, without either your request or the least recommendation of you, to offer you the place of Brigade-Major. You told me that, provided Colonel Pinckney had no objection, you would, during the existence of actual service, cheerfully accept it, because you might, by that means, have an opportunity of obtaining a knowledge of discipline, which would render you useful to your country as a militia officer; but that you did not desire to derive either emolument or reward from the appointment. You, accordingly, served me in South Carolina and Georgia, I believe, about five months; in the first of these you not only acted as Brigade Major, but did a great deal of duty in the militia; in the latter, you served Gen. Lee, in the absence of Col. Bullet, in the capacity of Adjutant General, without in the least neglecting the duty of your particular appointment; and it is but justice to you to say, that I found you active and capable in a post both difficult and fatiguing, and that you acquitted yourself to my entire satisfaction. The General often spoke of you in terms of approbation, and strongly recommended to me to keep you in the army if possible. When he returned to Charleston, and all actual service had ceased, you requested leave to resign, and, upon my earnestly urging you to continue with me, you reminded me of the conditions upon which you had been appointed—repeating, that as your principal view, in entering the regular service, was to gain a knowledge of discipline that would render you serviceable as a militia officer, in which capacity you conceived you could be most useful to your country, you were desirous of returning to your duty in the corps to which you belonged, where you would, with pleasure, exert yourself to the utmost of your ability.

These, sir, are all the circumstances I can just now recollect, and I have been thus particular because you desired it. The manner of my expression you will excuse, as I write in a hurry.

I am, dear sir, your most obedient servant,

ROBERT HOWE.

A. WM.SON TO COL. JAMES WILLIAMS.

[Original MS.]

WHITE HALL, April 19, 1778.

DEAR SIR:

In consequence of letters from his Excellency the President, to raise a certain number of men for the defence of this State, or to march into the State of Georgia, and assist the Georgians if the service requires it, I have wrote to Colonels Thomas Liles and Beard, and taken the liberty of appointing them to meet at your house on Saturday, the 25th instant, then and there to concert and put such plans into execution as may be adequate to the present emergency. You will please to invite such of your field-officers to be present as you think proper. I would recommend to you to secure all the provisions within your limits that you possibly can, as nothing can be done without a supply of that article.

I am, dear sir, your obedient humble servant,

A. WM.SON.

P. S.—I have desired them to be early in the day at your house.

A. WM.SON TO CAPT. JOHN IRVIN.

[Original MS.]

WHITE HALL, April 21, 1778.

SIR:

In consequence of orders from his Excellency the President, to forthwith embody a certain number of men for the purpose of defending this State, and to assist and march into the State of Georgia if the service requires it, or any other service the safety of this State may require.

I hereby empower you to raise, with all expedition, for three months, certain, or longer, if the service requires them, a company of horsemen, to consist of thirty privates—stout, able-bodied men—to be officered by yourself, captain, two lieutenants (for the first to have my approbation) and three sergeants. The pay of the sergeants and privates, and to draw provisions, to commence from the day of their enlistment, and the officers in completing their companies from the time of their beginning to enlist. The privates to take the oath of abjuration and fidelity, and to sign an agreement subjecting themselves to all pains and forfeitures of the militia law now in force in this State, in times of actual alarm.

I am, sir, your most obedient servant,

A. WM.SON.

N. B.—When you have returned twenty men, you will report the same to me, and then you will receive further orders.

A. WM.SON TO COL. GOODWYN.

[Original MS.]

CAMP NEAR CHEROKEE HILL, June 20th, 1778.

Col. Goodwyn to proceed with one hundred horsemen in quest of any enemy that may be about—the men to be taken from Col. Winn's, Col. Williamson's, Col. Goodwyn's, Col. McRary's and Maj. Brandon's detachments; to be conducted by Maj. Joseph Walker to such place or places as from information Col. Goodwyn shall judge it most expedient for furthering the intentions of such enemy, and for the benefit of the service to annoy, repel, kill or take prisoners. If the detachment should want provisions or carriages, they must be hired or impressed and after performing this duty, to join me at or near Fort Barrington or Sunbury by the nearest and most expeditious route. The men to have strict orders not to injure or molest any of the inhabitants on their march.

If any thing material occurs Col. Goodwyn will send an express to Col. Williamson, he will also take up and secure all deserters he may meet.

A. WM.SON.

ORDERS FOR LIEUT.-COL. JONAS BEARD, LIEUT.-COL. ROBERT McRARY AND MAJOR THOMAS BRANDON, LIEUT.-COL. JOHN WINN, COL. ROBT. GOODWYN AND MAJ. ANDREW PICKENS.

[Original MS.]

CAMP AT CAT HEAD, JULY 25, 1778.

You are to proceed with all expedition by the following rule of march with the different detachments under your command to the State of South Carolina, taking with you and under your escort all the waggons belonging to the districts of your respective regiments, letting the men and horses have the necessary provisions and rest, at such places as you shall find convenient. If any horses belonging to the waggons should tire, so as to render it inconvenient or prejudicial to your detachments to wait for them, such must necessarily be left after getting into the settlements in Georgia or South Carolina, with the driver or owner, until the horses are refreshed. The line of march, after separating the army to be observed so as to make it equally convenient to each detachment, so that if the detachments in front by any kind of delay are passed by the others, they must necessarily fall in the rear. All the provisions in the army will be divided in just and equal proportions to the different detachments according to the number of men in each. The commanding officer will order the proper returns to be made for this purpose and send their Quarter-Masters to receive it. Orders on the Governor of Georgia will be given by the commanding officer for the necessary supplies to the detachments on their march through this State. If any 'difficulty in getting such should happen within this State, or in South Carolina, the commanding officer of such detachment will impress what may be absolutely necessary, appointing proper persons to appraise such necessaries upon oath, that a just recompense may be made to the owners.

Col. Williamson having the greatest confidence in the care and diligence of the field officers, their zeal for the service, the honor of the State to which they belong, and the reputation of the troops, that he relies upon them for the preserving of good order and preventing the men from committing any depredations or injuring or insulting any person whatever on their return through this State or South Carolina; and, although the expedition to which they have been called has not been attended with the wished for success, he returns them and the officers and men under them his thanks for their perseverance and alacrity on so trying and difficult a service.

ORDER OF MARCH AT DETACHING THE ARMY.

1st. Col. Winn with his detachment; 2nd. Col. Williamson's detachment; 3rd. Col. Goodwyn's detachment; 4th. Col. Beard's detachment; 5th. Col. McRary and Maj. Brandon's detachment.

A. WM.SON.

ANDREW PICKENS TO CAPT. JOHN IRVIN, OR IN HIS ABSENCE TO
HIS LIEUTENANT.

August 29, 1778.

SIR:

By order of Col. Williamson, you are hereby required to embody the
State draft from your company, and march with them, well armed and
accoutred, with three days' provisions, to the place where the Long
Cane road crosses Little River, near the Rev. Mr. John Harris'. You
will be at the above place of rendezvous punctually on Friday, the 4th
day of September next, as the situation of the distressed people in
Georgia, to whose assistance we are to march, will admit of no delay.
There will be wagons at the place where we meet, to carry the men's
baggage, as the horses must be sent home if the men bring any from
home.

I am, sir, your most humble servant,

ANDREW PICKENS.

N. B.—Order every man to bring a good hatchet. Since I wrote
the above I have got intelligence that a party of Indians are on their
way to our frontier. I desire you would, with all possible speed, march
up to John Cameron's old place with five or six days' provisions.

A. P.

———

W. WARDLAW TO A. WM.SON.

[Original MS.]

LONG CANE, December 7, 2 o'clock, P. M., 1778.

SIR:

I have just received information that the Indians have carried away
Thos. Stevenson and his family, and three others that were there, and
robbed his house. They were tracked some distance, and seemed to
bear up the other side of Barker's Creek. This conduct seems unusual,
but from the signs it appears that there are Indians in company. I am
also informed that on yesterday there were several guns heard from the
Corner. The alarm is sufficient to direct you how to proceed. Please
to forward the other letters as directed.

I am, your humble servant,

W. WARDLAW.

P. S.—Our company is met this morning by day at the Corner, to
proceed as necessity appears.

A MUSTER ROLL OF THE GRENADIER COMPANY IN THE SECOND REGIMENT OF SOUTH CAROLINA INFANTRY, ON THE CONTINENTAL ESTABLISHMENT, COMMANDED BY COLONEL ISAAC MOTTE.

[Original MS.]

August 25, 1778.

NAMES.	DATES OF COMMISS'NS	REMARKS.
Commissioned Officers.		
Thomas Dunbar, Captain,	November 9, 1777,	Present.
Albert Roux, 1st Lieutenant,	December 15, 1777,	Do.
Staff-Commissioned Officers.		
John Downs, Adjutant,	March 12, 1778,	Absent with leave.
Rev. Henry Purcell, Chaplain,	May 7, 1776,	Do.
John Hall, Quarter-Master,	July 1, 1776,	Do.
Henry Gray, Pay-Master,	December 16, 1777,	Do.
Jeremiah Thews, Surgeon,	August 2, 1777,	Present.
John Henry Rusche, 1st Mate, do.,	June 11, 1778,	Do.
Silvester Springer, 2d Mate, do.,	June 27, 1778,	Do.
Staff Non-Commissioned Officers.		
Lewis Coffer, Sergeant-Major,	June 16, 1778,	Discharged July 9, 1798
John Wickom, Sergeant-Major,	October 5, 1778,	Present.
William Fletcher, Qr.-master Sergeant,	July 15, 1778,	Discharg'd July16,1778
Daniel Simpson, Qr.-master Sergeant,	During the war,	Sick in Gen. Hospital,
James Arnold, Drum-Major,	September 16, 1779,	Present. [Charles Town
Hugh Campbell, Fife-Major,	June 16, 1778,	Discharged July 1, 1778

NAMES.	ENLISTM'T TIME.	TIME OF SERVICE.	REMARKS.
Non-Commissioned Officers.			
SERGEANTS.			
William Jasper,	July 8, 1775,	July 8, 1778,	Discharged,
John Marlow,	June 26, 1775,	June 26, 1778,	Discharged July 9, 1778.
John Gemmell,	July 18, 1775,	July 18, 1778,	Discharged July 21,1778
Robert Watt,	August 5, 1777,	During the war,	Present.
William Brown,	July 6, 1778,	July 6, 1781,	Present.
CORPORALS.			
Samuel Butler,	July 7, 1775,	July 7, 1778,	Discharged.
John Roberts,	Nov. 26, 1776,	Nov. 26, 1779,	Preferred in another Com-
Robert Watt,	August 5, 1777,	During the war,	Preferred. [pany.
Frederick Simons,	July 27, 1777,	During the war,	Present.
DRUMMERS.			
John Wheeler,	July 1, 1775,	July 1, 1778,	Discharged.
Peter Uptegrove,	July 18, 1778,	Jan. 18, 1780,	On the recruiting service.
PRIVATES.			
William Ashford	July 11, 1777,	During the war,	On Outpost.
William Arnold,	July 8, 1775,	July 8, 1778,	Discharged July 15,1778.
Barnaby Bryan,	August 5, 1777,	During the war,	Present.
John Cook,	July 13, 1775,	July 13, 1778,	Discharged.
Charles Cox,	July 1, 1778,	March 1, 1779,	On the recruiting service.
John Baptist DeLaney,	June 25, 1775,	June 25, 1778,	Discharged July 1, 1778.

7

NAMES.	ENLISTM'T TIME.	TIME OF SERVICE.	REMARKS
Owen Griffin,	July 11, 1777,	During the war,	Present.
Silas Gibson,	July 16, 1778,	July 16, 1781,	Present.
Loami Husbands,	August 2, 1775,	August 2, 1778,	Discharged.
John Humphreys,	June 18, 1775,	June 18, 1778,	Discharged July 1, 1778.
Aaron Harris,	January 31, 1777,	Jan. 31, 1780,	Present.
James Hooper,	August 5, 1777,	During the war,	Sick at Quarters.
William Jones,	July 7, 1777	During the war,	On Garrison guard.
Robert Ivey,	July 8, 1775,	July 8, 1778,	Discharged.
Charles Lucas,	July 19, 1775,	July 19, 1778,	Discharged July 1, 1778.
Joseph Martin,	July 10, 1775,	July 10, 1778,	Discharged July 18, 1778.
Martin Moore,	July 8, 1775,	July 8, 1778,	Discharged.
Jacob Murph,	July 8, 1775,	July 8, 1778,	Discharged.
John McCaid,	August 5, 1777,	During the war,	On the recruiting service.
John McDowell,	June 16, 1778	During the war,	Preferred in another Company.
James McClean,	August 5, 1775,	August 5, 1778,	Discharged.
Archibald McDonald,		During the war,	Present.
James Oliver,		During the war,	Present.
Edmund Penrice	July 2, 1775,	July 2, 1778,	Discharged.
David Parsons,	August 1, 1775,	August 1, 1778,	Discharged.
Richard Richardson,	August 3, 1777,	During the war,	Present.
William Roberts,	August 7, 1775,	August 7. 1778,	Discharged.
Frederick Simmons,	July 27, 1777,	During the war,	Preferred.
Thomas Stafford,	January 4, 1777,	During the war,	On Duty.
John Steele,	July 9, 1778,	During the war,	Present.
Anthony Uhthoff,	July 6, 1775,	July 6, 1778,	Lischarged.
John Whitely,	July 11, 1777,	During the war,	Present.
Robert Whiley,	March 11, 1778,	During the war,	On Duty.
Shadrack Williamson,	July 8, 1775,	July 8, 1778,	Discharged.
Richard Williamson,	July 9, 1777,	During the war,	Confined.
John Kelly,		During the war,	Present.

PROOF OF THE EFFECTIVE.

Present.—Captains, 1; 1st Lieutenants, 1; Surgeons, 1; Surgeon's Mates, 2; Sergeant-Major, 1; Drum-Major, 1; Sergeants, 2; Corporals, 1; Privates, 10.

Absent.—Adjutants, 1; Chaplains, 1; Quarter-Master, 1; Pay-Master, 1; Quarter-Master Sergeants, 1; Privates, 8.

We do swear the above Muster Roll is a true state of the Company, without fraud to the United States or any individual, according to the best of our knowledge.

THOS. DUNBAR, *Captain.*

ALBERT ROUX, 1*st Lieutenant.*

Sworn before me this 25th August, 1778.

FRANCIS MARION, *Second Colonial Regiment.*

Then mustered, as certified by

THOS. JERVEY, *Deputy Muster Master.*

A. WM.SON TO COL. ROBERT GOODWYN.

[Original MS.]

WHITE HALL, November 28, 1778.

DEAR SIR:

My having been continually employed in Georgia since the Southern expedition, prevented me being able before this period to attend to and examine and adjust the expenses arising from that service. I would therefore request you will, as soon after the receipt of this letter as you possibly can, furnish me with the pay-bills and amounts of your detachment employed in that service, in order that I may examine and adjust them, and be able to take the proper and necessary steps to obtain payment for the people for their good services. Some information I have just received makes me apprehensive that the disaffected meant again to collect, and join the enemy, who are said to have landed on this side the Altamaha, to the amount of 800, and penetrated into the lower parts of Georgia. You will perceive from this intelligence how cautious we should be to guard against our internal enemies, who, during this struggle, have demonstrated themselves the most cruel and rancorous enemies. McGirt, it is said, landed in Georgia at the same time, but has taken his course higher up the country; no doubt but he will endeavor to visit his old range. I wish you may be fortunate enough (if he comes your way) to secure him, or give him a proper dose, to prevent his inroads in future.

I am, with great regard, dear sir, your most obdt. servant,

A. WM.SON.

LIEUT.-COL. HENDERSON TO CAPT. BUCHANAN.

[Original MS.]

RECRUITING ORDERS.

CAMP PURYSBURG, February 5, 1779.

SIR::

You are to set out immediately on the recruiting service. You are to recruit anywhere within the State; you are to enlist no man under the age of sixteen nor above forty-five; you are to enlist no notorious rogue if you know it; you are to bring all the men you enlist to Headquarters or cause them to be brought; all the men you enlist, you are to give five hundred dollars to—fifty in hand and the rest when you gain Head-Quarters—for the first month after the 29th of January last; for the second month four hundred dollars; for the third month three hundred and fifty dollars, and the same pay and rations as usual; you are to enlist no man for less time than sixteen months. But as many as you can for during the war; you are from time to time to let the commanding officer know what success you have and what part of the country you are in; you are to go from here to Charlestown; you are not to stay there more than three days before you set out—from which time, you are to join Head-Quarters in six weeks, unless you have strong reason to believe you will have good success, in which case you are to stay some days longer. You are to deceive no man to enlist him. All reasonable expenses will be paid for bringing recruits to Head-Quarters.

WM. HENDERSON,

Lieut.-Col. 6th Regiment.

J. RUTLEDGE TO COL. ROBERT GOODWYN.

[Original MS.]

CHARLESTOWN, S. C., February 10, 1779.

SIR :

You are immediately to detach two hundred and fifty men, rank and file, of your regiment, properly armed and accoutred, with the necessary number of officers, the whole under the command of a field officer, to join and put themselves under the orders of Brig.-Gen. Williamson, to assemble and encamp the remainder of your regiment at Friday's Ferry, on the twenty-third day of February, inst., there to wait any further orders.

Your men may be assured, that any arrears of pay shall be very soon settled and discharged; that, in future, they will receive their pay with more regularity than heretofore; that, in all probability, the pay of privates will be augmented by an ordinance now before the Legislature, to a dollar per day, and that everything in the town shall be done to render their situation, on service, as comfortable as possible, and I trust that I shall be readily and cheerfully obeyed.

I am, sir, your very humble servant,

J. RUTLEDGE.

INTRODUCTION OF THE MINISTER TO A FREE CONFERENCE IN A
COMMITTEE OF THE WHOLE CONGRESS.

[Notes by W. H. Drayton.]

MONDAY, February 15, 1779.

He informed the Committee that his master, actuated by the most
friendly regard to the United States, had ordered him to acquaint them
that a great revolution had taken place in Great Britain respecting the
question of their independence; that there had been a great party in
the Cabinet Council of that nation in favor of that independence; that
they were willing to grant that independence with certain conditions;
that those conditions were somewhat similar to those proposed by the
late commissioners; that they principally respected a kind of Federal
Union, such as that the United States should assist Great Britain in
her wars; that, however, this measure had been laid aside, the Cabinet
being impressed with the representation of the Commissioners that
divisions prevailed among the members in Congress, and between the
Congress and some of the States; that by the operations of the Commissioners a foundation was laid upon which discord would arise between
the United States and France in the ensuing campaign; that in its
operation it would be sudden and critical, and that there was a powerful party against the independence of the United States; that the
British Court, as they had always done, propagated and spread these
suggestions throughout Europe, and were the more at large in the
calumny, that some impressions might remain in consequence of the
heat of the calumny; that although his most Christian Majesty paid
no attention to these suggestions, yet he most strongly recommended
concord without meaning in any manner to look into or interfere in the
internal measures of the United States.

That such being the disposition of the Cabinet the beginning of
October, the Court of Spain had thereupon taken her final resolution,
as expressed by her remonstrance to the Court of London the end of
that month, respecting her hostile operations against France, making
the independence of the United States the preliminary article to a
general pacification; that it was possible this would lead to a general
peace, and that the negociations would necessarily be rapid, as peace or
war must finally be determined upon before the season for opening the
campaign came on. That as the Court of France had no object in view
but the independence of the United States, if this was to be obtained
there was a great probability of peace; but if it could not be obtained,

his most Christian Majesty would exert all his powers in the next campaign in prosecution of the war. That the Congress ought to lose no time in appointing a proper person to take a part in the expected negociations; that he should be furnished with ample powers, as well as the desires of Americans as her ultimatum, relaxing in the first as in his discretion he should see fit, the distance being too great, and the crisis too pressing, to admit of applications to Congress for instructions; that the United States should consider their resources and their abilities on the one hand, and the probable advantages and disadvantages arising on the other, by continuing the war; that moderate terms might, perhaps, be now obtained; that the pride of Great Britain was too high, and her abilities too great, to submit to extraordinary demands at present. She might be able to continue the war for some years yet. France desired no aggrandizement by conquest, the Independence of America being alone such a debilitating of Great Britain, as to secure her effectually against the haughtiness of that nation.

That the Court of Great Britain had endeavored to form alliances upon the Continent; that twenty months ago she had applied to the Empress of Russia for a body of her troops for the American service; that she replied she had not been raised to empire by Providence for such a purpose; that she would not send her troops against a people who asked only for justice and liberty; she would not engage in such a bloody work. In short, she answered with such disdain, that the British ambassador retired from Court till he received instructions on that head from London; that these instructions were in such mild terms, that he returned as if nothing had happened; that afterwards he applied to the Empress that her Majesty should act in strict conjunction with the British, and that a large district in America would be assigned to the Empress; but she answered this in such a manner, as discouraged a renewal of the application. That Britain had also proposed to the King of Prussia to loan an army of observation, with the view of collecting to it such forces as were against the interests of the Emperor; that the King, the Emperor, and the Queen of Hungary, had applied to his Master to mediate in the disputes relative to Bavaria; that he being in alliance with Vienna, had not chosen to be alone the arbiter, but had called upon Russia to be a co-umpire, to which the King of Prussia and the Emperor had consented; that the Empress of Russia had desired of the King of France to mediate between her and the Porte; that thus it appeared none of the Great Powers of Europe would take part against France, and that Great Britain was destitute of alliances against his Master; that Spain wished to have the territorial claims of the United States terminated. She wished to have the navigation of the Mississippi shut, and possession of the Floridas; that she disliked the neighborhood of the British in that quarter, who were too restless and enterprising, and preferred that of the United States; that if the war continued, a subsidy might be obtained of Spain in aid of the pecuniary wants of the United States; that this aid was most honorable to protect States to obtain under the mark of a subsidy; that it might at a loose rate call for 6,000 men, when not more than 3,000 would be expected to be embodied for the reduction of the Floridas, to be relinquished to Spain when conquered; that Spain might obtain that territory independent of the States; that if a peace now took place, Spain would have no claim upon the United States, nor would they have any upon the Floridas; that if this subsidy took place, the money might be lodged in respectable private hands in Paris, and if prudently managed would give the States a credit in Europe equal to their wishes; that at all events the United States should exert themselves to prepare for another campaign, and put on the appearance of aiming at more than they meant to strike at; for such an appearance would accelerate the negociations, especially if the United States could strike a blow, which, though not important, might be brilliant; that peace was the time for the United States to recover their finances; that France had just begun to recover hers when hostilities begun between her and Britain; that had those hostilities been postponed two years, she would be more competent to the war; that, however, France had made every necessary arrangement for the next campaign. But that, as her exertions, and the maintenance of 60,000 men on the frontiers of Germany, to enforce her umpirage, would occupy all her resources, she was not able to afford those aids to America, which she was disposed to do, considering as she did the interests of America as her own.

AN ORDINANCE TO PREVENT PERSONS FROM WITHDRAWING FROM THE DEFENCE OF THIS STATE TO JOIN THE ENEMIES THEREOF, PASSED 20TH FEBRUARY, 1779.

[Original MS.]

STATE OF SOUTH CAROLINA.

At a General Assembly begun and holden at Charles Town, on Monday, the fourth day of January, in the year of our Lord one thousand seven hundred and seventy-nine, and from thence continued by divers adjournments to Saturday the twentieth day of February, in the year of our Lord one thousand seven hundred and seventy-nine.

Whereas, it is absolutely necessary in well regulated Governments that every person who has received protection from, should be aiding and assisting in the defence of the State wherein he lives; and whereas several persons, inhabitants of this State, forgetting their allegiance thereto, have gone over to the enemy, treacherously to bear arms against their country, although their families remain peaceably under the protection thereof. Therefore, to prevent such criminal conduct in future, Be it ordained by the Honorable the Senate and House of Representatives now met and sitting in General Assembly and by the authority of the same, That if any person or persons from and after passing this Ordinance shall withdraw him or themselves from the defence of the State, and attempt to join the inveterate enemies of the same, or shall actually go over to them, every such person and persons shall be declared guilty of treason against the State and upon conviction thereof, in any of the Courts of General Sessions of the Peace, Oyer and Terminer, assize and General Gaol delivery in this State, or in any special court of Oyer and Terminer, to be held by virtue of an Ordinance passed the thirteenth day of February, one thousand seven hundred and seventy-nine shall suffer death as a traitor, without benefit of clergy; and the estate of such person or persons, real and personal, shall be confiscated and forfeited for and to the use of the State.

And be it further ordained by the authority aforesaid, That if it shall appear to the Governor or Commander-in-Chief, for the time being, on the oath of two creditable witnesses that any person or persons hath or have withdrawn himself or themselves from this State, and joined the enemies thereof, it shall and may be lawful to and for the Governor or Commander-in-chief to issue his Proclamation, thereby requiring every such person or persons to return to this State, and surrender himself or themselves to some Magistrate thereof within forty days after the issuing of such proclamation, and in case of his or their non-appearance, within the time aforesaid, he or they shall be deemed outlawed, and all the estate, real and personal, of such person or persons shall be sold by proper persons for that purpose to be appointed by the Governor or Commander-in-chief, and the monies to arise therefrom deposited in the public Treasury of this State, there to remain for the disposal of the Legislature thereof. And be it further ordained by the authority aforesaid, That the Governor or Commander-in-chief, for the time being, is hereby authorized and required to appoint one or more Commissioner or Commissioners for the sale of such estates, and to cause the families, or such of the families of every absentee, outlawed as aforesaid, to be sent off without delay, if it shall appear upon trial to be duly had at any of the Courts of Sessions, Oyer and Terminer, Assize and General Gaol delivery, on a Bill of Indictment that the remaining of such person or persons in this State shall be dangerous to the safety of the community. And be it further ordained by the authority aforesaid, that all and singular, the matter and things in the foregoing clause contained shall be construed to extend to the families of such persons as have been sent off, or have quitted, or shall quit this State, for having refused or neglected to take the oath or oaths required by any Act or Ordinance of the Legislature of this State. And be it further ordained by the authority aforesaid, That this Ordinance shall continue and be of force for six months, and from thence to the end of the then next sitting of the General Assembly and no longer.

Ratified by the General Assembly, in the Senate House, the 20th day of February, 1779.

    CHAS. PINCKNEY, *President of the Senate.*

    JNO. MATHEWS, *Speaker of the House of Representatives.*

7TH MARCH, 1779.

Compared with the original under the Broad Seal by Thomas Winstanley and Jacob Read.

BOUNDARY OF CAPT. ANDREW HAMILTON'S COMPANY.

[Original MS.]

Beginning at the mouth of the Reedy Branch, and up said branch to John Cambels; from thence to Rocky Creek, including Joseph Able, the Boggeses, Arthur Dickson and the Thomsons, north west course beginning at the mouth of Reedy Branch; from thence up Long Cain to the waggon-ford at Mathew Edward's plantation; from thence to Wm. Little's; from thence to Crocket's Old Place on John's Creek; from thence to Simon Tuckers's; from thence to Robert Adair's; from thence to Wm. Thomson on Cowhead; from thence to Patrick Gibson's; from thence to Edward Brannon's; from thence to the Thomson's on Rocky Creek.

ANDREW PICKENS TO CAPT. JOHN IRVINE.

[Original MS.]

FEBRUARY 20, 1779.

SIR :—You are hereby desired to be at White Hall on Wednesday next with one third of your Company—they to be horsemen—and one Lieutenant, and one other third of your Company to continue at White Hall until further orders.   You will receive further orders on that day.

I am, sir, your most humble servant,

ANDREW PICKENS.

C. PINCKNEY' JUN., TO MRS. C. PINCKNEY.

[Original MS.]

CHARLESTON, February 24, 1779.

HONORED MADAM :

I embrace with pleasure an opportunity of complying with the request, you made me when I left Santee, of transmitting such intelligence as I thought worthy your notice, though the presence of our active officers (General Moultrie and Col. Pinckney) renders the subject somewhat barren.   My cousin and the General returned to town on Tuesday by desire of Gen. Lincoln, who was of opinion that unless the assembly took some effectual measures to oblige the militia to do their duty, and placed them under the same articles as those from North Carolina, our situation would soon be discouraging, even to those who had voluntarily resigned their lives and fortunes, in our defence, though at a great distance from danger and who were merely actuated upon this occasion by a love to their country.   They opened the matter very fully; related several facts of which we were ignorant; were exceedingly warm; and roused the spirit as well as the indignation of the House so much at the conduct of their fellow-citizens, that notwithstanding they had, some little time before, reprobated the idea of subjecting the militia to martial law, yet an Ordinance being prepared and brought in for that purpose passed both Houses without opposition.   The reluctance of our militia to continue at Purysburgh longer than the 1st of March, frustrated one of the best laid schemes, that our affairs have yet given Gen. Lincoln an opportunity of concerting. A detachment of the enemy having taken possession of Augusta, Gen. Ash was immediately detached to reinforce Gen. Williamson; these corps when joined consisted of between two and three thousand men. Gen. Moultrie was ordered to march with his division, consisting of 1,600 Continentals and some regiments of militia; and had he occupied the post to which he was ordered and was then proceeding to, the enemy would have been completely surrounded and either obliged to hazard a battle on the disadvantageous terms of three to one or have surrendered themselves prisoners of war—but after marching six or eight miles up the river for this purpose, he received an order from Gen. Lincoln to return to his former post; but I am happy in acquainting you that our officers pledge themselves, that they will, with the assistance of only a small part of our militia, free Georgia from the present invasion; indeed, the enemy themselves confess that they have erred in not marching immediately to Charlestown, after the rout at Savannah; and the late precipitate retreat from Augusta, where they left their Hospital, with a letter recommending their sick and wounded to the care and humanity of Gen. Williamson, convinces me that they either mean to evacuate Georgia very soon, or to confine themselves to Savannah and its environs—but it is a matter of doubt with me, whether they will be even able to maintain their post there, as I am informed that the reinforcement which G. M. carries with him, will enable our forces to act offensively. Lincoln is anxious and uneasy at being obliged from the enemy's superiority, or at least equality of numbers, to remain so long inactive, and will assuredly take the first opportunity of paying them a visit. The long expected express from the northward arrived on Monday. Messrs. Laurens and Drayton acquaint us that it is impossible to spare any Continental troops, as a secret expedition now on the carpet, will demand their whole force. They say that Congress in consequence of our application, have granted us every assistance in their power, and refer the Governor to the President's letter on that subject, which has not yet come to hand. As to a further aid from North Carolina, they have agreed to send us 2,000 more men immediately. We have now upwards of 3,000 of their men with us; and I esteem this last augmentation, as the highest possible mark of their affection for us and as the most convincing proof of their zeal for the glorious cause in which they are engaged; they have been so willing and ready upon all occasions to afford us all the assistance in their power, that I shall ever love a North Carolinian, and join with Gen. Moultrie in confessing that they have been the salvation of this country.

I expect Col. Horry will be in town in a few days, as he was on Friday last elected Colonel of a Regiment of light dragoons, which are to be immediately raised for the public service.   Maham is Major—there was an opposition in favor of Major Huger, but by no means a serious one, as the Colonel carried it by a majority of 44; Huger will soon be promoted in the Continental service as a Commission arrived yesterday appointing Col. Huger, a Brigadier General.

There is almost a total stagnation of every kind of business; and we daily expect a Proclamation from the Governor and Council for stopping the Courts of Justice and prohibiting all commercial proceedings whatsoever until the removal of the enemy from Georgia.   The people of this country were scarcely roused to a sense of their danger, till within this fortnight, but I believe I may now venture to assert that Carolina, will in a short time (comparatively speaking) be as tenacious of her freedom and as forward in defending her liberties as any State on the continent, though, from her internal disputes and natural weakness, she may not be able to bring as many men into the field.   Our town, once the seat of pleasure and amusement, is now dull and insipid; a sameness prevails through every thing, and the duty of the remaining militia is full as fatiguing as that of the regulars.   We have very few men left here, notwithstanding which they are daily reducing us, and should a fleet and army appear at our bar, God knows what we should do.   If the enemy should prove unable to penetrate into this State, and I can get leave (for no one is suffered to leave the town without it under a heavy fine) I purpose paying you a visit at Santee for a few days.   I am fond of variety, and changing the scene now and then is I think very agreeable.   I hope the little bantling and my friend Daniel are well.   Should the weather continue good, my uncle and family will be at Santee on Thursday.   I shall expect an anwer from you by your next express, and you may depend upon my writing you as often as I can find a conveyance for a letter.   My compliments to Miss Howarth and our Santee friends (in which my mother joins me).   Conclude me

Your affectionate nephew,

CHARLES PINCKNEY, Jr.

P. S.—Mr. Bee being elected Lieutenant-General, and E. Rutledge refusing to go to Congress, Mr. Lowndes and William Henry Drayton (who carried it against Daniel Huger by one vote) were elected in their room.

ANDREW PICKENS TO CAPT. JOHN IRVINE.

[Original MS.]

March 12, 1779.

SIR :

On receipt of this immediately march, with twenty-five men of your company, to Ninety-Six, and join Col. Williams, in order to guard the prisoners while on trial. You will receive orders from Col. Williams when you arrive at Ninety-Six. Dinborough is to supply you with provisions while on duty. You will have Lieut. Joseph Wardlaw and any others of your company that were prisoners with the Tories, and can be any evidence against any of them. Elijah and Samuel Moore, that were with me at the battle of Kettle Creek, I am well informed have some horses and two rifle guns that were taken at that battle, and as that property belongs to the people in general, you will order them, without loss of time, to bring those effects to me, or they may depend on being prosecuted for the same.

I am, sir, your humble servant,

ANDREW PICKENS.

A MUSTER ROLL OF CAPT. RICHARD B. ROBERTS' COMPANY OF THE SOUTH CAROLINA CONTINENTAL CORPS OF ARTILLERY, COMMANDED BY COL. OWEN ROBERTS.

[Original MS.]

HEAD QUARTERS, Purysburgh, March 19, 1779.

COM. OFFICERS' NAMES.	RANK.	DATE OF COMM'N.	REMARKS.
Richard B. Roberts,	Captain,	June 4, 1777,	Present.
John Gorgan,	Capt.-Lieut.,	May 30, 1778,	Do.
Frederick Von Plater,	1st Lieutenant,	October 28, 1778,	Do.

NON-COMMISSIONED AND PRIVATE NAMES.	DATE OF ENLISTMENT.	TIME OF SERVICE.	REMARKS.
John Smith, Sergeant,	June 3, 1777,	3 years,	Absent on Guard.
Brice Mathews, do.,	Nov. 24, 1777,	3 years,	Present.
Joseph Hull, Corporal,	June 25, 1777,	The war,	Do.
John Sessions, do.,	June 29, 1778,	3 years,	On Detachment.
Edward Conner, do.,	June 29, 1778,	3 years,	Present.
Robert Goodall, Gunner,	Sept. 17, 1777,	The war,	De.
Benjamin Williams, do.,	June 2, 1777,	3 years,	Do.
Alexander McMullan, do.,	Feb. 3, 1779,	16 months,	Do.
Aaron Baroth, do.,	June 3, 1777,	3 years,	Absent on Duty.

Non-Commissioned and Private Names	Date of Enlistment.	Time of Service.	Remarks.
Matrosses.			
David Cunningham,	June 3, 1777,	3 years,	Present.
John Driver,	July 14, 1778,	3 years,	Do.
Joseph Johnson,	June 2, 1777,	The war,	Do.
John Causey,	Sept. 5, 1778,	3 years,	Do.
John Murrow,	July 16, 1778,	3 years,	Do.
Samuel White,	Sept. 25, 1777,	The war,	Do.
Jacob Paul,	June 2, 1777,	The war,	Do.
John Porter,	June 19, 1777,	The war,	Do.
Aquilla Sing,	July 18, 1778,	3 years,	Sick in Fix Hospital.
John Colby,	Aug. 10, 1778,	The war,	Present.
James Roe,	July 22, 1778,	The war,	Do.
Lewis Cornyorck,		The war,	Sick in Fix Hospital.
Charles McIver,	Aug. 2, 1778,	3 years,	Present.
James Hughes,	June 1, 1777,	3 years,	Do.
John Conner,		The war,	Do.
Nicholas Glossom,		The war,	Do.
James Lewis,		3 years,	Do.
Michael Lewis,	Sept. 17, 1778,	The war,	Do.
Isaac Garrick,	Feb. 16, 1779,	16 months,	Do.
Wm. Maloy,		3 years,	Do.
James Causey,	Sept. 5, 1778,	3 years,	Do.
Denis Ch loque,		The war,	Deserted.
Joseph Antonio,	Sept. 17, 1778,	The war,	Do.
Samuel Hickman,	July 21, 1778,	3 years,	On Detachment.
Robert Wil iam,	May 28, 1778,	The war,	Do.
Hill Hewet,	June 2, 1777,	3 years,	Do.
Nicholas Prince,	Aug. 3, 1778,	3 years,	Absent on Duty.
Samuel Jefft,	July 16, 1778,	The war,	Sick in Gen. Hospital.
William Read, Drummer,	Sept. 21, 1777,	The war,	Sick in Fix Hospital.
Wm. Fleming, Fifer,		The war,	Present.

Present.—Captains, 1; Capt.-Lieutenants, 1; 1st Lieutenant, 1; Sergeant-Major, 1; Sergeants, 1; Corporals, 2; Fifers, 1; Gunners, 3; Matrosses, 19.

Absent.—Sergeants, 1; Corporals, 1; Drummers, 1; Gunners, 1; Matrosses, 7.

I do swear that the within Muster Roll is a true state of the Company, without fraud to the United States, or to any individual thereof, according to the best of my knowledge.

    R. B. ROBERTS, *Capt. Artillery.*

Sworn before me this 19*th March,* 1779,

  J. WISE.

Then mustered as certified by

    F. BREMAR, *Deputy Muster Master.*

C. PINCKNEY, JUN., TO MRS. C. PINCKNEY.

[Original MS.]

CHARLESTON, March 28, 1779.

HONORED MADAM:

This is the second or third time that I have wrote you without hearing a word from you or of you, only in general that you are very well. The last was on the 20th, by your servant, Moses, which I hope you have received. Since that General Lincoln has thought proper to remove the army from Purysburgh to the two Sisters (except about three hundred left as a guard to their camp under the command of Col. Pinckney) where it seems the enemy have assembled their whole force, and from whence an easy transition may be made into this State—this movement is if possible to prevent their crossing, and keep them at bay until our army is reinforced, either by the arrival of some auxiliaries from the northward, or by a body of our militia from Orangeburgh. I am led to believe the Governor's presence will have a good effect in inducing the militia to turn out more cheerfully than they have hitherto done. We must now or never turn our thoughts entirely to war; we must rouse our spirits and sacrifice with pleasure part of our estates to secure the rest; in short we must be wanting to ourselves in nothing that may be requisite to the common safety—have we any reason or the least pretence to be excused from so doing? In what fatal tranquility did we remain when we received the intelligence of the enemy's being in possession of Savannah, the defeat at Augusta, the taking of our gallies, and other affairs of less importance. We are now sufficiently punished by the consequences of our insensibility; for had we sent speedy relief to Savannah when besieged, which the common rules of policy and prudence required the enemy would not perhaps have been in possession of it at this day; but by perpetually neglecting the present and vainly hoping, that time would adjust matters and bring them to a better issue; we have established them in a situation, that they never could have hoped to have arrived at. And yet we need not despair if we have still courage and perseverence enough to make use of the present opportunity, and by properly reinforcing our General, enable him effectually to prevent their crossing. We must all be sensible of the particular protection of Providence, in blessings so often offered; and if we make a just estimate of its repeated favors, who is there but must be touched with the highest gratitude, for our losses are only to be imputed to the little concern we have shown to prevent them; while a superior power never ceasing to protect us, does yet point out a short and secure way of repairing all our former mistakes, by every man's resolving to do his duty, thereby providing for the safety of his country, and doing all in his powor to retrieve her reputation.   Those who neglect or do not improve the favorable opportunities offered by Providence, forget the acknowledgments that are due to her, and the same imprudence which makes them unfortunate, makes them ungrateful; for in the minds of men, the last accident commonly impresses the character of misfortune or happiness upon the whole.   It is time for us to reform our false mode of reasoning and to be truly ashamed of our want of public virtue.   We should preserve at least what remains to prevent an eternal stain upon our reputation.   Nor is our interest less at stake.   For Georgia being now in their possession, what barrier have we to secure us from the conquerors?   I could mention a number of little skirmishes, that we have lately been unsuccessful in, but as the recital is disagreeable, I will pass them over.   We must surely be convinced by this time that we have been exceedingly remiss in suffering these encroachments upon our neighbours; that we have a restless and enterprising enemy to deal with, that all their present designs are levelled against this town, and that all opposition to them, tends in some degree to the safety of the State—for can any one be so weak as to imagine that they would undergo all the fatigues and hazards of a winter campaign merely to possess a few paltry posts on Savannah river, and rather not with an eye to this place?   Will they suffer us (if they can prevent it) to enjoy the advantages this town affords, and take up their quarters in a swamp? No! they endure the one that they may possess the other.   We should in time reflect, what must be the last fatal scene of the bloody tragedy, if while they act the parts of indefatigable conquerors, we remain the patient and gentle spectators of their unbounded violence.   Can any be so weak-sighted as not to see that the war is hastening to us?   It must be blindness in them, who will not perceive that the calamities, the Georgians now endure, are the same that are preparing for themselves— I fear we shall sometime or other pay very dear for those soft and easy moments we now enjoy through the fatal remissness of our present disposition.   You will perhaps say, how easy it is to find fault—that censuring is every body's talent; but that few do their duty, and that those who censure most do the least—they who deliver this opinion are commonly right; however, I shall endeavor as long as I am able to do my duty, and hope that in a little time the major part of my countrymen will do the same.   My compliments to my cousin, conclude me

Your affectionate nephew,

CHARLES PINCKNEY, Jr.

ANDREW PICKENS TO CAPT. JOHN IRVIN.

[Original MS.]

April 12, 1779.

SIR :

It is the Governor's orders that two-thirds of the militia of this State be embodied, and Gen. Williamson's orders to me, to embody the same number of this regiment. You will, therefore, order one-third part of your company, with yourself, to join me on Friday, the 16th inst., on horseback, at Cowan's Ferry, well armed; and those who neglected going with your lieutenant when ordered, you will bring with you, that they may be dealt with as the law directs. You will bring an exact list of your company, as I am ordered to make a return of the payment.

I am, sir, your most humble servant,

ANDREW PICKENS.

ANDREW PICKENS TO CAPT. JOHN IRVIN.

[Original MS.]

March 14, 1779.

SIR :

I wrote you a few days ago to reinforce Colonel Williams at Ninety-Six with twenty-five men from your company; but, as I have just got orders from Gen. Williamson to march a strong party of my regiment to Cowan's Ferry, on Savannah river, you will, therefore, march with two parts of your company to that place, to be there on Wednesday next, the 17th inst., armed and accoutred, with good horses. I have wrote to Col. Williams to let your men come home, though you had better see him yourself. I hope you will be spirited in this matter.

I am, sir, your most humble servant,

ANDREW PICKENS.

[Original MS.]

We, the subscribers, being duly sworn, have appraised and valued the undermentioned horses at the price opposite each proprietor's name, being on scouting duty under Col. Benj. Garden, 26th May, 1779:

8

Jacob Wincklers, 1 horse,..	$ 400
Abraham Bininger, do.,..	450
David Hardstone, do.,..	500
Mr. Philips, two mares, at $400 cach,....................	800
J. J. Hardstone, 1 horse,....................................	650
Robert Brown, do.,...	500
Josiah Dupont, do.,..	450
Henry Talbird, ditto,..	800
Major Butler, two horses,...................................	2400
G. Hipp, two horses, $450 and $600,.......................	1050
Mr. Ferguson, one horse,....................................	450
Mr. Irvine, do.,..	750
Richard Dawson, do., P. B.,.................................	200
Chas. Devant, do.,...	250
Chas. Rankins, do.,..	700

A. CHIFFELLE.

JAS. BAILLEY.

JAMES WILLIAMS TO HIS WIFE.

[Original MS.]

CAMP, HEAD-QUARTERS, June 3, 1779.

MY DEAR:

I have nothing more than I have enclosed of the 1st instant. As to the news, our army is very strong, and in high spirits. There was a probability of an action the other day, and it appeared to be the hearty desire of every man to come to action; but it was not thought expedient by the General, and we returned to camp. We are now laying in camp, where I expect to lay for several days. As to particulars, I refer you to Major Gillam. 1 desire that Daniel will use his utmost endeavors to have the mills in the best order against harvest. I was speaking to him in regard to trying to plant that field over the road in corn; but that I submit to him, and he may do as he pleases. I hope that the utmost care will be taken by him to save the crop that is planted. My wagon that I rode in with, is at Ninety-Six; send Daniel to bring it home, and have it put under a shed. I purpose to sell it when I return home. I desire you, my dear; to send me about half-a-pound of cloves and cinnamon by Major Gillam; what I brought I have used, and find it a great help to me. The water is so bad that I make as little use of it as possible. Major Gillam has come to bring a relief for the men that are here. If it is possible, I should be glad that you could send me an under jacket, for the two that I brought with me are breaking before.

I am, dear wife, with respect, your ever loving husband till death,

JAS. WILLIAMS.

J. RUTLEDGE TO COL. GADSDEN.

[Original MS.]

CHARLES TOWN, June 12th, 1779.

SIR:

I presume the draught has been made of a fourth part of your regiment, for patrol duty, according to the directions I gave some time ago, and expected that the remainder would have been in town e'er now. I think it necessary, that a field officer should be here with them—you will be pleased to repair hither, with such of the regiment as are not to do patrol duty, as soon as possible. The persons belonging to your regiment, who have taken protection, are to be tried here by a court from that regiment. It is therefore necessary, in order that their case may be decided, that a part of the regiment should be here—you will suffer such other as Mr. Harden names to go with him on a particular piece of business, which I have committed to his charge; you will order all the evidences against the plunderers you've sent down, to repair hither immediately, that they may be brought to trial for their offences before a Court Martial.

I am, sir, your very humble servant,

J. RUTLEDGE.

JAMES WILLIAMS TO MR. DANIEL WILLIAMS.

[Original MS.]

CAMP, HEAD-QUARTERS, June 12, 1779.

DEAR SON:

This is the first chance I have had to write you. I am, by the care of Providence, in the field in defence of my country. When I reflect on the matter, I feel myself distracted on both hands by this thought, that in my old age I should be obliged to take the field in defence of my rights and liberties, and that of my children. God only knows that it is not of choice, but of necessity, and from the consideration that I had rather suffer anything than lose my birthright, and that of my children. When I come to lay down in the field, stripped of all the pleasure that my family connections afford me at home—surrounded by an affectionate wife and eight dear children, and all the blessings of life—when I reflect on my own distress, I feel for that of my family, on account of my absence from their midst; and especially for the mother, who sits like a dove that has lost its mate, having the weight of the family on her shoulders. These thoughts make me afraid that the son we so carefully nursed in our youth may do something that would grieve his mother. Now, my son, if my favor is worth seeking, let me tell you the only step to procure it is the care of your tender mother— to please her is ten times more valuable than any other favor that you could do me in my person. I hope that when you come to reflect on the duty of a son to a tender parent, you will take every step to establish that connection, which will add to my happiness; for it is a pleasure to me to know that I have a son who is able to manage my business and plantation affairs. Make it your study to be obliging to your mother, being careful not to do anything that may grieve her. Take the utmost care of every thing that falls under your care, so that you may receive, on my return, my thanks, and have the blessing of being a faithful and dutiful son to his trust. I would have you to consider yourself filling one of the most important posts that could be confided in you; and if you should manage well, it will greatly redound to your praise. After these serious thoughts, I beg that you will take these hints. In the first place, consider that the eye of God is on you, and to secure His blessing is the only way to make yourself, and those that are concerned with you, happy; for to fear God is the first and great command.

The next command is, to honor thy father and mother. Now, the only way to do this, is not to do anything that will grieve or oppress them. Be kind to your brothers and sisters, and careful to manage the business to the interest of the family. Your care and good conduct in the management of my plantation adds greatly to my happiness; and I can promise you, that you shall feel the good effects of it, for I have the pleasure to hear by your tender mother's letter to me, that you are doing very well, and business goes on well. I am happy to hear it. I have wrote several times about trying to get a few good horses. I expect by this time you have made the trial; if you have been success-

ful in procuring some, I shall be glad to hear how many, and what sort
they are, and I will send some good man to bring them down—if unsuccessful in your effort, no matter.   I want Nancy brought to me at that
time to ride.   Try to have the mares in as good order as possible; be
careful that they are all well fed; let them be used as little as possible.
I have traded for a fine English mare, which is on Fishing Creek, at
Mr. Wm. Adair's; the order is enclosed for her.   I wish you could
get a man to go for her, or spare the time to go yourself, as she is a
valuable animal.   If you go, Mr. Adair will, doubtless, be saying something about her.   She was taken from McGirth by Capt. Moore, and I
bought his right of her; she is a young, full-blood mare, and has no
brand on her unless Adair has branded her since she has been to his
house.   He took her up in favor of Capt. Moore, and since she was
carried from camp I traded for her.   I want her got home with as little
stir as possible, and branded on both cushions with my branding iron;
and let it be said that I bought her of a man on Fishing Creek, and paid
$1,000.   My reason for begging you to go for her is, that it may not
be known she is a plunder mare; and when we have the pleasure of
meeting, I will put you in possession of all the particulars regarding
her.   I shall be glad if you put her to the horse as soon as you get her.
On all necessary occasions get Mr. Griffin to help you about the plantation.   Regarding the horses I wrote you about, you may either come
or let it alone, just as you please, as I can send for them if you have
any agreeable to my direction.

I am sorry I have to inform you of the melancholy death of Anthony
Griffin, which took place on the 11th instant, while out with a scouting
party.   Alighting from his horse, and leaning on his gun, it accidentally went off, shooting him through the head.   He never spoke after
the accident.   This is the fatal consequence of handling guns without
proper care; they ought to be used with the greatest caution.   The
uncertainty of life ought to induce every man to prepare for death.

As for news, I have nothing more to communicate than what I wrote
last to your dear mother.   I hope every thing will be done to have the
mill in as good order as possible, to grind up the wheat; and as soon
as you can, supply the saw mill with timber, as I desire it put in operation.   In regard to whiskey, I think you must raise the price of it, in
order to have things as much on an average as possible.   I think you
ought to sell it at two dollars a quart; if by retail, one dollar a half
pint.   Secure all you can at £35 per 110 gallons.   I am in hopes of
being at home by the 1st July, to see my family.   I shall be glad to
hear from you by every opportunity.   Son, I think if you manage mat-

ters well, and I am spared, I can put affairs in such a state that, under the blessing of God, we may stand in as good a position as any family in the State. Pray, let no pains be spared to make every edge cut, and have the crops secured in the best manner, as much depend on them.

Now, my son, I must bid you farewell. I commit you to the care of Providence, begging that you will try to obtain that peculiar blessing. May God bless you, my son, and give you grace to conduct yourself, in my absence, as becomes a dutiful son to a tender mother and the family. I am in reasonable good health at present, and the regiment as much so as could be expected. The death of Griffin is much lamented. I hope in God this will find you, my son, and your dear mother and the children, all well. My best compliments to you all, and all enquiring friends.

I am, dear son, with great respect, your affectionate father,

JAS. WILLIAMS.

J. RUTLEDGE TO COL. GARDEN.

[Original MS.]

JUNE 17, 1779.

SIR :

It will be necessary that you send down as soon as you can, the witnesses against the several prisoners brought by Lieut. Cone, that they may be brought to trial, by a Court Martial, which they cannot be without the witnesses being here. Be pleased to cause the proclamations herewith sent to be made known in the district of your regiment.

I am sir, your humble servant,

J. RUTLEDGE.

TO COL. BENJAMIN GARDEN.

[Original MS.]

SALTKETCHER, June 26, 1779.

SIR :

I have sent you down two prisoners, one Gunrod Beasinger, a deserter from the third regiment, and has been deserted for this twelve month and better, and by what I can learn was at the taking of our guard at Savannah River. The other is one John Martias, a Spaniard, who has lately stole a beef from Thomas Bass, and was found in his possession and by the account of this Beasinger, has supplied the out-lyers with beef for this sometime past. I have an account of two companies of out-lyers in the swamp, and will do my endeavor to have them taken or killed this week. I shall be much obliged to you, if you will send me up two or three pounds of lead, as I am in great want at present, and also to acquaint me in what manner I can get provisions for my horses, as I know of a great deal, but can't get it without a proper authority from you.

I am, sir, your most obedient humble servant,

JOHN CONE.

P. S.—As you desired me to take an account of the women and children in distress for provisions, I know of a great many families that are entirely out; therefore would be glad if you would send me word how they may be supplied.

J. FURGUSON TO COL. B. GARDEN.

[Original MS.]

JULY 4, 1779.

SIR :

I herewith send by the bearer for some powder, ball, buck-shot and flints; likewise the rum you mentioned to me yesterday. Our people here complain very hard of their duty being every night on guard and then they say if they were safe from the enemy they would not think much of the duty, hard as it is, but every night expect to be surprised. They go so far as to declare they will not stay without more assistance, so that they may have three sentries of a night. I am willing to comply with any orders whatever, but at the same time I can't think but there is a good deal of danger in our situation, there being no guard in all the Creek but ours, and if Mrs. Page once knows our situation, she will do her endeavors to let the enemy know, and I don't know of any way to prevent her from sending, as the river is so wide she may send in the night and our sentry never the wiser of it.

I am, sir, your most obedient humble servant,

J. FERGUSON.

P. S.—Send some paper for cartouches.

GEORGE HIPP TO COL. BENJAMIN GARDEN.

[Original MS.]

JULY 10, 1778.

SIR:

Your last orders to me was to keep only one fourth of the company on duty; the rest were sent to you, now most of them are returned (as they tell me from Charles Town); should be glad to know what is to be done with them. I have ordered them on duty in different parts of the district, and shall be glad to have your approbation; we are surrounded on all sides by the enemy. I have put a Sergeant and six men at Shubrick's Cliff; a Sergeant and ten men on the river May; and am myself with ten men at Colleton's Bluff, the mouth of Oakety Creek. Mr. Guerard's school master has lately come over to the Barony, and carried off a handkerchief full of indigo, and told the negroes he intended coming for the whole shortly. I have ordered a patrol of six men to keep a look out for him; another officer is much wanted to take post on May river, from whence I have reason to think a correspondance is carried on between some of the inhabitants and Georgia. I have ordered Mr. Pendarvis to you for trial. He has certainly taken the oath, and there are some returned from town that have taken it—say Joseph Sealey, John Kerr, and Thos. Scott—they took protection from Capt. Thacher at Purysburgh, and all that took protection from him were sworn as likewise those that went to stone the Capt. of the Galley at Purysburgh. None mind the oath but those that went to Major Vanbram at Ebenezer, and they all got printed certificates. There is a continual concourse of small craft (such as sloops and schooners) going to and fro, through Scull Creek. A small galley (such as one of the trading boats would make that are laying in New River) would annoy them much and might have a safe retreat up to Pring's Creek, should any thing too hard for her come against her.

I am sir, your most obedient humble servant,

GEO. HIPP.

J. RUTLEDGE TO COL. GARDEN.

CHARLES TOWN, July 27, 1779.

SIR:

As your regiment may be more usefully employed at present near Savannah river, to guard their settlements and prevent the depredations of the enemy in that part of the country, than by acting with the continental troops under Col. Pinckney; you will be pleased to make the best disposition of it, for that purpose.

I am, sir, your most humble servant,

J. RUTLEDGE.

DR. RAMSAY TO HON. WILLIAM HENRY DRAYTON.

[Original MS.]

CHARLESTOWN, September 1, 1779.

DEAR SIR:

Your favor of July 18th,.came safe to hand on the 16th of August. A hurry of business prevented my acknowledging the receipt of it sooner.

Our Assembly is now drawing near to the close of a long session. Little business is yet completed. A tax bill of twenty-one dollars a head has been read twice. A bill for filling our regiments by giving a negro bounty to every volunteer recruit, has also been read twice. This measure is now our *ultima spes.* Money will not procure soldiers. The militia will not submit to a draught; it has been once carried in the House to put them under Continental articles; but the friends of this measure, fear that it will be lost on the next reading. The patriotism of many people is *vox et præterea nihil.* The measure for embodying the negroes had about twelve votes; it was received with horror by the planters, who figured to themselves terrible consequences. Next Friday is set apart to choose a new delegate in the room of Mr. Lowndes, when it is probable that Mr. E. Rutledge will be chosen. Mr. A. Middleton will set out in a few weeks. Most people expect the enemy here in October or November, and yet we are half asleep. When the campaign closes to the northward, it will be easy for them to send a few thousands of a reinforcement to their troops in Savannah. Our back country is much disaffected especially at the high price of salt, which is 60 dollars a bushel. We mean to solicit aid from the grand army. I wish you would send us two thousand Continentals immediately. You know the importance of Charlestown; it is the *vinculum* that binds three States to the authority of Congress. If the enemy posses themselves of this town, there will be no living for honest whigs to the southward of Santee; at present, nothing is wanting to put them in possession of it, but vigor and activity on their part. A spirit of money-making has eaten up our patriotism. Our morals are more depreciated than our currency. It is with great pleasure I receive your letters, and I shall be always ready to acknowledge them.

Yours,

DAVID RAMSAY.

W. CROGHAN TO MR. GRATZ.

[Original MS.]

CAMP SMITH'S CLOVE, Sept. 13, 1779.

DEAR SIR:

We arrived in those disagreeable mountains about two weeks ago, from the mouth of the Clove, where our chief employment is to repair the roads, and keep them in good order, which is a very difficult task.

By various accounts from New York, we have every reason to believe the enemy intend an embarkation of a great part of their troops. It is generally believed they are destined for the West Indies, from the quantity of summer clothing the officers are getting made, and other reasons.

I much fear if the enemy don't soon embark that it won't be in my power to accompany you to Virginia, as a number of officers have applied for leave of absence for a few months, but to no effect; they can't get liberty until the close of the campaign. Indeed, 'tis very few who would ask for it, if their business was not very urgent. If you think my going to Virginia would be of any service with respect to the Colonel's claims, let me know as soon as you can, by post or otherwise, and in what respect I can be of assistance, as it might be necessary for me to show that part of your letter to the General which would mention the necessity of my going. I had a few lines from the Colonel's man, James, informing me of his being very unwell. Pray, let me hear from you soon, and say how the old gentleman is, and if he purposes going to Virginia. I am, dear sir, your most obedient humble servant,

W. CROGHAN.

COL. WILLIAMS TO MRS. WILLIAMS.

[Original MS.]

CAMP 40 MILES FROM SAVANNAH, Sept. 30, 1779.

DEAR WIFE:

I wrote a letter last night to you, my love, that gave you the best intelligence that I have been able to get. I have every reason to believe that the matter is settled before this; and as you may in confidence depend that whenever I am able to get the truth of matters I will transmit it to you, by express. I beg that you may bear with fortitude my absence; and let us with humble confidence rely on Him that is able to protect and defend us, in all danger, and through every difficulty; but, my dear, let us, with one heart, call on God for his mercies, and that his goodness may be continued to us, that we, under his blessing, may have the happiness of enjoying each other's society once more.

I mentioned in my last letter about the salt. I beg that you may have it well dried and ground in the mill and then you are to sell it for one hundred dollars per bushel. Let Sam have the wheat sown as soon as possible, and I beg that you may take a little time to see about the plantation, and make Samuel do what is best to be done. As to Lea, I hope you will let no one have her without an order from me in writing, and signed by me. My compliments to you, my dear, and my children and friends.

I am, dear wife, with great respect,
your ever loving husband, until death,
JAS. WILLIAMS.

COL. JAMES WILLIAMS TO GEN. WILLIAMSON.

[Original MS.]

MOUNT PLEASANT, January 4, 1780.

DEAR SIR:

I received your favor by master George, and have carefully observed the contents. I have had a Captain, one Sergeant, and 8 picked men out in the upper part of my regiment for some time, in order to prevent those fellows from plundering the good people, and to have them taken and brought to justice. I am about to try to embody a part of the regiment to send to town; how they will turn out I can't tell, but I fear but poorly. I have made it as public in these parts, as possible, about the Governor promising to get salt for the back country; and it has given some satisfaction to the people—but at present it is bad, for many a poor man is obliged to turn out his hogs for the want of salt. To my knowledge some people must suffer greatly. I have sent a pay bill of Capt. I. Gray's with Mr. McNear to get the money, and should take it as a singular favor if it could be got. The Captain deserted his country, and the men will probably lose their money, and I am likely to be a great loser by it myself. I have advanced a great part of their wages to them myself. If I could get the money, I am going to that part of the regiment, and will settle with every man myself. If it is possible, I should be glad to get the money, as I am going to that part of the regiment the latter end of this week.

I am, dear sir, your most respectful and humble servant,

JAS. WILLIAMS.

————

JOURNAL OF THE SIEGE OF CHARLESTON BY THE ENGLISH IN 1780. THE ARMY COMMANDED BY GEN. SIR HENRY CLINTON, AND THE FLEET BY ADMIRAL ARBUTHNOT. THE GARRISON BY MAJOR-GENERAL LINCOLN.

[Original MS.]°

February 9, 1780.

The English fleet arrived in Stono Inlet; the alarm was fired in Charlestown.

10th.—The troops landed.

March 9 and 10, 1780.

Seven vessels were sunk near the mouth of Cooper River, and cables fixed from one to the other, to prevent the entrance of this river.

13th.—The enemy took possession of the land on Ashley River opposite the town, constructed a battery near the mouth of Wappoo, on the prolongation of Tradd street.

21st.—The English fleet passed the bar, and anchored in Five Fathom Hole.

25th.—Our armed vessels before Fort Moultrie returned to town; their cannon were transported into the land batteries.

29th.—The English army crossed Ashley River twelve miles above the town.

30th.—The advanced guard of the enemy came within two miles of Charlestown, when a party of two hundred men, under Colonel John Laurens (and a little while after two field-pieces), went out against them, who, after a skirmish of some hours, returned towards sun-set. The fortifications of Charlestown were, even at this time, very incomplete. All the negroes in town were impressed, who, together with the parties detailed from the garrison, were henceforth employed upon the works.

31st.—At day-break we observed that the enemy had opened his trenches in three places.

————

* The original is in French, and was kept by DeBrahm, an engineer. The translation was made and furnished me by Col. Jas. Ferguson, of Dockon.

April 1 and 2, 1780.

The enemy's works were a little extended, and ours augmented.

3d.—This morning the battery was discovered upon a height,. at Hampstead. A battery of four pieces was constructed on our right to oppose that of the enemy, from which, as well as from all the others, a continued firing of shot and bombs was kept up the following night along the lines.·

4th.—This morning, daylight discovered to us the enemy's battery very much injured.

5th.—Last night's fire of our batteries was kept up as heretofore. The enemy's galley approached the town, and fired upon it all night. We began to dig wells in our front, and to close up the gorge of the horn work.

6th.—The fire of the batteries and the works continued as before. To-day the reinforcement under General Woodford arrived.

7th.—Very little fire from our batteries last night, and more on the part of the enemy. The enemy has prolonged the right of his first parallel. All our workmen employed digging wells.

8th.—Last night the enemy commenced a battery of six pieces. All our workmen employed making traverses. A quarter of an hour before sun-set, the English fleet passed Fort Moultrie, under a heavy fire on both sides, and anchored in a line near Fort Johnson. Nobody wounded or killed in Fort Moultrie. The fleet consisted of the following vessels:—One of 50 guns, two of 40, four frigates, two vessels armed *en flute,* and two other smaller ones; one of these armed *en flute* grounded on a bank called "The Green."

· 9th.—The vessel which grounded was abandoned, and burnt by the crew last night. This morning the commencement of a battery appeared in front of our left. Our workmen employed as heretofore.

10th.—The works of the enemy were advanced. Our negroes employed in making a battery of five pieces in redoubt, and the soldiers on fatigue in making traverses. This evening a parley was received from the enemy, demanding the surrender of the town; it was refused.

11th.—Our batteries kept .up a great deal of fire last night. The enemy had repaired his batteries, and mounted some cannon. Finished the battery in the redoubt. Our workmen employed in making traverses, and strengthening the profiles of some works. This evening Major Gilbank was accidentally killed, making some experiments with shells.

12th.—Very little firing last night. The enemy.had more cannon mounted. The workmen employed as before. Our sailors employed in elevating the parapet near Exchange Battery, and making embrasures to it. At 12 o'clock, meridian, three chalops passed Fort Moultrie, and joined the fleet, although fired upon all the time by the Fort.

13th.—Very little firing last night. This morning one of the batteries of the enemy was finished, the others not quite; the trenches extended. This morning, at 9 o'clock, the enemy opened his batteries, firing bombs, carcasses and hot balls, which were returned with all our force from the batteries. This lasted about two hours, when the firing was abated on both sides, till about 5 o'clock, when all the fire was on the side of the enemy. We had one 18 pounder dismounted, and two houses burnt in town. Our workmen employed as before.

14th.—A slow fire was kept up on both sides last night. The approaches of the enemy a little advanced. The enemy's galley fired all night. He commenced another battery opposite the town, on the banks of Ashley River.

15th.—Fire from the batteries and works as before. The enemy had a bomb battery. His second parallel commenced, and manned by the Chasseurs, who kept up a continued fire upon our lines.

16th.—In addition to his usual fire, the enemy opened his new battery. Last night we extended from our redoubt a counter-mine with a small parallel whence we could return the fire of the enemy's musketry. This evening one of our Gallies ascended Cooper river to a place whence she enfiladed the English camp for several hours, which was briskly answered by field pieces from the camp.

17th.—The enemy enfiladed the town on all sides last night and threw a great quantity of bombs—sometimes from fifteen to twenty at once. We worked upon our counter mine. We received intelligence from our detachment at Lamprieres, that one thousand or fifteen hundred of the enemy under General Lord Cornwallis had passed Monk's Corner, Strawberry, Bonneau's Ferry, and Wappetaw, and actually arrived within six miles of the said post. This morning the enemy's second parallel was prolonged towards our left, supplied with bags of earth and full of Chasseurs.

18th.—Fire from the batteries as heretofore, and a shower of musketry all day; this day like last night very rainy.

19th.—Fire from the batteries as heretofore. This evening three of the enemies Gallies descended from Wappoo down Ashley river to the Fleet under a heavy fire from our battaries; one lost her main mast. This night the communication is made from the battery of the French sailors to the town.

20th.—Fire from the batteries as ordinary. This evening the Ravelin commenced in front of the horn work.

21st.—Fire from the batteries as ordinary. This morning the enemy had commenced two batteries, near his second parallel.

22d.—Fire from the batteries as ordinary; and from the musketry more than ever. This morning a parley was sent to the enemy and the answer returned about 9 o'clock in the evening.

23d.—Fire from the batteries as ordinary. The enemy extended the saps of his second parallel.

24th.—Fire from the batteries as ordinary. This morning at daybreak, a party of two hundred men under Col. Henderson made a sortie upon the enemies works which caused a general fire of musketry on both sides. The party returned in a little while with twelve prisoners. Our loss was one Captain and one soldier killed.

25th.—As ordinary. Last night Col. Parker of the Virginia line was killed by a musket shot.

26th.—As ordinary. The enemy commenced his third parallel. Troops from a vessel and four gallies, landed at Mount Pleasant, and took possession of a battery of one piece, losing one galley in this affair.

27th.—As ordinary.

28th.—As ordinary. Last night our Fort at Lamprier's was evacuated, and taken possession of by the enemy to-day. It was not until this moment that Charlestown was completely invested; the enemy having possession of James Island, Wappoo, Charlestown Neck, Hobcaw Point, Lamprieres, and Haddrell's Point; and his fleet anchored in the Road-stead before the town.

29th.—As ordinary. The enemy's third parallel almost finished, and a battery commenced; as likewise a redoubt on our side.

30th.—As ordinary.

May 1st, 2nd, and 3rd.—As ordinary. Our hospital ship taken by the English and carried higher up the river.

4th, 5th, and 6th.—The enemy employed in making three batteries upon his third parallel. And we to make two redoubts.

7th.—This morning at eight o'clock Fort Moultrie capitulated. A sixty-gun ship joined the English Fleet.

8th.—As ordinary. Another redoubt was commenced last night in rear of our left line. This morning the enemy sent a parley again to demand the town—the truce was prolonged throughout the whole day. In a Council of War composed of all the officers of the General Staff, it was resolved by a majority of votes, to propose a capitulation.

9th.—The enemy had cannon mounted in the batteries of his third parallel.* The two commanders not agreeing upon the terms of capitulation the siege commenced this evening at nine o'clock with greater warmth than ever.

May 10th.—As ordinary.

11th.—As ordinary. The enemy's trenches are extended under the abbatis of the advanced battery. This afternoon a parley was sent to the enemy to propose fresh terms of capitulation.

12th.—The terms were accepted, and the English army took possession of the town. The English have worked very hard upon the fortifications. All that I can learn is, that they have strengthened the profiles of the lines; that they have constructed a Fort at Hampstead very nearly upon the plan herewith, marked with dotted lines; and some redoubts more advanced; they have also commenced a battery on Shultz's Folly—but the foundation is scarcely raised.

J. RUTLEDGE TO B. G.

[Original MS.]

CHARLES TOWN, Feb. 12th, 1780.

SIR:

I desire that you will immediately embody one-third of your regiment and procure as many volunteers as you can from it, properly armed and prepared to proceed, and send a Field Officer with them to Charles Town, with the utmost despatch.

I am in haste, sir,
your most obedient servant,
J. RUTLEDGE.

P. S.—Volunters serving as drafted militia shall have the same pay and allowance of salt, as these militia. Pray have the inclosed resolutions generally and speedily made known throughout your regiment.

---

* That it was for the purpose of mounting these cannon that the English proposed the truce I do not pretend to say, but this much is certain, that had it not been for the truce, this would have been a very laborious and dangerous job, and almost impracticable.

J. RUTLEDGE TO COL. GARDEN.

[Original MS.]

CHARLES TOWN, March 2, 1780.

SIR :

I desire that you will immediately cause the contents of this letter and the enclosed Proclamation to be circulated, and generally made known throughout the district of your regiment, in order that deliuquents and offenders may be made known of the consequences which will ensue from a neglect or refusal of their duty to the State. You are to order one-half of your regiment immediately to this town, and transmit to me as soon as possible a list of those who are, or may be drafted or ordered to march, to the end that it may be known who are defaulters to be effected by the Proclamation, which they may be assured will be carried into execution. People may be satisfied that the small pox is not in town, but if it was, I should not admit the circumstance as an excuse for the militia not coming down when ordered; if they will not come, they must abide the present as well as future consequences. I repeat in the most positive and peremptory terms, that I must have one-half of your regiment here, with the utmost expedition; that part of the regiment which remains in the district are to do patrol duty, for keeping the negroes in order, and be employed in suppressing any insurrections of the disaffected and in apprehending and securing persons who go about (as I am informed many do) making it their business to propagate false news, spread groundless reports, and sow discontent among the people; such persons are to be safely conveyed to me, with the witnesses against them. I shall expect the utmost exertions of yourself, and the officers under you, to carry every part of these orders strictly and speedily into execution.

I am, sir, your very humble servant,

J. RUTLEDGE.

W. CROGHAN TO MR. MICHAEL GRATZ.

[Original MS.]

CHARLESTOWN, S. C., April 8, 1780.

DEAR SIR :

I arrived here about ten days ago, when I had an opportunity of seeing the enemy at one view, both by land and water. We had one

9

small skirmish with the infantry, but nothing of consequence done. They have been throwing up works, and making nightly approaches on this city for some nights past; their lines are now about six hundred yards off; but I expect they are now approaching much nearer, as eleven sail of their line, this afternoon, with a fair wind, passed Fort Sullivan (now Fort Moultrie), under an exceeding heavy fire. We don't know what injury they sustained, further than our seeing one of their masts shot away. They now lay just out of cannon shot from town; but we expect if the wind continues fair, that they and their army will attack us early to-morrow morning, when they, doubtless, will meet with a very warm reception from our batteries, which are well constructed, have heavy metal, and well pointed, which we have convinced their army of for some days past, having fired pretty constant at their new works. The army and citizens are in high spirits, and have no doubt of their being able to defend the city, and make Sir Henry again give up the thought of taking it. I am uncertain where your brother is, otherwise should write him. Please present my best compliments to Mrs. and Miss Gratz. I am much fatigued, and determined to try if the enemy will let me sleep half-an-hour. I fear they won't, for now a heavy fire begins at Fort Moultrie. I am at a loss to know the reason.

I have wrote Col. Croghan, and hope he may receive the letter, as I have enclosed him one from his son-in-law, which a Mr. Cowen, formerly of Lancaster, gave me.

I am, your most obedient,

W. CROGHAN.

THOMAS PINCKNEY TO HIS MOTHER.

[Original MS.]

FORT MOULTRIE, April 10, 1780.

HONORED MADAM:

When I went to town yesterday, I found our works as strong as the high ideas which had been raised of them by report had made me figure them to myself. I likewise saw every part of them thronged with men, and matters in general in the best posture for a vigorous defence. I heard it reported that the Governor is shortly to take the field and draw down as many of our country militia into a camp to be formed somewhere on this side of the country as he can collect, as our militia in general cannot be prevailed on to come into town, and it is hoped this measure will be productive of very good consequences. The enemy continue their approaches but slowly; none of their works are nearer than 600 yards from our lines. Their men-of-war continue opposite to Fort Johnson. Their Admiral's ship was so much damaged as to be obliged to continue on the careen, part of two days, in order to repair.

The North Carolina and Virginia troops which cannot now be at a very great distance, together with such of our country militia as the Governor may collect, will, it is thought, be sufficient to oblige the enemy to raise the siege, or at all events will much incommode them and in the end render their repulse the more certain.

I remain, dear mother, sincerely your affectionate and dutiful son,

THOMAS PINCKNEY.

[Original MS.]

April 14, 1780.

SIR:

As I think it proper to form a respectable camp on the north side of Santee River, at Col. Macdonald's plantation, called Wright's Bluff, near the road leading from Manigault's and Gaillard's ferries to Camden, as soon as possible, (not only to cover and secure the country, but to proceed towards Charlestown, in order to compel the enemy to raise the siege of that place), I desire you will use your utmost endeavors to meet me there with as many volunteers as you can collect; but if they should not amount to a third, with one-third (to be drafted) of your regiment, properly armed and accoutred, as soon as they can be resembled. I persuade myself that a consideration of the important service which this measure may render, will induce you to use your utmost exertions to procure the men, and then to turn out cheerfully and speedily on this occasion, especially as the circumstances to which the country militia seem averse, viz.—the being confined in town, will not happen—for I don't mean to lead them thither. There are, I hope, men enough in town to defend it against an attack; but I think we should relieve our brethren there by obliging the enemy to give up the siege, and deliver the State from the calamities of war, by forcing the enemy to abandon the country, which, as I expect considerable aid from the northward, I doubt not they will soon be under the necessity of doing, if our militia will exert themselves as they ought. You will bring with you all the waggons, cattle and provisions, you can collect, but don't delay your march unnecessarily to wait for them. Dispatch is essential.

I am, sir, your very humble servant,

J. RUTLEDGE.

J. RUTLEDGE TO COL. GOODWYN.

[Original MS.]

GEORGE TOWN, April 24, 1780.

SIR:

I think it proper to acquaint you, and I desire that you will immediately make it known, throughout your regiment, that I expect to be
met by the full number which I have called for, from it, at Wright's
Bluff, with the utmost expedition, and that every defaulter may be
assured, that my Proclamation of last month, shall most certainly be
carried strictly into execution against him. As a further means of putting those who may not incline to come out, in a way of rendering service to their country, which perhaps, they may do, when they have left
their own homes, and joined the army, that I hope to have soon collected, I desire that you will cause those, who from love and zeal for
their country, march readily to bring with them, as many as they possibly can, of such as are lukewarm, or desirous of remaining inactive,
rather than of defending the State. I rely on your utmost exertions to
procure the force required, as soon as possible.

And am, sir, your most obedient servant,

J. RUTLEDGE.

P. S.—You will immediately appoint Commissioners (men of integrity and judgment,) in the district of your regiment, to make provision,
at the public expense, for the subsistence of such families as may suffer
by their parents or husbands being absent on militia duty.

———

[An Old Orderly Book.]

April 24, 1780.

In the morning, at the appearing of day-light, 300 men from Gen.
Hogan's and Gen. Woodford's and Gen. Scott's brigades, and twenty-one
men from the South Carolina Continentals, sallied out on an intrench-
ment which the enemy had thrown up in the night, and killed and took
prisoners to the amount of sixty men, only twelve of whom were brought
alive into lines, three or four being mortally wounded with bayonets.
Col. Henderson, from Virginia, had the command of our troops, and
made the men march up to these works, with their priming thrown out,
and gun cocks let down. Our men behaved with the greatest bravery
and good conduct. Our loss consisted of only 1 colonel
killed, and three privates wounded.   THOS. ——

W. CROGHAN TO MR. MICHAEL GRATZ.

[Original MS.]

CHARLESTOWN, May 18, 1780.

DEAR SIR:

I am just now going to cross the river to Haddrell's Point, where I am to remain on parole within the space of six miles—our army being under the necessity of surrendering this town to the British forces the 12th of this month. The bearer, Major Rice, is aid-de-camp to Gen. Lincoln, and can give you every information concerning this town. I suppose you will be informed of our supporting this town while we had provisions to live on, or a prospect of a reinforcement of troops. We have no Continental troops but the Virginians, Hogan's, and three South Carolina regiments. We had but very few militia. The majority of them are citizens of this town. We had a heavy and pretty constant fire from our side six weeks, and from the enemy twenty-nine days; not many lives lost on our side. The second day after the enemy took the town, their magazine blew up by accident, which destroyed all the arms they received from us, and near a hundred lives.

Pray, present my best compliments to Col. Croghan, and let him know I have wrote the Major, his son-in-law. Compliments to Mrs. and Miss Gratz.

I am, with much respect, your most obedient servant,

W. CROGHAN.

RETURN OF THE NUMBERS OF THE SOUTH CAROLINA LINE WHO APPEARED ON PARADE AND WERE MUSTERED MAY 27, 1780.

	No.	Pres. May 30.		No.	Pres. May 30
Pulaski's Dragoons,	6	4	Artillery, South Carolina,	43	28
Horry's Dragoons,	22	19	Artillery, North Carolina,	20	18

FIRST REGIMENT OF SOUTH CAROLINA TROOPS.

	No.	Pres. May 30.		No.	Pres. May 30
Light Infantry,	28	7	Capt. Gadsden,	14	13
Capt. Turner's,	18	15	Capt. Williamson,	23	14
Capt. Theu's,	18	8	Capt. Levarher,	15	11
Capt. Elliott,	23	18	Capt. Jackson,	18	6
Capt. Linning,	25	21			

SECOND REGIMENT OF SOUTH CAROLINA TROOPS.

	No. May 30.	Pres.		No. May 30	Pres.
Light Infantry,	30	12	Capt. Mason,	9	4
Capt. Mazyck,	17	4	Capt. Grey,	19	13
Capt. Shubrick,	19	11	Capt. Baker,	15	8
Capt. Prevaux,	18	9	Col. Company,	21	9
Capt. George Warley,	20	11			

THIRD REGIMENT OF SOUTH CAROLINA TROOPS.

	No. May 30.	Pres.		No. May 30	Pres.
Light Infantry,	26	8	Capt. Baker's,	15	5
Capt. Felix Warley's,	24	9	Capt. Faran's,	15	2
Capt. Joseph Warley's,	16	2	Capt. Liddell's,	17	5
Capt. Goodwyn's,	19	4	Capt. Pollard's,	9	7
Capt. Buchanan's,	17	5			

W. CROGHAN TO MR. MICHAEL GRATZ.

[Original MS.]

CHARLESTOWN, S. C., June 12, 1780.

DEAR SIR:

I before informed you that this day month we were under the necessity of surrendering this town to the British army. I suppose you are furnished with the articles of capitulation, and our reasons for giving it up, ere now. We flatter ourselves our friends to the northward will say we maintained the post as long and well as people in our situation could. I am on parole at Haddrell's Point (with the other Continental officers who were taken prisoners) in sight of town. I came here a few days ago to see Major Provost, who has set out for Savannah for Mrs. Provost, who is to remain here with him.

Colonel Nevill is lying in sight of me, bad with the gout.

I expect to have my parole extended to go to Pennsylvania very soon. Please present my best respects to Mrs. and Miss Gratz.

I am, dear sir, your most obedient servant,

W. CROGHAN.

THOMAS JEFFERSON TO COL. WILLIAM CAMPBELL.

[Original MS.]

IN COUNCIL, June 22, 1780.

SIR:

Orders have been sent to the county lieutenants of Montgomery and Washington, to furnish 250 of their militia to proceed in conjunction with the Carolinians against the Chickamoggas. You are hereby authorized to take command of the said men. Should the Carolinians not have at present such an expedition in contemplation, if you can engage them to concur as volunteers, either at their own expense or that of their State, it is recommended to you to do it. Take great care to distinguish the friendly from the hostile part of the Cherokee nation, and to protect the former while you severely punish the latter. The Commissary and Quarter-Master in the Southern department is hereby required to furnish you all the aid of his department. Should the men, for the purpose of despatch, furnish horses for themselves to ride, let them be previously appraised, as in cases of impress, and for such as shall be killed, die, or be lost in the service, without any default in the owner, payment shall be made by the public. An order was lodged with Col. Preston for 1,000 lbs. of powder from the lead mines for this expedition; and you receive herewith an order for 500 lbs. of powder from Col. Flemings for the same purpose, of the expenditure of which you will render account.·

I am, sir, your very humble servant,

THOS. JEFFERSON.

MR. WILLIAMS TO MRS. WILLIAMS.

[Original MS.]

CAMP CATAWBA, OLD NATION, July 4, 1780.

DEAR WIFE:

My anxiety for you and my dear children, far exceeds anything that I am able to express; not knowing your distress but I trust in God that His guardian care has been over you for your protection; I have earnestly requested the favor of heaven on you. I have had some accounts from you, but they were very imperfect. I pray God that I may have the happiness of seeing you my love at Mount Pleasant in the course of this month, with a force sufficient to repel all the Tories in the upper part of South Carolina. I have been informed that many false stories are in circulation in our country to the disheartening of our friends in that quarter of the State. I give the true state of things touching our army, and you, my love, and all my friends, may depend on it to be the truth. I was at my brother's and settled my family on as good terms as possible, and left him well with his family. I left there on the 29th of last month; that day, Major General DeKalb and General Wayne and Smallwood, with the Maryland and Pennsylvania troops to the amount of 3,000, and 2,500 from Virginia, are on the march from Roxbury in order to join Major General Caswell with about 2,000 North Carolina militia, and about 200 regular light horse; on the whole, 7,700, that is now in motion, and will be at Camden in the course of six or seven days, which may put a different face on matters. And there are 5,500 Virginia militia marching that will be here shortly, (and 2,000 North Carolina militia, under General Rutherford, that is to march to Ninety-six,) with some South Carolina militia commanded by Col. Sumter, to the amount of 500, now in camp at this place, and are expected to cross the river to-day, with about 500 of the Mecklenburg militia. Over and above all these, there are 4,000 more North Carolina militia to march as soon as harvest is over. On the whole, I expect we will shortly meet the tories, when they must give an account of their late conduct. I can assure you, my dear, that there is a large French Fleet and army on our coast. I think, from these circumstances, that our affairs are in a flattering condition at present. I expect you have heard of Moore's defeat, in the fork of the Catawba by a detached party from General Rutherford, under Capt. Falls, not exceeding 350, that defeated 1300 tories, and took their baggage, with about 500 horses and saddles and guns, and left 35 on the field dead. Since that General Caswell has defeated the English at the Cheraws, and cut off the 71st Regiment entirely. I can assure you and my friends that the English have never been able to make a stand in North Carolina yet, and they have slipt their time now, for they or retreating to Charlestown with all rapidity. From this you may see, under the blessing of God that we will soon relieve our distressed families and friends; so bear up with fortitude till that happy day comes. I hope in God this will find you, my dear wife, and my children all well. My compliments to you and my children and friends that inquire after me. Myself and Capt. Hays; Daniel and the boys are all hearty; God be blest for His mercy to us.

The uncertainty of your situation is my great mortification; but let our joint prayers meet in Heaven for each other and our bleeding country. The Rev. Mr. Simson has had his house and every thing he had but the clothing the family had on destroyed, and he is in camp with me and Mr. Croghead, and is part of my family in camp. Mr. Simson, Mr. Croghead, and Capt. Hays, join me in our compliments to you, my love and friends.

1 am with great regard your loving husband till death,

JAS. WILLIAMS.

N. B.—As for family affairs do as you may think best.

GENERAL GEORGE WASHINGTON TO MAJOR LEE.

[Original MS.]

HEAD-QUARTERS, PEEKSKILL, August 5, 1780.

DEAR SIR :

I received your letter from Eastown of the 31st ult.

Before this the Quarter-Master General will have transmitted you orders. I have to request after their execution, that you will immediately repair to the main army at Dobbs' ferry, by way of the two bridges.

I am, dear sir, your obedient and humble servant,

GEORGE WASHINGTON.

WILLIAM PRESTON TO COL. WILLIAM CAMPBELL.

[Original MS.]

August 24, 1780.

I have ordered the Montgomery troops to assemble at the lead mines as soon as possible. As you are to take the command of the whole, you will please to give orders to the officers accordingly, who, with the soldiers, are hereby strictly commanded to obey such orders as they may receive from you on this tour of duty.

You may continue them on this service as long as you judge it absolutely necessary for the safety of this and our sister State of North Carolina.

I wish you every success in suppressing the internal enemies of the State.

I am, sir, your very humble servant,

WILLIAM PRESTON.

A. NASH TO COL. JAMES WILLIAMS.

[Original MS.]

HILLSBOROUGH, September 8, 1780.

SIR:

You are desired to go to Caswell county, and to such other counties as you think proper, and use your best endeavors to collect any number of volunteer horsemen, not exceeding one hundred, and proceed with them into such parts as you judge proper, to act against the enemy, and in this you are to use your own discretion. You may assure the men who turn out with you that they shall be entitled to all the advantages and privileges of militia in actual service, and that it shall be considered as a tour of duty under the militia law, they serving the time prescribed by law for otner militia men. All Commissaries, and other staff-officers, are required to grant you such supplies as may be necessary.

In getting your men, you are to make no distinction between men already drafted and others; and, in case of need, you are to impress horses for expresses, and other cases of absolute necessity.

A. NASH.

RECEIPT TO COLONEL GOODWYN.

[Original MS.]

STATE OF NORTH CAROLINA.

Received, 18th December, 1780, of Col. Goodwyn, one negro man, named Doctor; one sorrel gelding, one saddle and bridle, one cutlass, nineteen silver dollars, for the use of the public. Unless it should appear when a full investigation can be made, that Col. Goodwyn's conduct has been nowise injurious to the liberties of America, in which case I promise to have the above articles returned to said Col. Goodwyn; and I further promise to give up to said Col. Goodwyn his negro man, named as above, upon his (the said Col. Goodwyn's) depositing in my hands the sum of two hundred guineas, or twenty thousand Continental dollars, or loan-office certificates to that amount—which money shall also be returned as above.

THOS. SUMTER.

COL. CAMPBELL TO REV. MR. CUMMING.

[Original MS.]

September —, 1780.

DEAR SIR:

I got home last Monday evening from my little excursion into South Carolina, and had the happiness of finding my family in good health.

I imagine you have already heard the particulars of the action at Whitsill's Mill, on the 6th instant; and I make no doubt but those of the action near Guilford C. H., upon the 15th, will be agreeable to you. General Greene having collected an army of 4,500 men at the High Rock ford of Haw River, began his march from that place on Monday, the 12th inst., determined to give battle to the enemy on the first opportunity. General Cornwallis lay at that time within two or three miles of Guilford C. H., on a branch called Buffaloe; and upon Gen. Greene's advancing towards him, he retired into a fork of Deep River, about eight miles above the Court House. Our army, upon the evening of the 14th, got up to Guilford C. H., and encamped about a mile above it that night. Myself and Col. C. Lynch, having each of us the command of a corps of riflemen, with Lieut.-Colonels Lee and Washington, of the Light Dragoons, were that evening advanced about a mile in front of the army, and about seven miles from the enemy. Next morning early, we had intelligence of their being in motion, and marching towards us; upon which Col. Lee, with his legion, and about thirty of my riflemen, under the command of Capt. Tate, of the Augusta militia, went out to meet them, while the rest of the riflemen, and Col. Washington's horse, formed at our encampment, to support them in their retreat back. They met with the enemy near two miles from our encampment, and immediately began to skirmish them, and continued fighting and retreating for about half-an-hour, which disconcerted and retarded the enemy very considerably. In the meantime, the main body of our army was formed about three-quarters of a mile in rear of us; and upon the legions rejoining us, we were ordered back, to take our position in the line of battle. We had not been formed there above ten minutes, before the cannonade began in the centre, which lasted about twenty minutes, in which time the enemy were forming their line of battle, by filing off to the right and left, and then immediately advanced upon our troops, upon which the firing of the small arms began. The Virginia regulars and militia, with the first Maryland regiment, behaved with the greatest bravery, and the riflemen who acted upon the wings, have done themselves honor; but, unhappily, a whole brigade of the North Carolina militia, of about 1,000 men, abandoned their party from the first onset. Many of them never fired their guns, and almost the whole of them threw away their arms, and fled with the greatest precipitation. To this misfortune is attributed our being obliged to quit the field, though the battle was maintained long and obstinately. All agree that it lasted two hours and a half, and I think myself it was considerably more. The enemy followed us no further than the heights just above Guilford C. H., and our army retreated in tolerable order to Speedwell Furnace, which is about ten miles below. There the most of the troops, who were dispersed in the action, assembled next day. The enemy lay at Guilford C. H. from Thursday till Sunday, 12 o'clock, (being employed in burying their dead, and taking care of their wounded,) and that evening retreated to New Garden Court House, where they left a number of their wounded, and wrote to Gen. Greene, requesting that they might not be ill-treated by the Americans. The next day (Monday) they continued their retreat to Centre Meeting House, and next morning I left camp, and have not had any certain intelligence from them since, though I make no doubt but there has been another battle, as every person seems to believe that Gen. Greene intended a pursuit.

Very truly yours,

W. CAMPBELL.

COL. WILLIAM CAMPBELL'S ACCOUNT OF THE BATTLE OF KING'S MOUNTAIN.

[Original MS.]

WILKES COUNTY, CAMP ON BRIAR CREEK, October 20, 1780.
DEAR SIR:

Ferguson and his party are no more in circumstances to injure the citizens of America.

We came up with him in Craven county, South Carolina, posted on a height called King's Mountain, about twelve miles north of the Cherokee ford of Broad River, about two o'clock in the evening of the 7th instant, we having marched the whole night before.

Col. Shelby's regiment and mine began the attack, and sustained the whole fire of the enemy for about ten minutes, while the other troops were forming around the height upon which the enemy was posted. The firing then became general, and as heavy as you can conceive for the number of men. The advantageous situation of the enemy—being the top of a steep ridge—obliged us to expose ourselves exceedingly, and the dislodging of them was equal to driving them from strong breast-works; though, in the end, we gained the point of the ridge, where my regiment fought, and drove them along the summit, nearly to the other end, where Col. Cleveland with his country men were. There they were drove into a huddle, and the greatest confusion. The flag for a surrender was immediately hoisted; and as soon as the troops could be noticed of it, the firing ceased, and the survivors surrendered themselves prisoners at discretion.

The victory was complete to a wish. My regiment has suffered more than any other in the action. I must proceed with the prisoners until I can some way dispose of them. Probably I may go on to Richmond in Virginia.

I am, &c.,

WM. CAMPBELL, Col. Com.

COL. CAMPBELL TO THOMAS JEFFERSON.

[Original MS.]

HILLSBOROUGH, October 31, 1780.

SIR :

I came to this place last night to receive General Gates' directions how to dispose of the prisoners taken at King's Mountain, in the State of South Carolina, upon the seventh instant. He has ordered them to be taken over to Montgomery county, where they are to be secured under proper guards. General Gates transmits to your Excellency a state of the proceedings of our little party to the westward. I flatter myself we have much relieved that part of the country from its late dis-tress.

I am your Excellency's most obedient and very humble servant,

WILLIAM CAMPBELL.

RESOLUTIONS OF THE SENATE OF VIRGINIA.

[Original MS.]

IN THE SENATE, November 15, 1780.

Resolved, nemine contradicente, that the thanks of this House are justly due to Col. William Campbell, of Washington county, and the brave officers and soldiers under his command, who with an ardor truly patriotic, in the month of September last, without waiting for the call of Goverment, voluntarily marched out to oppose the common enemy, at that time making depredations on the frontiers of North Carolina, and on the seventh day of October, by a well-timed judicious. and spirited attack, with a force inferior to that of Maj. Ferguson, then advantageously posted on King's Mountain, with upwards of eleven hundred men, and by a perseverance and gallantry rarely to be met with, even among veteran troops, totally defeated the whole party; whereby a formidable and dangerous scheme of the enemy was effectually frustrated.

Test,   WILLIAM DREW, C. S.

MARTIN ARMSTRONG TO COL. WILLIAM CAMPBELL.

[Original MS]

FEBRUARY 25th, 1781.

DEAR COLONEL:

Yesterday I had an express from Col. Lock's camp; he is at the High Rock Ford on Haw River. Gen. Perkins is near Hillsborough, and by this time considerable strong; General Greene on his march towards the enemy with a number of the Virginia militia and regulars; General Butler, with the Orange district militia, lies below Hillsborough, and by every intelligence, the enemy are penned up in that town. It is generally supposed that a reinforcement is on their march to the assistance of the British; our people are gathering from all quarters, and the enemies pickets are constantly harrassed by our reconoitering parties. The arrival of your troops would add vigor to us and discourage the enemy, who, no doubt, have heard of your being on your march towards them. Pray send back this express as quick as possible; I shall endeavor to have some meat for you at Bethabara—meal and corn you can have a plenty, but meat is scarce. However, I shall try my best. This day Col. Preston, I think, will join Gen. Pickens; if any extraordinary news comes to hand before you arrive at Bethabara, I shall let you know by another express.

I am in haste, sir, your humble servant,

MARTIN ARMSTRONG.

* WILLIAM MOULTRIE TO CHARLES MONTAGUE.

HADDRELL'S POINT, March 12, 1781.

MY LORD:

I received yours this morning by Fisher. I thank you for your wish to promote my advantage, but am much surprised at your proposition. I flattered myself I stood in a more favorable light with you! I shall write with the same freedom with which we used to converse, and doubt not you will receive it with the same candor. I have often heard you express your sentiments respecting this unfortunate war, when you thought the Americans injured; but am now astonished to find you taking an active part against them; though not fighting particularly on the Continent, yet the seducing their soldiers away to enlist in the British service is nearly similar.

My Lord, you are pleased to compliment me with having fought bravely in my country's cause for many years, and, in your opinion, fulfilled the duty every individual owes to it; but, I differ very widely with you in thinking, that I have discharged my duty to my country, while it is still deluged with blood, and over-run by the British troops, who exercise the most savage cruelties. When I entered into this contest, I did it with the most mature deliberation, and with a determined resolution to risk my life and fortune in the cause.

The hardships I have gone through, I look back upon with the greatest pleasure and honor to myself; I shall continue to go on as I have begun, that my example may encourage the youths of America, to stand forth in defence of their rights and liberties! You call upon me now, and tell me, I have a fair opening of quitting that service with honor and reputation to myself, by going with you to Jamaica! Good God! is it possible that such an idea could arise in the breast of a man of honor? I am sorry you should imagine I have so little regard for my own reputation, as to listen to such dishonorable proposals! Would you wish to have that man, whom you have honored with your friendship, play the traitor? Surely not! You say, by quitting this country, for a short time, I might avoid disagreeable conversations, and might return at my own leisure, and take possession of my estates for myself and family; but, you have forgotten to tell me, how I am to get rid of the feelings of an injured, honest heart, and where to hide myself from myself! Could I be guilty of so much baseness, I should hate myself,

* Autograph letter in possession of Dr. E. Brailsford, Charleston.

and shun mankind! This would be a fatal exchange from my present situation, with an easy and approved conscience of having done my duty, and conducted myself as a man of honor.

My Lord, I am sorry to observe, that I feel your friendship much abated, or you would not endeavor to prevail upon me to act so base a part! You earnestly wish you could bring it about, as you think it will be the means of bringing about that reconciliation we all wish for. I wish for a reconciliation, as much as any man; but, only upon honorable terms! The repossessing my estates; the offer of the command of your Regiment, and the honor you propose of serving under me, are paltry considerations to the loss of my reputation! No! not the fee simple of that valuable Island of Jamaica should induce me to part with my integrity!

My Lord, as you have made one proposal, give me leave to make another, which will be more honorable to us both. As you have an interest with your commanders, I would have you propose the withdrawing the British troops from the Continent of America! allow the Independence; and propose a peace! This being done, I will use my interest, with my commanders, to accept the terms, and allow Great Britain a free trade with America.

My Lord, I could make one more proposal, but my situation as a prisoner circumscribes me within certain bounds—I must, therefore, conclude with allowing you the free liberty to make what use of this you may think proper. Think better of me.

I am, my Lord,

Your Lordship's most obedient humble servant,

WILLIAM MOULTRIE, *Brigadier General.*

WILLIAM HENDERSON TO MR. WILLIAM BUTLER.

[Original MS.]

CAMP BEFORE NINETY-SIX, June 13, 1781.

SIR:

By information I have the greatest confidence in your exertions to facilitate the peace of this country; and also hearing that there is no officer in Capt. Watson's old company, you are authorised to take command of the said company, and gather them together. With one-half you will immediately repair to camp, with the others you will lay under the charge of an officer, to guard that country from the depredations of the enemy, and to gather the grain of the whole, as I make no doubt but the harvest is on hand. All the said company are ordered and required to pay due obedience to your orders.

From your humble servant,

WILLIAM HENDERSON, *Lieut.-Col. D.*

A LIST OF MY COMPANY, MALE AND FEMALE, OLD AND YOUNG.

[Original MS.]

	For duty.	Women.	Children.	Old Men.
John Irwin, Captain,	3	2	3	0
Andrew Warnock, Lieut.,	1	2	7	1
Wm. McMahen, Lieut.,	1	1	2	0
James Buchanan, Sen.,	1	2	3	0
Alexander Moor,	0	1	1	1
Widow Thomson,	1	2	4	0
John Loagen,	3	3	4	1
Widow Loagen,	0	2	7	0
Widow Forbes,	0	1	3	0
James Huston,	1	1	1	0
Alexander McAlister,	2	1	6	0
Andrew McAlister,	0	1	2	1
Hugh Douglas,	1	1	2	0
John Buchanan,	1	1	1	0
James Moor,	1	1	0	0
James Buchanan, Jun.,	1	1	5	0
John Beaker, Sen.,	0	2	5	1
John Beaker, Jun.,	1	1	0	0
James Beaker,	1	1	2	0
John Wardlow,	2	2	11	0
William Brown,	1	4	3	1
William Thomson,	1	0	0	0
Widow Brown,	0	1	2	0
Edward Forbes,	1	1	5	0
Jacob Brondoway,	1	1	1	1
Widow Parker,	2	1	1	0
Quintan Moor,	0	1	0	1
	27	38	81	8

JOHN IRWIN.

10

WILLIAM CHRISTIAN TO COL. WILLIAM PRESTON.

[Original MS.]

MAHANAIM, Saturday June 30, 1781.

DEAR SIR:

The Assembly adjourned on this day was a week. Mr. W. Madison came from Staunton but one day before I did, and, I suppose, has given you nearly all the news I have, but, as John Young is going over, I'll write what occurs to me. Several laws are made respecting the war. The militia law is amended—martial law declared in force for 20 miles around our army and also around the enemy's—all the powers of Government necessary for calling out militia, and resources of every kind are vested in the Executive—persons suspected of disaffection may be sent to the enemy after twenty days to dispose of their property—a law is passed allowing ten thousand dollars for voluntary recruits for two years or the war. I think there are twenty-two Acts in all, but the above are the most material, except one, I just remember, for punishing those who may oppose the laws by an armed force, declaring them to be civilly dead, and their estates to descend to the next of kin.

The lowland people are as true and firm, in the interest of America as any people in it. All I saw seem to disregard property, and only talk of independence. None despair in the least. They are more engaged for the fate of South Carolina at present than Virginia. Notwithstanding the anxiety for Carolina we had no certain accounts since the 24th of May—at that time Gen. Greene lay before Ninety-six, and expected twelve days would determine its fate. Col. Knox took down a report about ten days ago that it was actually taken, and that the General with his whole army and prisoners were then at Salisbury. Capt. Sagers took down an extract of a letter said to be written by G. G. to Col. Armstrong, saying that all Carolina had fallen but Charles Town. Since I came home last Tuesday I can hear nothing at all. The Marquis de LaFayette, retreated into Culpepper, near the Court house, to meet Wayne, to save 2,500 stand of arms, coming towards Fredericksburg, and to try to save Hunter's Works. Lord Cornwallis, was steering for Fredericksburg until he took some of our Expresses, giving information about our stores at Point of Fork, soon after which he turned about to that place. The Marquis crossed the country again to Alligre's, and followed down. The last and best accounts we had this day week were that Lord Cornwallis was in Richmond, and the Marquis at a church twelve miles on this side up the Goochland road.

The Marquis said he would fight if pushed hard, but if not would wave it longer. Baron Steuben it was supposed joined last week with six hundred newly raised regulars, and as many militia raised on the south side of the river. He had retreated as far as Dan from the Point of Fork, intending for Greene, but returned as we heard. Some stores are saved, some lost. We had no certain accounts, how much either way. At Charlottesville, the damage was not great; perhaps, about three hundred guns destroyed, and some stores, but the greatest part had got out of town, and Tarlton followed but one mile up the road. Col. Boone who was with Lord Cornwallis and since paroled, thinks the enemy about 6,000. Reports call ours 7,000, and increasing. Our strength in regulars, is about 2,200—to wit : the Marquis' men, 800, Wayne's 800, and Steuben's 600. When we got a return from the Marquis, of the militia, they fell greatly short of what was reported, near half. Deserters from Lord Cornwallis, call his force 4,500 and 5,000. Reports call his horse, 700. We were told that there are companies formed for trading in negroes and shipping them to the Islands, and East Florida. The midde country will be eat out between the two armies. I think there is an equal chance for peace next winter. The Spaniards seem to be bending their whole force at Gibralter and the French at the Islands. The French had fifty and the English thirty-five line of battle ships before St. Lucia. An engagement was looked for as the French would try to take that Island. I expect none of them here now. Let me deal in Latin like A. B. and desire you to ask D. R. to English—*uti possidetis.*

Adieu,

WILLIAM CHRISTIAN.

AN ACCOUNT OF GOODS RECEIVED OF COL. WADE HAMPTON, BY THOMAS JACKSON, FOR COMPLETING HIS REGIMENT.

[Original MS.]

January 5, 1782.

Forty yards of blue flannel, twenty yards of red flannel, twenty yards of home-spun.

Made use of part of the above by order, and for the use of said Col. Hampton.

Eight yards of red flannel for lining for Colonel Hampton's cloak; six yards ditto, Thos. Singleton; four yards of home-spun, Major Boykin; two yards ditto for lining Colonel Hampton's portmanteau.

REMAINS OF THE ABOVE DUE TO COL. HAMPTON.

	£	s.	d.
Forty yards of blue flannel, at 2s. 4d.,	4	13	4
Six yards of red ditto, at 2s. 4d.,	0	14	0
Fourteen yards of home-spun, at 2s. 4d.,	1	12	8
To an account that Mr. Wm. Boykin paid to Mr. Gaunt,	10	10	0
Six gallons of train oil, at 14s.,	4	4	0
Received of John Boykin,	3	3	0
To cash you paid to David Westcott,	8	8	0
Total,	£38	5	0

ACCOUNT OF THE CASH PAID TO THE WORKMEN, AND SUNDRY ARTICLES, FOR EQUIPPING COLONEL HAMPTON'S REGIMENT OF CAVALRY.

[Original MS.]

	£	s.	d.
Paid to James Perry, saddler,	6	15	0
Paid to David Tucker,	2	2	0
Paid to John Hall, for six months' work,	18	0	0
To ten dozen of bosses, at 2s. 6d.,	1	5	0
To twelve dozen of large buckles, at 3s. 6d.,	2	2	0
To fourteen dozen of small buckles, at 3s.,	2	12	0
To eight thousand tacks, at 9s. 4d.,	3	14	8
To thirty weight of wool, at 2s. 4d,	3	10	0
To twenty-five weight of fat, at 8d.,	0	16	8
To six weight of thread, at 9s. 4d.,	2	16	0
Paid for taking the negroes when run away,	3	14	8
Paid to Mr. Gregory for ironing the negro, Quake,	0	9	4
Left unpayed for the accoutrements,	10	3	0
Balance between Quaco and Malbery,	16	0	0
Total,	92	0	4
Deduct,	18	0	0
Half,	74	4	0
	£37	0	2

GOVERNOR MATTHEWS TO GENERAL MARION.

[Horry MS.]

CANE ACRE, April 1, 1782.

SIR :

I received your letter of the —— and ——, and I now enclose you a copy of a letter from Governor Burke, which explains what Ganey has been for some time past complaining of. I hope you will pay particular attention to Gov. Burke's requisition, that none of the disaffected of his State may be suffered to harbor with Ganey and his party; and it would be well to apprize him that if, when driven out of North Carolina, they are sheltered by any of his party in this State, it will be deemed an infraction of the truce, and consequently the North Carolinians will have a right to enter the neutral ground, and apprehend the fellows wherever they are found. If it can be clearly proved that the truce has been violated on their part, how far it might be advisable for you to co-operate with the North Carolinians, and by one decisive blow crush this infamous banditti, I must leave with you to determine. As to the proposal you make respecting Maham's and Horry's corps, Gen. Greene and myself having fully considered that matter, have given you our opinion thereon, which I suppose you have received ere this. But should there be any great difficulty in carrying our determination into execution, I have no objection to adopting the mode you now propose, if Gen. Greene approves of it, except that part "to recruit Maham's corps to one hundred and twenty men," as the time of service of the men will expire in July, therefore, it would not be worth while to incur the expense. I am very glad you have got some negroes for the recruiting service. I wish Col. Grimke would continue to furnish you with them, and not wait for my orders, which I can give him hereafter, when I know the quantity delivered to you. The orders you have lately received from me renders it unnecessary to say anything now respecting Mr. Philip Porcher.

Since writing the above, I have seen Gen. Greene, and he approves of Horry's corps being continued as infantry, agreeable to your proposal.

I am, sir, your most obedient servant,

JOHN MATTHEWS.

MAJ. BURNET, AIDE-DE-CAMP, TO COL. LAURENS.

[Horry MS.]

HEAD-QUARTERS, April 2, 1782.

MY DEAR SIR:

Since the General wrote you, this morning, he has conversed with the person mentioned in his letter; he is impressed with the idea of the enemy's intending to advance immediately; preparations are making to accomplish it as early as possible. The movement towards the Santee was probably to draw the attention of part of our force to that quarter. You will join the army with the troops under your command as early as possible. Be pleased to communicate to Gen. Marion on the subject. Gen. Greene wishes to hear from you this night.

I am with sincerity yours,

J. BURNET, *Aide-de-Camp.*

GEN. GREENE TO COL. LAURENS.

[Horry MS.]

HEAD-QUARTERS, April 2, 1782.

DEAR SIR:

I have just received the enclosed note from Mrs. McQueen, and have been talking with ————. It appears the enemy have it in contemplation to attack us in our divided state; they must inevitably ruin us. You will join the army, therefore, without loss of time. I wish it was possible for Gen. Marion to take a position near Monk's Corner, that he might join us in cases of necessity. Please to write to him on the subject. Let me hear from you to-night. I did not know until this morning that you had Major Moses' command with you. I thought they had joined the line.

Yours, &c.,

NATHANIEL GREENE.

COL. MAHAM TO GEN. MARION.

[Horry MS.]

STRAWBERRY, April 4, 1782.

SIR:

I take the liberty of informing you that we pursued the enemy with my cavalry down to Haddrell's. They had all got over not more than two or three hours before we got down. I was on my return to you the next day as far as Ball's Wambaw, when I received an express from Col. Laurens, to join him as quick as possible at Strawberry Ferry. Col. Laurens has rendezvoused at Strawberry. I still remain at Col. Harleston's, near the ferry, until I hear from Col. Laurens again.

I have the honor to be your most obdt. humble servant,

W. MAHAM.

SECRET CORRESPONDENT TO GEN. MARION.

[Horry MS.]

APRIL 4, 1782.

SIR:

I forwarded you yesterday a small packet by Mr. M'Dowle, to which I refer. I am now in the country and at liberty. I must, therefore, thank you again for your kindness and attention in forwarding me a protection and for saving me from impending destruction. Your late worthy brother, whose memory I shall ever revere, I considered as my father and best friend, and esteemed him beyond all other men and yourself, by your generous conduct have laid me under such obligations as entitles you to my affection and best services. I now answer your favor of the 7th ultimo, received the 23d. When it came to hand, I resolved the subject over and over in my mind, and came to this con-clusion, that it would be impossible for me alone to carry your views into their full extent, for the following reasons:—first, Because as I followed no kind of business, the purchasing goods alone in any quantity would create suspicion; secondly, Because I am much suspected already, not by those in authority, but by busy people who are ever prying into other people's business. I have been told I am suspected, and that my conduct is watched; thirdly, Because I think I want resolution for such an undertaking, laboring as I do under a great infirmity

of face (having in all my concerns walked in a straight path), insomuch
if any danger arose, I should sink under it, if the truth was against
me.   These considerations determined me to consult a second person.
I knew of none so proper as my friend, Mr. Wm. Smith, No. 33 on
the Bay; I, therefore, in confidence made him acquainted with the
subject of your letter.   This produced a return of confidence from him,
and he acquainted me Capt. Theus had already wrote to him on the
subject, and that he had made the necessary applications; that the
answers were more favorable than he expected, and that he only waited
for an opportunity to write Capt. Theus.   I enclosed Mr. Smith's
answer to C. T. to you yesterday.   I wish it may be satisfactory.   In
my former letter I mentioned a Mr. Warrington, gone in a flag to
George Town.   He has a large stock, and I fancy has had large concerns in the country already.   I am of opinion good business may be
done with him if he is not returned.   I lament much I could not advise
you of this man before, but it was impracticable.   I am in hopes your
business may be done by mutual consent of parties; if it can, you will
be much better served, and there will be no risk, which always is great;
for only two or three days ago a vessel loaded with rum was seized at
Roper's Wharf; Capt. Keaton and Dickerson confined in the prevost,
and Mr. John McQueen obliged to abscond.   Excuse me, sir, for offering to give advice.   But, supposing Capt. Theus were to write to Mr.
Smith for such articles, as he wanted to be paid in produce, it will be
Mr. Smith's interest to serve you, or rather himself.   I, perhaps, may
succeed in a small concern, also, if you approve it.   Fresh meat sells
at an enormous price; a good animal would fetch in quarters twenty
guineas or upwards.   If permission could be had to bring proper goods
in return from town, a few animals would procure you a great many
necessaries, and bear trifling and temporary relief to the town.   I do
not know this can be done; but if you desire it, I will try, and desire
no advantage from it; at all events, I can get many goods out with
passes, as I did the hoes.   To conclude, I will render you all the services in my power, and when the plan and correspondence is settled,
the conveyance of letters from hence will be regular.   I could wish
Lieut. Capers might convey all letters, and accompany any person on
this business; as he is known by my people, and often here, it will not
create any suspicion, for I only wish to trust one negro.   I must now
beg leave to execute a commission in behalf of a very much distressed
man; I mean my worthy friend, Mr. Philip Porcher.   He is much
hurt by the late act that affects him.   I do think if ever man was deserving of favor, he is of the number.   As you know him well, I shall

only say, he is determined to throw himself on your protection, and I expect he is now on his way to you to solicit your kind offices to rank him amongst the number you have made happy. I am also desired to forward your letter from my friend Dr. E. He is a true penitent, and sincerely desirous of making his peace and of following your directions in all things. His lady is coming out to effect it, if possible. This freedom in me needs every apology I can make; my wish to serve my friends will, I hope, plead it. I shall only further add, that

I am, sir, your obedient humble servant,

ⵔ ✲

P. S.—Please to destroy this letter, for fear of accidents.

———

GEN. LESLIE TO GEN. MARION.

[Horry MS.]

April 4, 1782.

SIR:

It was with deep concern I viewed, on the proceedings of the last sessions of your Assembly, acts for amercing the property of some persons, and confiscating that of others, whose principles had attached them to the cause of their Sovereign. Yet, alarming as these public resolutions appeared, I was in hopes humanity, as well as policy, would have arrested their execution, and that I should not have been compelled to take measures for their counteraction, injurious to the country, and therefore painful to me; but when these hopes were disappointed, and I found the effects of the loyal and well-affected removed from their estates, and carried to parts far distant from them, I could no longer remain the quiet spectator of their distresses; but, in order to induce a more just line of conduct, have employed a part of the force intrusted to my charge for their protection, in seizing the negroes of your friends, that restitution may be thereby made to such of ours as may suffer under these oppressive and ruinous resolutions. This, sir, was the object of the late excursion towards Santee, and these principles will greatly mark the future operations of this army, unless a relinquishment of this assumed right on your part should justify less destructive measures on mine. To point out to you, or the world, the distinction between temporary sequestration and actual confiscation, would be impertinence; but, will by no means be so to observe on the opposite conduct, pursued by each party in carrying into execution these very different measures, for which you have endeavored to involve in perpetual ruin the persons and estates of those whose violent opposition to the King's Government compelled the withholding from them, for a time, their possessions in this province, for the great attention which has been invariably paid to their property—the connected state in which it was preserved, and the liberal allowances that were made to their families—insomuch, that whilst other estates were running to waste by the distractions of the country, these have greatly thriven at the expense of Government. Thus far I have deemed it necessary to urge the motives of humanity, policy and example, for your suspension of such rigorous procedures; and should you think a meeting of Commissioners on each side might tend to lessen the devastations of war, and secure inviolate the property of individuals, I shall have a peculiar happiness in embracing proposals that may accomplish such benevolent purposes. But if, notwithstanding this earnest representation, you should still persevere in executing these Acts of your Assembly, I trust this letter will hold me justifiable to the world for any measures which necessity may adopt, in counteraction of steps unjust in their principles, and personally distressing in their consequences; and that whilst I only endeavor to secure to those who, with respectable steadiness, have attached themselves to our cause, the full possession of their effects, or, in case of losses, to provide an equitable restitution for them, I shall be clearly exculpated from all the honors and calamities which the road you now point out unavoidably leads to.

I have the honor to be, sir, your most obdt. and humble servant,

ALEXANDER LESLIE.

COL. LAURENS TO GEN. MARION.

[Horry MS.]

J. WRAGG'S, NEAR STRAWBERRY, April 4, 1782.

DEAR GENERAL:

The letter and intelligence from Gen. Greene, enclosed herewith, although it was probably his first upon the subject of the enemies' movement, and the foundation of all his anxiety, did not reach me till late last night, I must confess I am not much inclined to believe that the enemy meditate any such enterprise as his information alludes to. However, it is possible, and the collecting our force within a proper distance, for a general re-union or co-operation, is a point of prudence, and cannot be attended with any ill consequences. Monk's Corner is said to be a very exhausted country; there is nothing to be had. Col. Maham's cavalry propose crossing Strawberry Ferry, where boats are provided, and light troops can always cover his return by the same way, which will save some distance in marching. I think it agreeable to the spirit of Gen. Greene's letter, that the part of your brigade now in this vicinity should cross Strawberry, and be somewhere in a position to communicate with us, and have given this as my opinion to him. Should anything serious happen, your counsel and support are too important not to be wished for by the General and army.

I am, with sincere esteem, dear General, yours,

J. LAURENS.

P. S. The enemy had not moved yesterday or discovered any signs of it.

GEN. GREENE TO GEN. MARION.

[Horry MS.]

HEAD-QUARTERS, NEAR DORCHESTER, April 8, 1782.

DEAR SIR:

Your letter yesterday to Col. Maham is this moment handed to me. Lieut.-Col. Laurens joined us the night before last, and I have heard nothing further of the enemy's attack upon us. While the light troops were absent, I was a little apprehensive; but on their return, I feel perfectly easy. Enclosed I send you a copy of a letter from General Leslie, by which you will see what the poor inhabitants have to expect. I gave no other answer to it than by informing him that I had no control over civil Government, and directed him to the Governor and Council, who alone possessed powers competent to the business, and who would give him such an answer as the honor and interest of the Government required. If you could subsist with a flying party in the neighborhood of Strawberry, or anywhere between Cooper River and Santee, it would afford great protection to that part of the country. Our present position is so favorable for affording you support by a rapid march of our cavalry, that I much doubt whether the enemy will venture any bold enterprise against you; and if they should, if you move from day to day, and with your usual caution and address, as you are so perfectly acquainted with the country, you can easily avoid them until our cavalry can join you, and by fixing upon some place to meet at, you may form a junction with certainty and despatch. But, if you think your party will be too much exposed, you will take any position you may think their safety requires, giving the inhabitants as full notice as possible—and all the negroes, also—of the enemy's intentions to steal all the latter they can, and carry them off. If the negroes are advertised of the enemy's intentions, I think they will get but few of them.

I am, dear sir, your most obedient humble servant,

NATHANIEL GREENE.

GEN. MARION TO COL. P. HORRY.

[Horry MS.]

ST. STEPHENS, April 9, 1782.

DEAR SIR:

I am informed that a Capt. Howell, in a N. W. cutter, has taken the flag schooner which Gen. Greene ordered to load with rice. I hope you have prevented her being carried away. You will confine Captain Howell for infringing a flag contrary to Gen. Greene's passport; his vessel and crew must also be secured and confined as plunderers until I have Gen. Greene's and the Governor's orders and directions, and the schooner be permitted to sail without delay for Charlestown. I have heard from Gen. Greene there has not been any action, as was reported; the firing heard was within the enemy's lines, and proved to be a field day with them. As it is possible the enemy may make another excursion in the country, you will send me every horse you have, that can be of the least service, as I am determined to oppose them at all events. There are only two officers, and twenty-eight non-commissioned and privates here; the rest have been sent away by the officers on frivolous pretences. Mr. Lesesne is absent without leave, Mr. Wragg also; if he is a volunteer he must be discharged, and not suffered in future to be on the Commissary Department. Mr. Guerry is absent without leave, and must be dismissed. I expect every officer and private will be sent me that is able to act. 1 have had no answer from the General respecting the reduction of the corps, and have again wrote him on that subject yesterday. You will go on in equipping and arming your men as usual; and as soon as I hear from Gen. Greene, will send you a power to impress horses to make up your losses. I wish you would procure the rum, sugar and coffee, formerly mentioned to you. If a stop is put to the injurious proceedings of the N. W. privateers, I shall be able to procure clothing, &c., &c., for our army, and again complete your men with those articles. I shall remain here some time.

I am, your obedient servant,

FRANCIS MARION.

GOVERNOR MATTHEWS TO GENERAL MARION.

[Horry MS.]

CANE ACRE, April 10, 1782.

SIR :

I received yours of the 8th instant late last evening. I now write to Heriot and Tucker about the indigo, which you will forward to them. I answered your former letter respecting Mr. Philip Porcher, by referring you to the orders I had given respecting those who should come from within the enemy's lines; lest any accidents should have happened to that dispatch, I now enclose it. These orders are general, therefore unnecessary to observe upon the other. I have already informed you that Gen. Greene and myself agreed to the last proposition you made respecting Maham's and Horry's corps, which was to continue Horry's dismounted, to act as infantry. If the matter can be accommodated upon this plan, I shall give myself no further trouble about it, as they have so little time to serve. Whilst I am on this subject, I must take notice of the conduct of Mr. Thomas Drayton, who was sent to the southward to impress horses. He has made so improper a use of the authority given him, that I have been obliged to order him on no account to impress another horse, and to return such as he had impressed. The reason of my ordering him to return those he had taken was, that at all events Maham would have Horry's horses, and consequently could not want more; however, whether the thing takes place or not, the impressing of horses is attended with such ruinous consequences, that I am determined not to countenance it. You will, therefore, sir, look upon the authority given you on the 6th of March last, for impressing horses, as hereby revoked. I have given no commissions in the second regiment. I did give Mr. Thomas Pinckney a certificate for a commission in the first regiment before I knew of the form observed for commissions in the regiments of this State. You say the application can only be made to the Colonel of the regiment. In this case the Governor, who has the sole right to appoint if he chooses to exercise it, becomes a mere machine. At all events, I shall expect a decent regard to be paid to any recommendation from me. This is a point I do not think I am at liberty to give up. I should be glad Mr. Hall's baggage was sent forward, as the public papers in it are much wanted.

I am, sir, with esteem and regard, your most obdt. servant,

JNO. MATTHEWS.

————

CAPT. HOWELL TO GEN. MARION.

[Horry MS.]

GEORGETOWN, April 10, 1782.

SIR:

Having the honor of bearing a Continental commission, I have, agreeably to my instructions from Congress, seized a certain vessel, now here under the sanction of a flag from Charlestown, for having contraband goods. As I have in all former cases of this kind applied to the Judge of the Admiralty, where civil Government was established, so I have in the present one wrote to the Judge of the Admiralty of this State, in order that she may be legally tried; but am apprehensive, from the behavior of Col. Horry (his ordering my cutter under the guns of the battery, when she might be at sea, and other matters which I conceive to be entirely out of his line), that the military mean to interfere with the civil authority. I think it needless to trouble you much further about he matter, as I conceive it to be altogether of a civil nature. I just beg leave to trouble you with the enclosed copies of my commissioned orders and instructions for your perusal, by which you see, and I hope readily agree, that I have only acted in the line of my duty, and that the vessel and cargo are lawful prizes, in consequence of her having on board goods for which no license or permission has been given; and do, therefore, request you will give orders for the discharge of my cutter, in order that I may send her to sea. I beg, sir, that you would not have that unfavorable opinion of my conduct as the misrepresentations of some people might induce you to entertain. I have always been a friend to my country, and have acted as such.

I am, sir, your most obedient servant,

JNO. HOWELL.

GEN. GREENE TO GEN. MARION.

[Horry MS.]

HEAD-QUARTERS, NEAR DORCHESTER, April 10, 1782.

DEAR SIR:

Your favor of the 8th was handed me yesterday. Lieut.-Colonel Laurens has given me an account of the enemy's last movement, and Gen. Leslie has explained the object to me in a letter, a copy of which I inclosed to you in my last. With respect to the incorporation of Horry's and Maham's corps, I have said all upon it that I can say. If you cannot effect the incorporation upon the first plan, pursue your second; and if you cannot accomplish that, employ the force in any manner you can most for the benefit of the service, and in a way most pleasing to the officers. The schooner that went to Georgetown for rice has the Governor's pass, and not mine; however, be it one or the other, tell Col. Horry not to let the cutter have anything to do with her; and if they attempt to carry her away by force, to repel force by force. Whatever position you take with your troops, it will be necessary frequently to change it, which will keep the enemy in the dark, and prevent their enterprising anything against you. Should the enemy move out after you, our cavalry shall form a junction with you at the place you mention, or any other you may advise, upon the spur of the occasion. Col. Pinckney has arrived in camp. With esteem and regard,

I am, dear sir, your most obedient and humble servant,

NATHANIEL GREENE.

GEN. GREENE TO COL. P. HORRY.

[Horry MS.]

No date, supposed about April 10, 1782.

DEAR SIR:

Your letter of the 8th April has been received; and as I have had no direct opportunity to give it an answer, and as the subject did not require it immediately, I have omitted it. I cannot decide on one part of your letter, that is, respecting half-pay. If you were entitled to half-pay on your former standing, you are entitled to it now; but, if you mean upon the present reduction proposed, there can be no half-pay establishment follow it, as I have no authority for the purpose, nor can I conceive the officers would have the least right to expect such a thing. Their services were due to the State, from the situation it was in, and those temporary corps afforded them a much more honorable and agreeable service than serving in the militia; and as the Continent takes the expense upon themselves until their reduction, it is all that can be expected—and, to continue them longer than they are useful, would be multiplying expense without sufficient object, for no country ever required economy more than ours to complete their independence. I left the business of reducing the regiments entirely to Gen. Marion; if it could be effected, well, but if not, let them remain as they were, until the men's term of service expires. He informs me that he has united all the horse under Col. Maham, and directed your men to do duty at Georgetown; this is perfectly agreeable to me, if so to you. I directed, a few days past, a company of artillery to join you at Georgetown, and to your orders, in defence of that place. I am much afraid the enemy will attempt something against Waccamaw, as I am told there is a great quantity of provisions there.

I am, with great esteem, your obedient servant,

NATHANIEL GREENE.

GEN. MARION TO COL. P. HORRY.

[Horry MS.]

April 10, 1782.

DEAR SIR:

Yours of the 8th ultimo came to hand. By the papers just sent me, it appears that Capt. Howell had the candles sold to the flag people, on purpose to have a plea of seizing her; you will, therefore, order the flag to sail immediately, and Capt. Howell and his vessel's crew to be detained, as I wrote you yesterday, until I hear from Gen. Greene or the Governor. If Botard should take her at sea, we have nothing to do with it. You will put Moore, Broderick and Myers on board the flag vessel, to return to Charlestown, with orders not to return within our lines. In answer to your last post, I wrote you yesterday; have not heard from head-quarters since. A letter from Capt. Pinckney, Cainhoy, says the British horse were crossing to Haddrell's on Saturday, but it comes by such a hand that I don't believe it. I shall hear more to-day.

I am, sir, your obedient servant,

F. MARION.

GEN. GREENE TO GEN. MARION.

[Horry MS]

April 12, 1782.

DEAR SIR:

I have been of opinion some time, and got intelligence last evening, that the enemy were preparing to come out and attack us. It seems the refugees are pushing the General very hard for the purpose. What serves to confirm me in opinion that the enemy have some offensive operations in view is, they have taken uncommon pains for a few days past to find out our position, by sending flag after flag, and by searching out and interrupting every channel through which we might get intelligence. The refugees are ordered to be embodied to do garrison duty, while the army takes the field. It may all end in smoke, but I seriously believe they mean to give us battle; and as they will have all their force collected, so I think it prudent to draw ours to a point until their intentions are better understood. You will, therefore, move over towards Dorchester with all your force as soon as possible, and let me know from time to time where you are. You will leave a very small patrole to watch the motions of the enemy in that quarter, and to forward intelligence of all matters of discovery. I would have you put your men in the best order for action, and send me a roll of the force you will be able to bring to our aid.

I am, dear sir, your most obedient servant,

NATHANIEL GREENE.

GEN. MARION TO COL. P. HORRY.

[Horry MS.]

ST. STEPHENS, April 12, 1782.

SIR:

Yours by Mr. Cest came to hand. I wrote per Dragoon respecting Capt. Howell and the flag. Messrs. Doughty and Ancrum are not to do duty your way. I shall have such men returned as have served their month. I cannot send you the militia law; have none by me. I wrote you before that Capt. Weyman had it, and you might get it from him. I sent Capt. Stephens to Georgetown, only to stay until his corps returned. I wrote the Governor respecting Mr. Wayne's account, and

11

think he is rather impatient. I have had no answer yet to my letters, and hope you will make yourself easy until I can fully satisfy you, which will be as soon as I get an answer from the General. I have some accounts of the enemy's coming over to St. Thomas', and wish I had every horse you have that can be of any service, as I find I am under the necessity of attacking them.

I am, your obedient servant,

FRANCIS MARION.

GEN. MARION TO COL. P. HORRY.

[Horry MS.]

April 12, 1782.

DEAR SIR:

Since I wrote the enclosed, I have received a letter from Gen. Greene. His orders are, not to suffer the flag schooner to be taken or detained. You will follow my orders respecting that business. I have answered Capt. Howell's letter by this opportunity. In respect to your corps, the General and Governor approves of the plan of dismounting them, to act in Georgetown as infantry; but will not impress any more horses for the service of either corps, as their time will so soon expire, and it seems not their intention of keeping them up longer. I shall write you fuller in my next.

I am, with esteem, your obedient servant,

FRANCIS MARION.

GEN. MARION TO COL. P. HORRY.

[Horry MS.]

April 13, 1782.

SIR:

Yours of the 11th ultimo is before me. If you suffer Moore and Broderick to remain, they must give bail for their good behavior; each to give two good sureties, bound in five hundred guineas each, and to do six months' duty in the militia; the bond to be executed before a Justice of the Peace. Mr. Lesesne must certainly pay his rent; but it is a matter I have nothing to do with; as it is a civil affair between citizen and citizen, there is a way pointed out by law. He never had any promises from me of a billet, which ought not to be done but on the greatest necessity, as it is a grievance to the people, which at all times ought to be avoided when it can. If it can be proved that Solomon Miller has cheated or defrauded the public, he should suffer agreeably to law, which is, to have a hearing before a Justice of the Peace, and, if found guilty, must go to jail, or give security to appear at the next sessions. Capt. Gough told me he had leave of absence for a month. As the Governor and Gen. Greene have come into the plan of dismounting your corps to act as infantry under you, if it is agreeable to you; if not, to remain as they are, without the liberty of impressing any horses for them, for their time of service is so short, it is not worth going to that expense, neither will they let Maham impress any more horses, and without more horses, &c., &c., the few you have cannot be of any service. I will make the proper arrangement, but will not do it without you signify your approbation, which I will wait for. The four barrels indigo, in the hands of Paul Trapier, Esq., you will take for public uses, and may procure clothing for our troops, and rum, sugar, &c. I wish the flag could sail, that Capt. Howell and crew may be dismissed. In my last I mentioned the British being up in St. Thomas', but believe it is premature, as my party of observation, who are down towards Cainhoy, have given me no account of it. For want of forage and subsistence, I shall remove to-day above Murray's Ferry, in St. Stephens'; indeed, I shall be obliged to move often, to prevent the enemy forming any plan against me. I am very sensible the trouble you must have in your command in Georgetown, but your well known abilities and zeal for your country will surmount everything.

I am, with esteem, your obedient servant,

FRANCIS MARION.

GEN. GREENE TO GEN. MARION.

[Horry MS.]

HEAD-QUARTERS, April 14, 1782.

DEAR SIR:

Your favor of the 13th inst. is this moment came to hand. The prospect of a general action is not so immediate as I expected a few days ago. You will, therefore, halt in the neighborhood of Strawberry

Ferry, and wait there, or in that neighborhood, until you hear further from me. I don't believe the enemy will make another excursion soon into St. Thomas', but they may. I should be obliged to you to get an account of all the forage in that quarter; with us it is scarce. I begin to feel afraid our cavalry will be obliged to cross the Edisto for subsistence.

I am, dear sir, your most obedient servant,

NATHANIEL GREENE.

GEN. GREENE TO GEN. MARION.

[Horry MS.]

HEAD-QUARTERS, April 15, 1782.

DEAR SIR:

I wrote you yesterday to return to Strawberry, but, as you are so near, before you return I wish to see you, provided you come to Mr. Blake's to-night; but, if you should meet with your first express, and halt short of Mr. Blake's, you may return to the position recommended in that letter. However, I am of opinion, from a variety of reports, the enemy means to take the field in a few days, and that they have little less than 700 negroes armed for the purpose. The British horse were at Dorchester yesterday, but returned last night.

I am, dear sir, your humble servant,

NATHANIEL GREENE.

GOVERNOR MATTHEWS TO GENERAL MARION.

{Horry MS.]

CANE ACRE, April 15, 1782.

SIR :

Your letter of the 10th inst. came safe to hand two days ago. The commanders of privateers, knowing their authority, and regardless of our unfortunate situation, are determined to add to our distresses, instead of contributing towards their relief; indeed, the men who usually command these vessels are needy and avaricious to the last degree, and come out with a view of making money by any means that does not subject them to be hanged; humanity is a thing they are totally unacquainted with. By a late Act of Congress, all British property, wheresoever found, is made liable to seizure. How far the vessel in question, having Gen. Greene's flag, might have violated, I will not pretend to judge, if it is put upon this issue; thus its rests with Gen. Greene to take cognizance of the affair. But in the light the matter at present strikes me, we have gone far enough in confining the captain and crew; more rigorous measures may probably bring us into a dispute with the State of North Carolina. What we have already done is a mere act of power, and in our circumstances highly excusable. I would, therefore, recommend that the captain and crew be discharged, and the vessel be permitted to depart as soon as the flag has sailed, and got beyond all danger of being taken. I should be extremely glad if you could contract for any quantity of clothing from the quarter you mention, and I will engage to have produce returned for it—that is, if it can be spared. I have employed Mr. Robert Heriot to take an account of the provisions in the district of Georgetown; as soon as I can get his return, I shall be able to let you know what rice is to be spared. All the southward parts of the country are stripped very bare, and it is very probable we shall be obliged to draw some provisions from Santee for this army. The same objection lies against paying Mr. Wayne's account. Until I can get the return above mentioned, I enclose you an order on Capt. Richardson, at the high hills of Santee, for 500 lbs. powder and 1,500 lead, 50 muskets and bayonets, 50 cartouch boxes, and 1,000 flints, which you may send for as soon as you please. As to cannon ball, I know not where to procure them; if you can point any mode that promises a probability of success, I will undertake to have the experiment made. I have already wrote you fully respecting Mr. Porcher; also, respecting Maham's and Horry's corps, and my determination about impressing horses. Mr. John Waring's situation at present being so exceedingly distressing, I have given him permission to remain at home, on his engaging to join you again as soon as possible. Mrs. Hall sends on a horse for his wagon; I, therefore, request you would furnish the necessary escort, and send it forward without delay.

I am, sir, your most obedient servant,

JOHN MATTHEWS.

GOVERNOR MATTHEWS TO GENERAL MARION.

[Horry MS.]

CANE ACRE, April 16, 1782.

SIR:

The bearer, Mr. Shrewsbury, you are better acquainted with than I, therefore, I shall say no more concerning him than recommend him to be disposed of as you shall think proper. If you think he can be use-fully employed in his profession, you will do so; if not, he must do his duty as a militia man. If you approve of neither, you may either send him back to town, or do what you please with him.

I am, sir, your most obedient servant,
JOHN MATTHEWS.

———

GEN. GREENE TO GEN. MARION.

[Horry MS.]

HEAD–QUARTERS, April 16, 1782.

DEAR SIR:

I am favored with your letter of this day. I know of no way of reinforcing you but by Col. Hampton's corps. I will speak with the Governor on the subject. At present, I believe we have no spare arms; however, I will make more strict enquiry, and let you know. Arms are expected from the Northward, but they will be a long time on the road, if we are to judge of the future by the past. To enable me to give my orders respecting the cannon at Georgetown, you must send the size of the calibres. Every measure should be taken to preserve the provi-sions, for I am very apprehensive there will be a scarcity. I thank you for the enemy's returns of rations drawn. I think it large, but, per-haps, their force may be greater than I imagine.

I am, dear sir, your most obedient servant,
NATHANIEL GREENE.

———

GEN. MARION TO COL. P. HORRY.

[Horry MS.]

FERGUSON SWAMP, April 18, 1782.

DEAR SIR:

I have got thus far in my return from the Southward. I have been within eight miles of Bacon Bridge, and have had a hard march for no purpose. The General imagined the enemy was coming out, and is still of the opinion they will take the field soon; but I think they will not without a reinforcement, which it seems they expect, as they have done for six months past. I hope the flag schooner is sailed; if so, discharge Capt. Howell's crew and cutter. Col. Moultrie is to stay in Georgetown, and collect his regiment; he will be of service to you—at least, will not keep you so much confined. I shall send Col. Maham for the horses of your corps as soon as I hear from you. I intend to leave you thirteen, but they must not be the best. I will send you arms as soon as I get them from the high hills of Santee.

I am, yours, &c.,

FRANCIS MARION.

GOV. MATTHEWS TO GEN. MARION.

[Horry MS.]

CANE ACRE, April 18, 1782.

SIR:

The manner in which you mentioned Mr. P——, gave me no kind of apprehension of his being on the confiscation list, therefore, wrote to you respecting him as one of those who had not been noticed by the Legislature. I am, however, very glad you have proceeded no further, and this mistake of mine will serve to make me more guarded in future. It is utterly out of my power to grant Mr. P—— any indulgence, as the Act in which he is included is clear and positive. Were I to suffer him to remain in the country, it would be a partial suspension of the law, which cannot be done; I must, therefore, desire that Mr. P—— be immediately ordered into Charlestown. An application has lately been made me in favor of Mr. Alex. Rose, who had been banished the town by the British, but I was obliged to refuse it; and, if Mr. Rose should come out, you must order him immediately to return. Before this reaches you, you will have received my order for the arms and ammunition you want. My reason for ordering the horses to be returned that were impressed by order of Col. Maham, was, that Horry's horses were to be turned over to his regiment. I thought it impossible that more horses could be wanted, after having those of a whole regiment. I am sorry to find that this regiment has proved so very insignificant, as not to be able to supply more than twelve horses; however, Maham's order was for no more than fifteen, which makes a difference of only three horses, consequently the service cannot suffer for want of so trifling a number of horses. Another reason was, that I found the authority put into very improper hands, instead of its being entrusted to very discreet persons. The thing in itself is odious, and ought to be avoided if possible; but, if such a necessity arises as renders the measure indispensable, it ought to be exercised with caution and lenity. If I am rightly informed, the gentlemen who had the press warrant did, by no means, confine themselves to taking horses from such only as showed no disposition to serve their country; and another reason that induced me to countermand the order was, that I found it created very great discontents, to find that horses, which were immediately to be attached to your brigade, should be taken out of another; and, as it was likely to be productive of many inconveniences, and having already full enough to struggle with, and not conceiving the horses to be substantially necessary, I thought it best to put a stop to any further embarrassments on this account. As to Col. Maham's threatening to resign, because he is not permitted to do as he is pleases, he must use his own pleasure. I can assure him these kind of threats are by no means calculated to operate with me in the manrer they are intended to do, but the reverse. I am very sorry to find so few of the Charlestown militia at Georgetown. There is now a newspaper regularly published. Suppose you issue general orders for those men to join their several corps within a certain limited time, and such as do not, to send a party to take them into custody; and if, on trial, they are convicted, send them to the Continental line—a few examples, perhaps, may bring them to their senses. It is disgraceful in the highest degree that men should require to be thus goaded to their duty. An express is this day arrived from Philadelphia, and brings letters from Gillon, who is arrived at the Havanna with five prizes, worth 150,000 hard dollars. It is not unlikely he may send a vessel or two to Georgetown—therefore, could wish a good look-out may be kept there, that if they arrive they may not be detained for want of a pilot. They talk much at the Northward of the French fleet coming either here or to New York, early this spring. Let either be the object, the issue will be highly important. I could wish Charlestown to be the first, not only as most interesting to us, but because I believe the attempt here would be successful, and I have very great doubts about the other; and, because I fear if our allies were to meet with a rebuff in one place, they will not be so ready to attempt another, as success is always a stimulus to encounter new dangers. I suppose you will think I have little to do, to write so much about politics—this is not the fact; but my pen naturally run into its old channel before I recollected myself. I wish I had time to give you these occurrences oftener than I do; however, if you will give me leave, I will subscribe to our newspaper for you, from whence you will stand a better chance of getting news than from my pen.

I am, sir, your most obedient servant,

JOHN MATTHEWS.

GEN. MARION TO COL. P. HORRY.

[Horry MS.]

St. Stephens, April 19, 1782.

SIR:

Yours of the 12th came to hand yesterday, on my march here. I wrote you before respecting Brodrick and Moore, to take bail for their appearance at court, and good behavior. The Georgia refugees must do duty, if they have been in this State three months. No excuse to be taken for not doing duty. Let me know if the flag has sailed; and, if you have not discharged Howell and crew, it must be done immediately. Send me the calibre of the different pieces of cannon you have, that I may procure shot for them; also, other articles which may be wanted. I wrote you yesterday by Col. Moultrie.

I am, your humble servant,

FRANCIS MARION.

P. S.—If you have any coffee and sugar, send a little by first opportunity. As you have rice and indigo, you may pay off small accounts, such as is enclosed.

———

GEN. MARION TO COL. P. HORRY.

[Horry MS.]

St. Stephens, April 22, 1782.

DEAR SIR :

I received yours of the 17th. The flag must be sent immediately back, with all her cargo, passengers, attendance, goods, &c., &c., except Mrs. Shad, Mrs. Barnes and Miss Simmons, and their attendances and property; and I positively order no other man, woman or servants, or any property, be landed, or suffered to come ashore—but the vessel ordered immediately to go out of the harbor, on pain of being made a prize in twenty-four hours after such notice be given; and you are hereby ordered to make prize of said vessel, cargo, &c., &c., and the captain, crew and passengers to put in close confinement, without suffering any person whatever to visit or speak to either of said prisoners, until my further orders. McClean, with his companions, must be kept in close confinement until a proper opportunity offers to send them to the Governor of North Carolina. Col. S—— is trading on his private account, and I am not surprised at anything he has, or can do; he is no friend. I wrote you respecting the pilots, and I left you to act as you pleased respecting the boat mentioned in my last. Mr. Chatelleat has my pass to go to the Northward. You will permit the flag to carry one barrel of rice, and a few poultry, for the relief of Mr. John Clements, a prisoner, and wounded in Charlestown; he is one of my brigade. No officer ever had a right to public horses; but those you have you will keep, and you have a right to them, until my further orders. The officers and men of your corps here must remain as yet. The report of galley or armed vessels to go to Georgetown, I do not think true, as I had a letter from Charlestown last evening, that says a French fleet is at Tybee; and, from the person it came from, I have reason to believe it may be true.

I am, with esteem, your obedient servant,

FRANCIS MARION.

P. S.—Since I wrote the above, I have perused the papers sent, and find Col. Ray is exchanged; he and the others mentioned in General Butler's pass are to be put on board the flag vessel, and suffered to proceed to Charlestown.

————

GEN. MARION TO COL. P. HORRY.

[Horry MS.]

St. Stephens, April 24, 1782.

SIR:

Enclosed is a return of the companies which are to do duty in Georgetown. Warden's and Long's will be sent to you. I also send you the militia laws. The Governor wrote you that Commodore Gillon has carried in five Jamaica prizes in the Havanna, worth 150,000 dollars. Two of the prizes are expected in Georgetown, and the Governor desires the pilot to keep a good look out for them. Several of your men wish to enlist in the infantry, on the new bounty. Such as have but two months to serve in your corps, may be discharged, on condition of enlisting for three years, or during the war. I send two men, with their attestations, which cannot be sworn to until your discharge is obtained, which please see done, and give them the enclosed orders to Swinton for their negroes, and grant them one month furlough. Mr. Shrewsberry will wait on you—he is a shipwright, and may be useful; but he must be watched, for he has been, and is, much suspected. He will want to send a boat to Dewees' Island for some goods, osnaburgs and Russian drab, which is for our soldiers. You will please give him a pass for that boat, and receive the goods; but he must not be suffered to go out of Georgetown. I will send fifty stand of arms, and pouches with ammunition. Col. Moultrie will want some of them, and you are to take what he may not want at present, until I get more from Gen Greene.

I am, your obedient servant,

FRANCIS MARION.

GEN. MARION TO CAPT. JAMES WITHERSPOON.

[Original MS.]

St. Stephens, April 24, 1782.

Sir:

Inclosed is a commission to command the King's Tree Company, and hope you will accept of it; and let no trifling matter induce you to refuse it. In these times when our country calls for men of bravery and ability, such as you, no good man, well-wisher to his country, ought to resign or shun the service, and it gives me great pleasure to see you at the head of a company, which I know will be led on by a man whose conduct and spirit I have been an eye-witness of, whom I have always had the highest opinion of, and the greatest regard for.

I am sir, your obedient servant,

FRANCIS MARION.

GEN. GREENE TO GEN. MARION.

[Horry MS.]

Head–Quarters, April 28, 1782.

Dear Sir:

From many different accounts the enemy threatens us with an attack. We have had no small uneasiness in our camp for want of pay, clothing and spirits. The discontent has reached the enemy, and it is confidently asserted that they are coming out to take advantage of it. I think it necessary, therefore, as I am not well informed of the full extent of the discontent, to call our force together from all parts, as well to awe the malcontents, if any there be, as to prevent the enemy from attempting anything in consequence thereof. I beg you will, therefore, march and join us as soon as possible, with all your force, except a small reconnoitering party; and, although this may expose a greater part of the country, yet it will serve to secure a greater object. I beg you will lose no time.

I am, dear sir, your most obedient servant,

NATHANIEL GREENE.

GEN. MARION TO COL. P. HORRY.

[Horry MS.]

APRIL 30, 1782.

SIR:

Yours of the 26th came to hand. You may do as you please with Mr. Shad's daughter. Let Col. Moultrie have four rations. I wrote you last night, and enclosed Meyer's account, but the letter is lost. You will pay him out of the indigo and rice you have in your hands; if not sufficient, he must wait. I am called to join Gen. Greene. You will keep a good look-out, lest the enemy form an attack against you; and let it be always a rule to be ready at a moment, if a retreat should be necessary, as my former orders. I shall be absent I fear some time. A wagon, with fifty stand of arms, is on its way from High Hills for you. Should you want ammunition, send to Mr. William Richardson. I am told your officers have public horses, and the best; they must be given up, and all your horses and men that are out must be called in immediately, when I shall send for such as may be for dragoon service.

I am, in haste, adieu,

FRANCIS MARION.

GOV. MATTHEWS TO COL. P. HORRY.

[Horry MS.]

CANE ACRE, May 1, 1782.

SIR:

I understand there has been some regulation of prices lately attempted at the port of Georgetown. Such a measure is highly impolitic, and must inevitably ruin the commerce that is attempted to be established there, in its very infancy. It is, therefore, my particular orders, that you give no countenance to any such measures; but, on the contrary, use your best endeavors to suppress it, and give every enouragement to a free uninterrupted trade.

I am, sir, your most obedient servant,

JNO. MATTHEWS.

GEN. GREENE TO GEN. MARION.

[Horry MS.]

HEAD-QUARTERS, May 1, 1782.

DEAR SIR:

I wish you to take a position in the neighborhood of camp, that we may join our force on the shortest notice, should the enemy attempt anything against us. The North Carolina troops were discharged this day; and it is highly probable that if the enemy attempt anything at all, it will be to-morrow, and more especially if they get intelligence that our force is collecting to a point. Col. Hammond is coming to join us with a body of militia, and I wish you to take command of the whole, and form a camp near to ours. If you will give orders for your troops to march in the morning, and come forward, we will look out a camp together; bring a small party of horse with you.

I am, dear sir, your most obedient humble servant,

NATHANIEL GREENE.

GEN. MARION TO COL. P. HORRY.

[Horry MS.]

NEAR BACON BRIDGE, May 3, 1782.

SIR:

I am posted here, two miles in front of the Continental army, within three-quarters of a mile of the above bridge. The General, according to custom, keeps me between him and the enemy. By what I can learn, we shall not move from here until the army move. Gen. Pickens' brigade is here under me; Capt. Gee's men are come here. You will relieve those at Cat Island by some other men. I hope by this you have received the arms. Send me by the first opportunity a general return of your corps, of men, horses, saddles and arms; as you have all the officers except Maxwell, you cannot be at a loss. If any officers or men are on a furlough, you must call them in, and give no more leave of absence on any account. I shall send a waggon for rum, sugar and coffee; please get it ready for me. This place is a starving hole, where nothing can be had, and nothing can be expected but hard knocks. Gen. O'Hara and seventeen empty· transports are arrived, and Gen. Leslie is going away, said for Jamaica. Deserters just come in say they are levelling their works, and are to contract their garrison; some say part of the troops are going with Gen. Leslie. I wrote you in my last that you may do as you please with Shad's daughter. Tell Capt. Roux he is retained in the service, and is in the second regiment. I have not time to write him.

I am, sir, your obedient servant,

FRANCIS MARION.

GEN. MARION TO COL. P. HORRY.

[Horry MS.]

BACON BRIDGE, May 11, 1782.

SIR:

You will deliver all the horses you have, with the saddles, bridles, halter, and swords, except 14 of the ordinary horses which you will keep for your crops. The officers must give up every public horse they have. Col. Maham will send an officer to receive them. Mr. Withers has permission to send to Charlestown some tobacco to procure necessaries for the army. You will give him passes when he applies for it, and receive whatever clothing he may get. I sent you a letter by Comodore Lockwood, informing that the British intend to go to Georgetown, under French colors and dress; you will, I dare say, prevent their deception from taking effect. I am apprehensive they will go to Waccamaw; you will keep some boats ready at the ferry above Wragg's to cross over a few men on Waccamaw. Should they go there, a fire or two on them may make them go away. The whole of the men around your post should be called for if they do attempt. We are perfectly idle here. Nothing new but that deserters from the British come in every day. `

I am, sir, your obedient servant,

FRANCIS MARION.

GEN. PINCKNEY TO GOV. MATTHEWS.

[Horry MS.]

Pon Pon, May 19, 1782.

Dear Sir:

By a letter this moment received from Gen. Huger, dated the 10th of this month, he desires me to inform your excellency, that a Col. Perkins, a trader from Virginia, has contracted for five or six hundred head of cattle on Pee Dee and the Cheraws, and which in a few days will be drove off for Virginia, if not immediately stopped; the couse-quences of such a speculation (for our commissaries have it not in their power to go to market with ready money) are truly alarming.

I am your excellency's most obedient servant,

CHARLES COTESWORTH PINCKNEY.

GEN. MARION TO COL. P. HORRY.

[Horry MS.]

Bacon Bridge, May 20, 1782.

Sir:

I send you two letters addressed to Gov. Martin, which you will send by express that may be depended on—it requires expedition. I send a letter for Ganey; please forward. Mrs. P—— has abused the trust reposed in her, in making use of the pass more than once. You may permit Mr. Dyer to bail for his future good behaviour. I am sorry to find the guard at Cat Island do not do their duty, in suffering boats to pass the Musketoe Creek. I hope some steps will be taken to prevent such an evil so much to the prejudice to our service. The few men of yours here are not to be spared yet, and hope you will make yourself satisfied, as it is not in the power of government to get money as yet to pay the troops in her service, but hope, it will be soon. Col. Moultrie will give you all the news here; I have not time just now to write them to you.

I am your obedient servant,

FRANCIS MARION.

GOV. MATTHEWS TO GEN. MARION.

[Horry MS.]

CANE ACRE, May 21, 1782.

SIR:

I enclose you the instructions for quieting the discontents of the people on Little Pee Dee, with whom you some time ago entered into a truce. The express brings you twenty commissions. I also enclose you an order for arms and ammunition. I think there is something else you mentioned to me in the course of our conversation to-day, but in the multiplicity of business I have engaged in since I came home, it has slipt my memory; you will, therefore, be pleased to repeat it to me by the return of the express I send you to-morrow.

I am, sir, your most obedient servant,

JNO. MATTHEWS.

P. S.—Be pleased to send me your opinion in writing before you go away, whether it will be best to sell the negroes, and recruit with money, or continue on the old plan of recruiting with negroes.

GOV. MATTHEWS TO GEN. MARION.

[Horry MS.]

CANE ACRE, May 21, 1782.

INSTRUCTIONS FOR GEN. MARION FOR OFFERING TERMS OF RECON-CILIATION TO MAJOR GANEY AND OTHERS, WITH WHOM GENERAL MARION ENTERED INTO A TRUCE, ON THE 17TH JUNE LAST.

First, You are to take with you four or five judicious, intelligent persons, to meet those appointed on the part of Ganey and others, to confer on the business herein committed to your charge, but they are not to be considered as joined with you in this commission. *Second,* The said Ganey and others, with whom such truce was made, are to lay down their arms as enemies to this State, and are not to resume them again until called on to do so, in support of the interest of the United States, and of this State in particular. *Third,* They are to deliver up all negroes, horses, cattle, and other property, that have been plundered from the inhabitants of this or any other State. *Fourth,* They are to engage to demean themselves as peaceable citizens of this State, and submit themselves in future to be governed by its laws, in the same manner as the rest of the citizens thereof. *Fifth,* They are to be allowed two, or, if you find it necessary, three months, to remain at home, before they are called on to bear arms in behalf of this State. *Sixth,* They are to engage to apprehend and deliver up all persons within their district, who shall refuse to accede to these terms, and contumaciously persist in rebellion against the State. *Seventh,* If these terms are accepted by the said Ganey and others, you are then to promise them a full pardon for all treasons heretofore committed by them against the State. *Eighth,* If these terms are rejected by the said Ganey and others before mentioned, you are then to have recourse to force of arms, or otherwise to compel them to submission. *Ninth,* You are authorized and empowered, if you shall deem it for the public service, to apprehend, and send within the enemy's lines, any of the families of persons who continue in arms against the State.

Given under my hand, at Cane Acre, this 21st day of May, one thousand seven hundred and eighty-two.

JNO. MATTHEWS.

GEN. MARION TO COL. P. HORRY.

[Horry MS.]

BACON BRIDGE, May 21, 1782.

SIR:

I have information the enemy intends to make an attack on your post; you will order all the militia around you to your assistance. I am this moment in motion to reinforce you; you must make every defence possible until I arrive. A flag came here yesterday from the enemy on important business to both armies; what, we have not yet learned. The officer which came says we shall very soon take one another by the hand in friendship. Some say there is a cessation of arms to take place, and that peace is actually on the carpet. Send per express the letters to Col. Baxter and Murphy. I hope you have the twenty-five stand of arms last ordered.

I am, your obedient servant,
FRANCIS MARION.

12

GOV. MATTHEWS TO GEN. MARION.

[Horry MS.]

CANE ACRE, May 21, 1782.

SIR:

Gen. Barnwell having desired to retire from the command of the brigade to which he has been appointed, and, as I think the service would be best promoted by its being continued under the command of a Brigadier, in preference to the regiments being independently commanded by the Colonels, I, therefore, desire you would take the command of that brigade, and consider it as annexed to the brigade at present commanded by you, until you receive orders to the contrary from me, or the Commander-in-Chief of this State, for the time being.

I am, sir, your most obedient servant,

JNO. MATTHEWS.

GEN. LESLIE TO GEN. GREENE.

[Horry MS.]

HEAD-QUARTERS, May 23, 1782.

SIR:

Capt. Skelly having stated to me the queries he had the honor to receive from you, respecting the papers I submitted to your consideration, and what official authority I had for proposing a cessation of hostilities, and believing a treaty for terminating the war was now carrying on, I have, therefore, to inform you that those papers were transmitted to me by his Excellency, Sir Henry Clinton, accompanied by the Right Hon. Welbore Ellis, then one of his Majesty's principal secretaries of State, referring generally for my conduct in this respect; and that, I suppose, not only from the weight of their authority, but likewise from the explicit terms in which they convey the sense of his Majesty and the British House of Commons. Fuller instructions I momently expect from our present Commander-in-Chief, Sir Guy Carlton, whose appointment and arrival in America has not yet been regularly notified to me. Thus, sir, I have explicitly stated to you the mode and circumstances under which these important papers have reached me; and as I can have no doubt from current report, and the nature of these documents, that a suspension of hostilities has taken place to the Northward, and that a treaty to conclude the war is now carrying on, I held it a duty I owed the rights of humanity, the welfare of this country, and the sentiments of the Legislature, of my own to propose, that such a cessation should take place here, and this proposal, from these motives, I again renew, and will depute, if it meets your concurrence, commissioners to settle the terms of it, and for securing the interests, as well civil as military of each party, in the present state, assuring you, at the same time, you will have the earliest notice of what instructions and advice I may receive on this head from New York.

I have the honor to be, sir, your most obedient, &c.,

ALEXANDER LESLIE.

MAJOR PIERCE TO GEN. MARION.

[Horry MS.]

HEAD-QUARTERS, May 24, 1782.

DEAR SIR:

The enclosed letter from Gen. Leslie you may make use of, to bring the Tories upon Pee Dee to a knowledge of their critical situation, and endeavor to convince them of the danger which impends, to cease their depredations, and beg pardon for their offences. Spare, if possible, the unnecessary effusion of blood; but, at all events, the General desires that the party be dispersed.

I am, dear General, with great esteem, your most obdt. humble sevt.,

WILLIAM PIERCE, JR., *Aid-de-Camp.*

GEN. MARION TO COL. P. HORRY.

[Horry MS.]

ST. STEPHENS, May 24, 1782.

SIR:

Yours of the 17th ult. came to hand. The men lately came out from the enemy for six months' duty. You must endeavor to seize Mrs. M——'s boat and negroes, and make prize of them, agreeable to the Governor's proclamation; a few men may do it easily. She has no pass from the Governor, Gen. Greene, or myself, nor no other person; they wish a stop put to it. I have taken steps with Mrs. T——. In respect to the regulation of trade, we must submit to superior power. I believe that scoundrel you mention has misrepresented to the Governor. I do not know any letters of yours I have not answered. Mr. Dillon, or any other Continental commissary, have nothing to do with the hides or tallow of the militia forces. Mr. Samuel Dwight is appointed by Gen. Greene commissary of issues, for the port of Georgetown, in the Continental line; White must act as commissary of purchases. I am sorry to see so few horses of your regiment to be had, out of so great a number. The officers must give a particular account how they are gone, or it can never be settled. Saunders is resigned. You certainly have a right to make what regulation you think proper in your corps. I shall march from here on Sunday for ———. The news is, that the Parliament have unanimously resolved that whoever advises the King to continue the war in America, shall be deemed a traitor and enemy to the country, and have petitioned him to discontinue the American war. His answer is, that he shall comply with the wishes of his Parliament. All the offensive ministers are put out, and Lord Rockingham is at the head of the administration, and it is expected peace will soon be concluded. The letter sent by Gen. Leslie to Gen. Greene proposes cessation of hostilities; it is said this has taken place at the Northward. It is believed that Count de Grasse and six ships of war were taken in the West Indies in the late fight; but the French and Spaniards have yet got the superiority of those seas. Please send the letters to Murrell, Allston and Long. It is necessary their companies should all be with you, to prevent the enemy from taking advantage when the troops are distant. I think there is little danger of the enemy attempting your post at this time.

I am, your obedient servant,

FRANCIS MARION.

P. S.—Postell's men I shall take with me. Warden, Murrell and Long, will send you half of their companies.

GEN. MARION TO COL. P. HORRY.

[Horry MS.]

St. Stephens, May 25, 1782.

Sir:

Yours of the 25th came to hand. I wrote you yesterday. It would be capital to take these Tories gone to town; about the mouth of Waccamaw will do it. I approve much of your sending Capt. Matthews in Santee. I am glad to hear the galley is got up. She must be fitted and manned for service as soon as possible, and stationed in the conflux of Waccamaw, Pee Dee and Sampit Rivers. I enclosed you brevets for Capt. Milligan and two lieutenants. The armed schooner will be a great addition to our strength and security at your post. All the sails and rigging, &c., belonging to the schooner Three Friends, must be to fit up the galley. The hulk, sell or dispose to the best advantage for the State. I dislike Col. Senff's plan of fortifying Georgetown. I shall visit it soon, and probably throw it wholly aside. I am sorry to see you have so few men, but I refer you to my last letter. I will acquaint the General and Governor respecting Capt. Putnam's vessel. The powder and lead from Capt. Putnam is seasonable. Let me know everything you learn of the Tories' movements and preparations, and take steps to know it by sending proper persons amongst them for the purpose. I believe your danger, if any, will be by water and Pee Dee.

I am, your obedient servant,

FRANCIS MARION.

CAPT. RICHARDSON TO GEN. MARION.

[Horry MS.]

May 26, 1782.

SIR:

By Mr. Harris' wagon you will please receive two chests, containing fifty muskets and bayonets, six pigs and part of a pig lead, quantity 618 lbs.; fifty cartouch boxes and one cask powder, weight 252 lbs. gross, in care of Lieut. Skilling. I sent to Georgetown agreeably to your former orders, twenty muskets and bayonets, by Capt. McClure, of the Artillery. 1 could not procure the baggage wagon you desired; neither of the gentlemen you mentioned had one. The one now sent with the stores I have contracted for, provided you take it, which you will please let me know by Mr. Harris' return. He is to proceed to Georgetown, and from thence return to me. I thank you for the good news you sent me, which portends a speedy peace. I hope the articles now sent will arrive safe, and most heartily wish you success.

I am, sir, your most obedient servant,

WILLIAM RICHARDSON.

GOV. MATTHEWS TO COL. P. HORRY.

[Horry MS.]

CANE ACRE, May 27, 1782.

SIR:

Yours of the —— (no date) I received the last evening. I did not know by whose orders the restrictions on trade at Georgetown had been adopted; but, it appearing to me to be founded on erroneous principles, induced me to give the order I did. As to the Charlestown militia, I have given orders so repeatedly about them, that it is needless to reiterate them. Except a very few, all these men are resident either in Gen. Marion's or Gen. Barnwell's brigade; and the latter being now under the command of Gen. Marion, he has sufficient power over them to do what you have requested of me. Gen. Marion has orders for the ammunition for your post, which, I suppose, he will deliver to you. I will attend to the agreement about the shot as soon as I get your account of it. I have directed Heriot and Tucker to apply to you for a party of men to take charge of some negroes to be brought from Mr. Smith's plantation on Santee. You will, therefore, be pleased to furnish them accordingly, on their application to you; and, also, have the negroes secured in Georgetown until the day of sale.

I am, your obedient servant,

JOHN MATTHEWS.

GOV. MATTHEWS TO GEN. MARION.

[Horry MS.]

CANE ACRE, May 27, 1782.

SIR:

I observe in your orders to Col. Saunders, he is directed to draft the whole of his regiment. I omitted to inform you that I had directed no draws should be made from the John's Island, Wadmelaw, Edisto and Stono companies—these companies being absolutely necessary to be kept at certain points to prevent the commerce between the country and Charlestown. I have, therefore, directed Col. Saunders to adhere to my former orders respecting these companies, and that I would inform you of the same. I suppose Col. Saunders has reported to you the refractory spirit that still prevails in his regiment. Unless vigorous measures are pursued to bring them to order, I am convinced they will do no duty.

I am, sir, your most obedient servant,

JNO. MATTHEWS.

GEN. MARION TO MAJOR GANEY.

[Horry MS.]

LYNCH'S CREEK, June 2, 1782.

SIR:

My last acquainted you that your letter was laid before the Governor and Council. Since that, I have received their instructions, and have sent Col. Peter Horry, Col. Baxter and Major James, to confer with you, and offer such terms as I can, and wish it may be acceded to, and prevent the effusion of blood and distresses of the women and children. The Colonels will give you a paper, in which you will find the determination of the British making peace with the Americans, which leaves you no hope of being supported by them. I have marched thus far with my brigade, for the purpose of either making terms, or prosecuting the war, whenever the term of the truce expires. And you may depend that I shall not infringe it until then; but wish that you may know your own interest, by submitting in time, and preventing ill consequences from obstinacy, which must terminate in your own and your people's destruction, and cannot be prevented when the North Carolinians come on, who are on the march, and are near at hand. Col. Horry, and the gentlemen above mentioned, will talk with you, and acquaint you with every particular with which they are charged. In the meantime, you will consider them under the sanction of a flag of truce; and you, or such men as will meet them at Birche's, shall be protected under that sanction.

I am, sir, your humble servant,

FRANCIS MARION.

Note by Peter Horry: "That Ganey and 700 men surrendered."

GOV. MATTHEWS TO COL. P. HORRY.

[Horry MS.]

CANE ACRE, June 2, 1782.

SIR:

I received your letter by Mr. King on the 31st ult. I approve of your appointment of Capt. Milligan to the command of the galley, and have accordingly enclosed him a commission, and another blank for a lieutenant, to be appointed by Milligan himself, as I think one lieutenant sufficient for the present. You must, by some means or other, procure Mr. Moore a horse, to come up to me; if it can be done by no other means, you must dismount one of your dragoons, and furnish him with his horse, as I have business of a very particular nature to transact with that gentleman. I have no other instructions for Milligan than to use his best endeavors to guard the harbor of Georgetown. The State has at present no particular service to employ Capt. Putnam in.

I am, sir, your most obedient servant,

JNO. MATTHEWS.

P. S.—Col. Lushington informs me there is a Mr. Edward Hair lately arrived at Georgetown, in a flag from Charlestown. This man's name is on the confiscation list, and is, of course, banished this State. You are, therefore, to order him immediately back to Charlestown, or at least within the enemy's lines, on pain of his incurring the pains and penalties of the Act before mentioned, if hereafter found within our lines. The same gentleman informs me there is one Wm. Graham, also within your command, who is looked upon as a dangerous person. If you should be of this opinion, give him the same orders you do Hair, for an authorised spy is the most dangerous enemy we can have to contend against.

J. M.

COLONEL THOMSON TO GENERAL HENDERSON.

[Original MS.]

AMELIA, June 2, 1782.

DEAR SIR:

I am very sorry to inform you that it is out of my power to get the officers of Col. R. Hampton's regiment to do their duty. When I saw you last, I thought it was the men's fault; but I sent a party of Capt. Rumph's men, under the command of Lieut. Wanamaker, to take all the delinquents of the third division, and bring them to me. He returned yesterday, and informs me that there is not a man in Capt. Dryer's nor Tateman's company, warned to go on duty. I find its the neglect of the officers, for they have had orders ever since the 18th or 19th of last month, for the men to meet at Beaver Creek on the 29th. If you arrest those officers, and have them broke, there is no other men that can, by any means, be entrusted with companies. I can't tell in what manner to act? Should esteem it as a singular favor if you would give orders to Col. Hampton, and let him try what he can do, and consider me no longer as an officer in his regiment. Capt. Rumph informs me Capt. House, and eight other prisoners, made their escape from Orange- burgh, the 31st May, and all the prisoners could have got away if they had tried. He likewise informs me that there are two parties of Tories in the Fork of Edisto; they consist of about fifteen each. If there could be about thirty or forty men to go and stay about in the Fork, they might be dispersed. I should be very glad to go with this com- mand. The command to stay about eight or ten days would be long enough. Capt. Rumph is in great want of ammunition.

I am, dear sir, your most humble servant,

W. R. THOMSON.

GEN. MARION TO MAJOR GANEY.

[Horry MS.]

June 3, 1782.

SIR:

Col. Richardson acquaints me that there was some men who did not, or would not, submit to the terms sent you. All such men will be allowed to go to Charlestown, and be considered as prisoners of war, to be exchanged for the American prisoners. Their wives and children, and such property as is theirs, they will be allowed to take with them, except stock and arms, and shall be safely conducted to town on Satur- day, or sooner, if possible. I shall be glad to see you at Mr. Burches'.

FRANCIS MARION.

GOV. MARTIN TO GEN. MARION.

[Horry MS.]

June 8, 1782.

SIR:

I am favored with two of your letters—one addressed to Gov. Burke, of the 13th of April, and one to myself, of the 20th of May—respect- ing the Tories on Drowning Creek and Pee Dee, and another from Gov. Matthews on the same subject. I beg leave to inform you I highly approve of your intentions, and I am happy that it is in the power of this State to co-operate with you in this undertaking. Accordingly, I have ordered Major Joel Lewis, or the Commanding Officer of the State legionary troops, now on Deep River in Randolph county, immediately tó proceed with that corps, consisting of 250 men, to Mr. Amey's, on Drowning Creek, where he will receive further information from you, and act as you will judge most conducive to the service. I have enclosed him a proclamation respecting such of those people who may be citizens of North Carolina, and join them, which you will please have attended to. If you think it necessary to have more men, Col. Owen, of Bladen county, is directed herewith to furnish you with what number you may think proper, to the amount of his regiment. Please to honor me with every intelligence of moment. In the meanwhile,

    I am, sir, with great respect and esteem, your most obdt. humble sevt.,

        ALEXANDER MARTIN.

GEN. HENDERSON TO COL. HAMPTON.

[Original MS.]

HAIG'S, June 3rd, 1782.

SIR:

    The inclosed is a letter from Col. Thomson respecting the state of your regiment, and his resignation. The former I refer to you, being yourself better acquainted with the circumstance than I can be.

    The latter I have not granted.

        I am sir, with esteem yours, &c.,

        WM. HENDERSON.

GOV. MARTIN TO CAPT. THOMAS OWEN, BLADEN CO. REGIMENT.

[Horry MS.]

WILLIAMSBOROUGH, June 8, 1782.

SIR:

    On application of Brigadier-General Marion, you will order out as many militia of your regiment as he shall judge necessary to be under his command in subduing the Tories on Drowning Creek and Pee Dee.

        I am, sir, your humble servant,

        ALEX. MARTIN.

GEN. GREENE TO GEN. MARION.

[Horry MS.]

HEAD QUARTERS, June 9, 1782.

DEAR SIR:

I had a line from you a day or two ago, and am glad to hear you are in a fair way of bringing the people upon the Pee Dee to a better temper. I wish the business was over, and you on this side the Santee. The Tories in that quarter are doing great mischief, and distressing all the good people in that quarter. By a person just from town, I learn the enemy are equipping three galleys for the destruction of the stores at Georgetown. Put the people there on their guard, and give every necessary order for the defence of the place. If there are any public stores in town that cannot be immediately sent to the army, for want of wagons, they had best be sent up the river to the place you mentioned to me. We have no news from the Northward. The enemy talk loudly again in Charlestown of a peace. In haste,

I am, dear sir, your most obedient humble servant,

NATHANIEL GREENE.

GEN. MARION TO COL. P. HORRY.

[Horry MS.]

BURCH'S, June 9, 1782.

DEAR SIR:

Yours of the 5th inst. came to hand. I am very sorry to hear you are yet sick. Yesterday, Major Ganey and myself signed a treaty. The principals are to submit it, and those who do not chose it are to be permitted to go within the enemy's lines with their wives and children, and their movable property, except stock, which they may sell. It seems all the officers will go, and a few men who are so notorious, as they will not be suffered to live. Col. Fanning, with thirty men, came a few days ago in the truce, and is thought will endeavor to make his way to Charlestown; but it is not unlikely he may make some attempt on your post, as his number is increased since he came. You will, therefore, guard against any sudden attack, by keeping a look-out at Wragg's and Black River Ferries. I am informed your troops receive rations of coffee and sugar—I mean the militia with you. I never knew that such articles were ever given to troops but in a besieged garrison, where provisions are scarce, and therefore must be stopped. Mutton, veal and poultry are not soldiers' food. I also am informed, that the officer who succeeds you in command, when you are absent, gives passes to men to go to Dewees' with articles for trading. You must give a general order to prevent it, and occasional commandants must be notified to take that liberty. Please send me some coffee by the bearer, as I am entirely out. You will let me know any particulars you may learn, for I find I cannot return soon, as we cannot finish here before the 25th ult., which is the time that these who are to go to town are to march, and possibly some few on the line, who never were subject to any command, may give us further trouble. I am with wishing you a speedy recovery,

Your obedient servant,

FRANCIS MARION.

GEN. MARION TO COL. P. HORRY.

[Horry MS.]

BURCH'S, June 12, 1782.

DEAR SIR:

Yours of the 10th came to hand the last evening, with the coffee, and shall be obliged to you to send me a few pounds of sugar per bearer. Provisions are so scarce here, that I am obliged to send boats down for rice. You will send by express thirty barrels, from whoever may have it, without regard of public or private property or engagements. If Heriot and Tucker have any by them, it must be taken from them, notwithstanding anything they may say, for without a supply I must move down, which would be of the worse consequence, until I can fully see the treaty properly executed. Mr. Fanning is very busy in recruiting men. On Friday next Ganey is to have a meeting of his people, to see who are to go to town, and who stay. I only wait until then, when I shall march over the river and overawe those who may be wavering, or will not give up or go to town. If Major Skelly is landed, I desire he may be parolled in a house where he may be genteelly and politely treated; and you will tell them I should have no objection to parole him to Charlestown, if he would get Lieut. Henry Ravenel parolled within our lines. I am told he is put in the provost; if so, Major

Skelly will be detained until he is liberated. You will give the Major a flag to Gen. Leslie, to effect that matter, and send his letters, after perusing them; this I wish may be done immediately. Enquire of the captain of the vessel who captured Major Skelly, if he found no letters or papers about him, as he must be charged with some important business to the Commander in Georgia. Three boats set out this day for the rice; if they can take more than thirty barrels, they must bring them. I beg the rice may be ready by the time they arrive.

I am, dear sir, your obedient servant,

FRANCIS MARION.

N. B.—Let me know if the man sent to Gov. Martin with my despatches has returned.

CAPT. CRAFTON (OF NORTH CAROLINA) TO GEN. MARION.

[Horry MS.]

CAMP AT CONNER'S DOWDS, June 13, 1782.

SIR :

I have received orders from his Excellency Gov. Martin, to march the State legion and join you at Sent's Bridge, on Drowning Creek, where I expect I shall be by the 16th inst., ready to receive any orders from you, either to act jointly or separately, as you may judge most advisable. The Governor informs me that you are to be at Mar's Bluff, on the 17th inst., which place I have sent the packet directed to you. If any orders or directions would be necessary to alter my route, you will be pleased to order them to meet as soon as possible, as I should wish to be down to the place designed for my destination. The State legion, now under my command at this place, consists of about 270 men, all well armed. I have some powder for the militia that may be ordered to join me. The Governor promised to order lead down from Salisbury by that part of the legion that is to join me from that district, but they have not yet joined. I have about three hundred dozen of cartridges already made up. I shall march from this place to-morrow morning.

I am, sir, with respect, your very humble servant,

BENNET CRAFTON.

GOV. MATTHEWS TO GEN. MARION.

[Horry MS.]

CANE ACRE, June 15, 1782.

SIR :

Your letter of the 9th inst., enclosing the articles of agreement entered into with Ganey and his party, came safe to me on the 13th. I
took the earliest opportunity of laying them before the Council for
their consideration, and, after weighing them with that circumspection
which was due to their interesting contents, they have signified their
unanimous approbation of the same. They also meet with my most
hearty concurrence; and permit me, sir, to express to you the high
sense I entertain of the services you have rendered to the State on this
important occasion. The measures adopted by you are so well calculated, that they could not fail to produce the favorable issue which has
attended them; and I think there is every reason to expect that the
advantages to be derived to the State from so happy a termination of
this matter, will be still more diffusive than they have   yet appeared to
be, and will, in a short time, work a total extinction of that spirit of
discord which has so unfortunately pervaded this State for some time
past. It is necessary I should have the names of the persons who are
parties to the agreement, as every man's name must be included in the
proclamation of pardon; I should, therefore, be glad you would forward
them to me as soon as you can, and, in the meantime, inform them of
the reasons for delaying the proclamation, as they might otherwise suspect an intention of avoiding it. I have no particular orders to give,
but I must earnestly recommend your earliest attention to be paid to
the militia of this brigade, who are the most incorrigibly obstinate and
perverse beings that I have ever met with, and who are absolutely a
disgrace to the State. I am convinced, from repeated experiments I
have made of them, that nothing but the most rigid execution of the
militia law with regard to them, can ever bring them to a proper sense
of their duty. In speaking of the brigade, it is necessary I should
inform you that the militia of the islands are by no means to be included
in the censure; on the contrary, they merit applause; for, notwithstanding their exposed situation, they early submitted, and, whilst the other
parts of the brigade were behaving in the most unwarrantable manner,
they cheerfully submitted to every order given them, and have repeatedly repulsed the attacks of the enemy on the islands, and, as far as I
have had occasion to employ them, they have done their duty. I have

this moment received your letter of the 16th inst. Most of its contents have already been observed upon. The mode in which you propose to treat Major Skelly, I think may be productive of very good consequences. I sent Mr. Wilson, the sheriff for Cheraws, his commission three months ago, and am surprised to find he has not received it. It must be lying somewhere at Georgetown; but, if he cannot get it, I will send him another. However, his not having the commission need not prevent him from acting. The appointment by the Legislature is the substantial part; the commission is more a matter of form.

I am, sir, your most obedient servant,

JOHN MATTHEWS.

GEN. MARION TO COL. P. HORRY.

[Horry MS.]

BURCH'S, June 15, 1782.

SIR:

Enclosed you will find Gen. Greene's information of the enemy's intention. You will, if possible, take your post in Georgetown, and follow the orders given to Lieut.-Col. Badley, as I do not know where you are, or if you can possibly take the command.

I am, your obedient servant,

FRANCIS MARION.

NATHANIEL GREEN TO MAJ. RUDULPH AND THE CAPTAINS OF THE LEGION.

[Original MS.]

HEAD QUARTERS, June 18, 1782.

GENTLEMEN:

Your letter of resignation of this day contains an accusation no less indelicate than unjust. You say, my orders contain such injustice, and are so repugnant to your feelings, that you cannot consistent with your established rights serve me any longer. I am not conscious of having done you injustice—I am sure I never intended it. You arrogate the sole right of judging and deciding upon privileges claimed but not authorised. You do not distinguish between what has been matter of indulgence and what are rights inherent from the constitution of your corps. I will not take upon myself to say positively that I have not invaded the privileges of your corps; but I am so fully persuaded of the propriety of my conduct upon the strictest military principles that I am perfectly willing to submit it to our superiors in Congress—the Board of War—the Commander-in-chief, or either of them. I have always conceived some privileges were intended your corps, not in common with the rest of the cavalry; but in that I may be mistaken. The late referrence to the Board of War will decide. I can see no necessity for the extraordinary step you are taking; if you think yourselves injured in matters of right and not of indulgence, represent the affair to Congress. Enclose a copy of my orders to Lieutenant-Colonel Lee, and let him bring the business to an explanation. If their decission corresponds with your sentiments, I shall be happy to confess my error. I am sure I have not a wish in my heart to retrench one privilege of the Legion, nor am I disposed to wantonly sport with the feelings of officers. But it is not in my power always to accommodate the service to the views of particular officers. Every person can judge of their own difficulties, but it is impossible to judge fairly for others without a collective view of all the circumstances. This you cannot have in the present case or I am persuaded you would not decide so hastily. The measure you are about to take may involve some disagreeable couse- quences to yourselves—perhaps to me. The world will judge of the propriety of your conduct not according to your way of thinking, but from the original principles of the matter in dispute; and I leave you to consider how unwarrantable a combination of this sort will appear in the critical situation of the Southern States, and how in- consistent with the character and dignity of your corps and the duty and obligation you owe to your country, and to the cause in which you are engaged. I readily confess you may have it in your power to hurt me as an individual, but let not little resentments plunge you into measures injurious to the public and unjust to yourselves. I am per- suaded upon a fair investigation of the matter and by reasoning more fully on the subject, you will be convinced that I have acted perfectly consistent with the duties of my station, with the established customs of armies and consonant to the rights of your corps. But be that as it may, let it be decided by those in power, whose determination shall govern my conduct; and to convince you that I am by no means dis- posed to do the least injury to your rights you shall see all I write both to Congress and Lieut.-Colonel Lee. If I am mistaken Congress will correct me; but if you are wrong, I presume you will have generosity enough to acknowledge it; and I am persuaded you will have the spirit of patriotism sufficient to continue your services to your country. I will add only one more observation and close this long and disagreeable letter. I have never known but very few officers leave the service in the progress of this war, but have repented of it. Combinations are always odious, and no character, however important, or set of men, however useful, can produce any great revolution in so great a cause. Let not secret insinuations mislead you, nor be so idle as others have been to think the public cannot do without you. I know your value and shall feel your loss, and wish you to reconsider the matter before you take your final resolution.

I am, gentlemen, with great respect,
your most obedient humble servant,
NATHANIEL GREENE.

MAJ. RUDOLPH TO GEN. GREENE.

[Original MS.]

JUNE 19, 1782.

SIR :

We are this moment honored with yours. We differ in opinion as to our rights, and can't think of waiting the decision of Congress laboring under the grievance.

You have already decided—our men are drafted *from us,* and of consequence you thought our services to our country no longer wanted.

As to our patriotism we beg leave to judge for ourselves.

We have the honor to be, sir,
your most obedient humble servant,
JOHN RUDOLPH, &c., &c., &c.

GEN. LESLIE TO MAJOR SKELLY.

[Horry MS.]

CHARLESTOWN, June 21, 1782.

DEAR SKELLY:

I am glad to hear you are well. Mr. Scott showed me a letter from you. I fear the Commandant of Georgetown cannot settle anything in

13

regard to your exchange, however, on your arrival in this city. I do assure you that Lieut. Ravenel shall be immediately parolled, and sent out of town. I am going to a grand German *fete champetre.* I hope you got mine by Mr. Bordeaux.

Yours, in haste,

A. LESLIE.

You shall hear from me very soon, if I don't see you.

GOV. MATTHEWS TO GEN. MARION.

[Horry MS.]

CANE ACRE, June 22, 1782.

SIR :

The evacuation of Savannah, and the highest probability that St. Augustine is likewise evacuated, offer so fair an opportunity of obliging the enemy to abandon the post they hold in this State, that it would be criminal not to make the attempt. I must, therefore, desire you would immediately draft one-half of your brigade, and as many more within eighty miles of Charlestown (agreeably to the law) as will be consistent with the safety of the country, and immediately put them in motion, and join the army under the command of Gen. Greene. If the men will now do their duty with cheerfulness and punctuality, I think I may almost venture to assure them this will be the last grand effort they will be called upon to make. I hope you have finished the business you are at present upon, before you receive this; if not, pray expedite it as much as possible, so that that may not interfere with the great object.

I am, sir, your most obedient servant,

JOHN MATTHEWS.

P. S.—It will be so long between the time of your receiving this and your orders respecting this brigade, and the service of, at least, a part of the men being immediately required, that I have given the necessary orders to these three regiments. The Commanding Officer at Georgetown is to forward this letter by express, with all possible expedition.

J. M.

WILLIAM PIERCE, JR., TO MAJOR RUDOLPH, AND THE CAPTAIN
OF THE LEGION.

[Original MS.]

HEAD-QUARTERS, June 23, 1782.

DEAR GENTLEMEN:

I have had a long conversation with General Greene respecting your resignations, and am happy to assure you that he discovered a disposition to accommodate the matter. He has, be assured, a proper idea of your merit, and upon all occasions speaks of the Legion in the warmest strains of panegyric. Your services are acknowledged with great generosity, and his friendship for you, individually, I know to be sincere.

Was the matter properly inquired into, and your rights fairly investigated, perhaps you would be of a different opinion to what you are now. From the information I have received, you did not fairly comprehend the order, and there appears to have been a mistake with respect to the disposition of the troops.

All this, I think, I can convince you of; and I shall feel myself the happiest man in the world to be able to restore to the service a set of officers whom I love and esteem. I think it can be done with satisfaction to yourselves, and with honor to the General.

You complain of having received a letter couched in terms improper and indelicate. I confess it struck me in the same point of light; but be assured I am authorised to say, that the General did not mean it as an insult, nor did he expect that it would meet with such a construction. The manner of resigning your commissions, in my opinion, was improper, and I think all combinations to oppose the measures of a commanding officer had better be avoided, because it inflames and irritates the mind more than it can well support. Had the commissions been sent separately, I think it would have been better. Your letter was rather violent. I wish it had been more moderate. The General is governed as much by prudence as almost any man I know; but in this instance, perhaps, he was carried too far, and in my opinion you have been too hasty. But the matter must be settled, and I beg you to throw aside every prejudice, and prepare your minds for a candid examination of the matter to-morrow. I will wait upon you at McQueen's, between twelve and one o'clock.

I am, dear gentlemen, with sincere friendship, your very humble servt.,

WM. PIERCE, JR.

Will Major Rudolph inform Roger Saunders that we will dine with him to-morrow?

COL. P. HORRY TO GEN. MARION.

[Horry MS.]

GEORGETOWN, June 29, 1782.

DEAR GENERAL:

I commissioned some days, Capt. Seamour, to send me out for our soldiers some clothing—say Russia drab; 70 yards coarse blue cloth, at 6s.; 22 yards red do., at 5s.; 5 dozen coarse hats, at 30s. a dozen; thread, coarse buttons, large and small; about 200 yards coarse linen for pants, from 6d. to 2s. per yard; 3 reams paper, wafers, ink-powder and shirt buttons, amounting in the whole to about £107 sterling, prime cost. These goods have arrived at Santee. My own men that remain are few, and their time nearly expired. I think it best to give them to your men, as very few of mine have only yet three or four months to serve. You desired me to endeavor to procure such goods for the troops. Capt. Seamour entreats you to give him rice, rough even will do; indigo and tobacco will not sell. Lockwood is here with orders from the Governor to load with rice for goods received; and, as you want goods, and they are present, I wish you may find it consistent to take these, and make payment agreeably to the adventurer. The boat waits your answer. The captain has risked these goods (and without a pass) to serve us, and is willing to send you any quantity you may commission him for.

I am, dear General, your obedient servant,

PETER HORRY.

GEN. MARION TO COL. P. HORRY.

[Horry MS.]

July 4, 1782.

SIR:

Since you left me, Mr. Dewees has shown me the bill for the goods you mentioned to me this morning. You will procure as much rough rice as will pay the amount, giving a receipt for it on the public account, and shall be glad you would send the goods to Capt. Roux. You will give what you think is a reasonable profit.

I am, sir, your obedient servant,

FRANCIS MARION.

GOV. MATTHEWS TO GEN. MARION.

[Horry MS.]

CANE ACRE, July 5, 1782.

SIR:

I am informed there is a number of seamen prisoners at Georgetown; I, therefore, desire you would endeavor to negotiate an exchange with the British Commander at Charlestown, for an equal number of American seamen, giving a preference to our own as far as we have a claim.

I am, sir, your obedient servant,

JOHN MATTHEWS.

GEN. GREENE TO GEN. MARION.

[Horry MS.]

HEAD-QUARTERS (Mr. Cattle's Plantation), July 9, 1782.

DEAR SIR:

Yours of the 16th June and 8th July I have had the pleasure to receive, and am made happy that you have brought Major Ganey, and his party, to submit to the laws of the State without making much use of force. Nothing reflects more honor upon an officer than accomplishing that by address which others could effect only by force; to save the effusion of human blood must be the wish of every humane and generous bosom. I fancy you must be mistaken about Mr. Ravenel's being in confinement. Capt. Warren, our Commissary of prisoners, was in town to examine the state of all the prisoners, as well militia as regulars; his report contains no such thing. Capt. Skelly is released in consideration of Judge Pendleton being set at liberty. The Judge has come out, and Capt. Skelly gone in. Should it be found that Mr. Ravenel is in confinement, which I cannot suppose, I will write to Gen. Leslie on the subject. It is evidently for the interest of those corps of Maham and Hampton to be incorporated. Neither would have existence long without it; but, by being consolidated, they will have, perhaps, a permanency during the war, and provision made for them accordingly. You will inform the officers thereof, that it is a matter settled between the Governor and myself, that the two corps be united, and that they are to be considered in future upon the State establishment. This was thought advisable after the fullest examination of the matter, and I hope the officers will make no difficulty in concurring in a measure equally beneficial to them, as necessary for the public good. The requisitiou for the militia was upon the supposition that the garrison of Savannah might come to Charlestown, and give the enemy such an additional force as to enable them to give a blow to our army. I believe Savannah is not fully evacuated, and therefore nothing to apprehend at present; you will remain, therefore, on the other side of Cooper River, between that and Santee, to protect the people from the daily depredations of little parties from Charlestown. If the garrison of Savannah arrives, I will notify you, and direct you where to form a junction with me. It is said that Fanning is determined to have you, dead or alive, therefore, take care of yourself. It is, also, reported, by a person in the enemy's secrets, that a large party of the enemy is to move out soon into St. Thomas' and St. Stephens' parishes.

I am, dear sir, your most obedient servant,

NATHANIEL GREENE.

July 10, 1782.

By a woman from town last night, I have just heard the garrison of Savannah is actually arrived at Charlestown. If it should prove true, you will hear from me again immediately.

COL. SAUNDERS TO GEN. MARION.

[Horry MS.]

July 10, 1782.

SIR:

Enclosed you will find a return of the defaulters of six companies. Not a single man has come to camp as yet, nor don't believe they will without being forced to it. I will send you a return of my regiment as soon as I can get the reports from the upper companies. I have sent for them repeatedly, but to no purpose. The Governor desired me not to order any man from the islands. I have got about fifty men on duty near Bacon Bridge, and don't expect any more will join camp without there is something done to make the men at home do duty.

I am, sir, your most obedient servant,

JOHN SAUNDERS.

GOV. MATTHEWS TO GEN. MARION.

[Horry MS.]

ASHLEY RIVER, July 18, 1782.

SIR:

I received your letter of the 16th late last evening. The officers of Col. Maham's corps seem to imitate the principle upon which the incorporation is founded. They appear to imagine it to be an admission of Major Conyer's corps into Col. Maham's; but this is not the case. There is a material difference between drafting one regiment into another, and consolidating two regiments into one. In the first instance, the drafted regiment is either disbanded altogether, or the officers sent out to recruit; in the second, there is an indiscriminate mixture of men, without giving a superiority in either one or the other, and the officers are commonly retained according to their rank; but sometimes the arbitrary rule of retaining them, according to their merit, has been adopted from this state of the case. The objection that Conyers is disliked by Maham and some of his officers, is frivolous, because Conyers can with equal propriety make the same objection to Maham and his officers; and these gentlemen deceive themselves very much when they set up a claim of superiority, for they have no manner of pretension to it, for the reasons I have given; and as to the abilities of Major Conyers, I believe, sir, you are no stranger to them, and that they entitle him to a claim equal to most officers; his merit stands confessed by every impartial man who knows him. If, after these considerations, gentlemen will suffer themselves to be guided by private pique, and rather resign their commissions than submit to the established rules of propriety and justice, why, they must do so, and we must endeavor to find men that will engage in the service from a pure, ardent zeal to love their country. Such will be less governed by passions, when they can't have their own humour gratified. I send you an extract of the minutes of the Council, from which time the commissions of Conyers and his officers are to bear date. It is true the corps was ordered by Gov. Rutledge to be raised in September; but, as it was afterwards rejected by the Legislature, the whole of that arrangement was done away, and can only be considered as commencing from the re-establishment by me after I came into office. On consulting Gen. Greene, I find Maham's must be considered as a State corps, on Continental pay. I should be very glad to be furnished with a return of Maham's and Conyer's corps as soon as you can procure it with accuracy.

I am very sorry to hear of poor Gough's fate; but it is astonishing to me that gentlemen will venture themselves in that part of the country, when they see we cannot afford protection to it, and that it is a nest for a great part of the devils in the British service. I have sent you an order for 100 stand of arms. I have some faint idea that there is some medicine at Richardson's, on the high hills of Santee. When you send for the arms, pray enquire if there is no one there. I know of no mode of getting them but from Georgetown; I, therefore, enclose you a letter to Heriot and Tucker, desiring them to endeavor to procure you a supply agreeably to such list as you may send them. The Continental hospitals here are but scantily supplied at present. Your presence is very much wanted in this quarter; indeed, every day renders it more and more necessary. I enclose you two brevets for Messrs. Huggins and Rothmahler, agreeably to your request, and have left the name blank. Savannah was completely evacuated on the 11th instant. Wayne, who is usually very sanguine, supposed, upon the commencement of the evacuation, it would have been pushed forward with great rapidity, and this led me to say to you that it was evacuated; indeed, it would have been so in three days, were it not for the Tories, and their negroes, whom they were obliged to carry off. Our prospects are flattering, and, if rightly improved, there is reason to expect we shall soon be at ease. It affords me very singular pleasure to hear you have finally settled the tranquility of the district of Little Pee Dee; so happy a conclusion to an affair, which, in its first stage, wore but a gloomy aspect, reflects great honor on you, sir, and promises lasting advantage to the State. Pray, is Ganey returned; I wish he may not be playing a fast and loose game. Mr. David Rumph has proposed to me to raise a party of militia horse for the protection of the part of the country he lives in. I have directed him to apply to you to know whether you approve of the plan.

I am, sir, your most obedient servant,

JOHN MATTHEWS.

GOV. MATTHEWS TO GEN. MARION.

[Horry MS.]

ASHLEY RIVER, July 19, 1782.

SIR:

I herewith send you two copies of the laws passed in the last sessions. There are several inaccuracies in the printing, but it luckily happens that there is not one in the law giving extraordinary powers. In my last letter I forgot to take notice of the circumstances of the prisoners. I had a complaint made me some time ago, of their severe treatment, and represented it to Gen. Greene, who, in consequence thereof, sent down the Commissary of prisoners to examine into the affairs, and on his return reported that he could find no marks of ill treatment of the prisoners, except that some of them were in want of clothing (which you know they are not obliged to find them). Whether he was deceived in his investigation of the matter, by false appearances, or what, we can't tell; but I have again spoken to Gen. Greene, and he will have a further enquiry made. As to his taking prisoners out of our hands, you know the law of Congress authorises him so to do, and, as one of the United States, we are compelled to submit to it, however disagreeable to our feelings. I have sent you thirty blank commissions, which are all I have. You will observe they are printed with Mr. Rutledge's name (and a few with mine); but, for want of others, I am obliged to make use of them, for our printer is sick, and I can get nothing done by him at present; nor has he printed any newspaper for some time past.

I am, sir, your most obedient servant,

JOHN MATTHEWS.

MAJOR BURNET TO GEN. MARION.

[Horry MS.]

HEAD-QUARTERS, Ashley Hill, July 24, 1782.

SIR:

I am directed by Major-General Greene to request you will be pleased to furnish fifty men as an escort to some wagons with clothing, waiting at Laurens' Ferry for the purpose. The General desires you will, as early as possible, furnish him with a return of the men you have, specifying the number, how they are armed, and how many days it will take you to join this army, after your receive this order.

I am, with respect, your most obdt. humble servant,

J. BURNET, Aide-de-Camp.

MAJOR BURNET TO GEN. MARION.

[Horry MS.]

HEAD-QUARTERS, Ashley Hill, July 26, 1782.

SIR:

I am directed by Major-General Greene to inform you, that the quarter part of the garrison of Savannah have arrived at Charlestown.

This reinforcement places the enemy in a situation to act offensively. The General begs you will order the troops under your command to Bacon Bridge with as much expedition as possible, as the advanced position of the army exposes it to be attacked by the enemy whenever they may think proper. Gen. Greene is fully persuaded that no time will be lost in taking the position at the bridge.—I have the honor to be, with much respect and esteem,

Your most obedient servant,

J. BURNET, Aide-de-Camp.

GEN. GREENE TO GEN. MARION.

[Horry MS.]

HEAD-QUARTERS, July 27,. 1782.

DEAR SIR :

I have this moment got intelligence that the enemy are embarking a body of troops to make a descent upon Georgetown, and in all probability will be there before to-morrow night. The stores there are immense. I wish you, therefore, to march immediately for the protection of that place and the stores. All the State troops and militia you have under your command, notwithstanding the orders you received yesterday, to join this army, after putting your troops in motion for Georgetown, you will repair there yourself as soon as you can, and take such measures the occasion may require. To send the stores up the rivers, appears the only probable way of saving them. 700 men go by land and water.

I am, dear sir, with great esteem, &c.,

NATHANIEL GREENE.

[Original MS.]

PHILADELPHIA, July 28, 1782.

I do hereby certify, that the bearer, Col. Richard Hampton of South Carolina, who is well known to me, is a steady friend to his country. Having occasion to go on business to the eastern States, it is hoped he will meet with no interruption.

J. RUTLEDGE.

To all whom it may concern.

GOV. MATTHEWS TO GEN. MARION.

[Horry MS.]

UXBRIDGE, Ashley River, July 30, 1782.

SIR:

I was not less surprised than concerned on receipt of your letter to-day, to find you at Wasmasaw, instead of being on the other side of Santee. Mr. Singleton, who was the express that carried the letter for you, deserves to be hanged. Pray, find him out, and have him confined, for he shall certainly answer for this infamous piece of negligence. Had you received the letter on Sunday morning, which was the time you ought to have got it, Georgetown might, in all probability, have been saved; but it must now, beyond all doubt, be lost. The last of the British troops, 170 in number, did not quit Charlestown until yesterday afternoon; you could, therefore, have been a full days' march ahead of them, besides, your then position being so much nearer the scene of action than that of the enemy's. On the contrary, they will now have a days' march of you, consequently the fall of Georgetown must inevitably follow, and which must be a dreadful stroke to us. The whole of the land forces said to be employed on this expedition is about 700. If any thing can be done to save the place, or any part of the stores, I am sure your utmost endeavors I can depend on. I am convinced the opportunity is lost. Pray, let me hear from you as soon as anything is done, and what is the fate of the place.

I am, sir, your obedient servant,

JOHN MATTHEWS.

GEN. GREENE TO GEN. MARION.

[Horry MS.]

HEAD-QUARTERS, July 30, 1782.

DEAR SIR:

I have just got your letter of this day, dated at Wasmasaw. Nothing ever surprised me more. I was in the highest hopes you were at or near Georgetown. Mr. Singleton, by whom I wrote, was fully informed of the contents of the letter, and the necessity of its being delivered with all possible dispatch. He had a letter for Col. Lushington, and promised to have it delivered in Georgetown the day following the date of your letter, by 10 o'clock, and yours I expected would have got to you by one in the morning, and you on your march before sunrise. Never did I feel such a vexatious disappointment in all the course of my life. I beg you will make enquiry into the cause of the delay, as you write that mine never got to your hands until this morning. Somebody deserves nothing short of hanging. I am afraid you will now arrive too late to be of any service, unless the goods should be got up the rivers, and your force deter the enemy from following them. Since I wrote you, the enemy's intentions have been again confirmed by repeated accounts. I need not urge you to use all possible dispatch in marching to the relief of the place, as your own zeal will stimulate you to do all in your power. I have not heard anything from the party that crossed to Haddrell's Point, whether they proceeded or not; but, in order to alarm their fears, I made a move in force towards James' Island, to induce them, if possible, to countermand the order. I beg you will let me hear from you respecting the progress the enemy has made, and if they have attempted anything, and how far they were successful. If the enemy has not made the descent, you will wait in the neighborhood of Georgetown until you hear further from me. I consider the disappointment of your not getting my letter the greater, as I find your force so respectable, as they appear by your returns.

I am, sir, your obedient servant,

NATHANIEL GREENE.

MAJOR PIERCE TO GEN. MARION.

[Horry MS.]

HEAD-QUARTERS, Ashley Hill, August 4, 1782.

DEAR GENERAL:

I am desired to acknowledge the receipt of your letter of the 1st August to Gen. Greene. The General is happy to find that you have arrived at Georgetown before the enemy. He is in hopes that the removal of the stores, and your being in the possession of the works, will prevent any serious attempt on that part. Should the British relinquish their design against Georgetown, and return back to Charlestown, I have to inform you that it is the wish of the General that you should re-cross the Santee, and take a position on Cooper River as speedily as possible. Every necessary step for the support of the town, and the effectual security of the stores, you will please to make particular objects of your attention.

I am, dear General, with much esteem, yours, &c.,

WM. PIERCE, JR., Aide-de-Camp.

GEN. GREENE TO GEN. MARION.

[Horry MS.]

HEAD-QUARTERS, Ashley Hill, August 9, 1782.

DEAR GENERAL:

I have just received your letter of the 5th. I am sorry the enemy is so situated as to give them an opportunity to carry off the produce of the country, without your having it in your power to injure them. Cannot small parties interrupt them, or is there any move that we can make that may tend to dislodge them. Great preparations are making in Charlestown for the evacuation of the place. I am persuaded it will take place soon, and the more scanty we can render their supplies of provisions, the sooner it will happen, and the fewer negroes they will have in their power to take with them. I am glad you have got through the disagreeable business of uniting Maham's and Hampton's corps. In the present form I am in hopes they will be useful. Should the enemy leave Santee, you will cross the river and move towards the Cooper. But it is necessary I should inform you that the enemy are advised of my wishes on this head, having taken Mr. Singleton with a number of letters—among others, one for you. With respect to the beef collectors, I am a stranger to it. We have no Commissaries of our own, they are all under the government of Mr. Hort, and by him appointed. But I should not suppose these people will dare to rise in the present situation of things, and it is necessary they should contribute to the support of the army as well as other parts of the State.

I am, dear sir, your most obedient humble servant,

NATHANIEL GREENE.

GEN. GREENE TO COL. P. HORRY.

[Horry MS.]

HEAD-QUARTERS, August 10, 1782.

DEAR SIR:

Your letter of the 20th July, came safe to hand. The dissolution of your corps, or rather embodying it with other corps, I think a prudent measure. At present, I have no commands which will interfere with your wishes for retiring. All the cavalry corps are incorporated into one, and the great probability of a speedy evacuation of Charlestown will, I hope, render your further services unnecessary. Whether you are a supernumerary or not, don't depend on my opinion; but if those letters are all you have to found your claim upon, I think you are not, however great your sufferings, expense and trouble, since I have been to the Southward. I flatter myself you feel yourself happy in the reflection that you have aided your country in the hour of her greatest distress, and that the efforts have contributed to her deliverance. I sincerely thank you for your polite attentions to all my wishes, and for the very essential service which you have rendered the public and me in the arduous struggle.

I am, with great esteem and regard, your most obt. humble servant,

NATHANIEL GREENE.

MAJOR WARLEY TO GEN. MARION.

[Horry MS.]

CAMP CONGAREE, August 11, 1782.

DEAR GENERAL:

I take the liberty of enclosing you the names of near 500 soldiers, belonging to the 3d regiment, most of whom were absent at the time Charlestown surrendered to the enemy. Many of them are entitled to their discharges; but the greater part are deserters, and I hope will be apprehended and made to serve their times over, at least. A few have already been taken up and tried by a court martial in camp, and sentenced to serve in the South Carolina line two days for every absent one. Whether this kind of punishment is right or not, I am at a loss to know; however, the men seem satisfied with it. I heartily wish this list may enable you to strengthen our line, which is still very weak, as you will see by the annexed return of the detachment under my command. I propose making out a few copies now, in order to send to Gens. Henderson and Pickens, and to some of the militia Colonels. Corporal Gambell unfortunately, a few days ago, killed one of the recruits from Georgetown, by the name of Charles Smith. He was soon after committed to Orangeburgh jail by a magistrate of this district. I have not heard what success the officers recruiting have had lately. Lieuts. Martin and Langford wrote Gen. Huger, about a fortnight ago, that they then had enlisted eight men for the South Carolina line, four of whom are in camp, the rest on furlough. Capts. T. Warley and Levercher have, also, sent from Georgetown nine recruits, and two other soldiers.—I am, with the greatest respect, dear General,

Your most obedient humble servant,

FELIX WARLEY, *Captain.*

GOV. MATTHEWS TO GEN. MARION.

[Horry MS.]

UXBRIDGE, Ashley River, August 14, 1782.

SIR:

Your letters of the 6th and 9th inst., are come safe to hand, but the paper containing the consolidation of Maham's corps you have not sent me, which I suppose was omitted by some mistake. I enclose you —— blank commissions. I very much approve of your plan of removing the rice from Santee to Georgetown, for Gen. Leslie has this day given official information that he is greatly distressed for want of provisions, and that unless I will furnish him, he must come and take it; therefore, you must expect another visit from him before he goes. As to your proposal to send rice to Charlestown for clothing, that is now rendered unnecessary, as we shall be in possession of it in the course of a month or six weeks. The rice, &c., which Mr. Selby has permission to send to town, is in payment for clothing furnished the officers of our line, and the supernumerary officers; therefore, his vessel ought not to be detained. I am much surprised at your mentioning that the time of Maham's men will all expire in a little time. I understood you, the last time we conversed on that subject, that very few were enlisted for one year, but most for two and three years. This circumstance has given me much uneasiness; and, to relieve my difficulties, I request you would forward me the return of the regiment without delay, that I might know what to determine on respecting that regiment. Although I am clearly of opinion there ought to be two Majors to a regiment, I should wish first to see before I make an appointment, that the state of the corps is such as to render the creation of another Major necessary. I must first see Gen. Greene before I can say anything to you about the exchange of prisoners you mention.

I am, sir, your most obedient servant,

JNO. MATTHEWS.

COL. BENTON TO GOV. MATTHEWS.

[Horry MS.]

ST. DAVID'S, Great Pee Dee, August 20, 1782.

SIR:

Though I have not the honor of a personal acquaintance with you, I am now under the necessity of humbly addressing you in this manner in behalf of the parish and regiment I have the honor to represent and command—a people that have ever stood foremost among those, by their inflexible attachment to their country; suffered many capital distresses, nor did not despair of success in our greatest extremity. Although we have so long been at such a distance from the enemy's lines, and suffering every murder, plundering and cruelty, that could be perpetrated by a banditti of the most desperate villains and mulattoes, immediately bordering on our settlements, we have, on all occasions, turned out, and kept in Gen. Marion's camp equal numbers with any in his brigade. Part of those who were under a truce that have not surrendered, and many other villains in this part of the country, that still continue their outrage, render the lives and property of the good citizens very unsafe; and this disorder, in all probability, must continue, and the re-establishment of good order and civil law hindered, except you, in your goodness, will indulge my regiment with a sufficient guard to the gaol, as it is insufficient of its use; with orders for supplies of provisions for that and the poor inhabitants; an armed party to detect and bring to punishment the refractory and disobedient, which my warm desire for that purpose will induce me to engage to have punctually performed, with all due moderation, for the good of this country, and agreeably to any instructions you may think proper to give me, which I could do, and keep one-fourth on the field on common occasions, and on extraordinary emergencies with cheerfulness turn out one-half. My feelings will not let me omit mentioning to you some characters among them of Mr. Ganey's truce men, who have been received by Gen. Marion as citizens, and are now doing military duty, and enjoying equal privileges with your best soldiers and citizens, who have borne the burden and heat of the day. Such I mean as were meant to be exempted by an Act of the late General Assembly at Jacksonborough —men who have burned, plundered, and in cold blood (after many of our worthiest men had surrendered as prisoners of war) in the most ignominious and cruel manner taken their lives, particularly Col. Abel Robb's, my worthy predecessor, and a gentleman formerly a member of the Assembly, a Justice of the Peace, a good officer and a useful citizen, and capital loss to this part of the country; and the very villains that perpetrated this wanton, horrid murder, burning and plundering, are now, in the face of his distressed family and friends, received and restored to equal privileges with the men who have suffered everything by them that it was in their power and savage disposition to inflict.

I am, sir, your most obedient and very humble servant,

LAMB BENTON, *Lieut.-Col. Com. Cheraw Militia.*

N. B.—Your answer and instructions I shall hope to receive by the bearer, Mr. Vinow, in regard to the above. I do not doubt but Gen. Marion will acquiesce in it, as I·mentioned the matter to him not long since, about provisions, men and ammunition.

If you will be so kind as to furnish us with the militia laws, passed by the last Assembly, it will be of singular service, and the people and myself will be instructed.

GOV. MATTHEWS. TO GEN. MARION.

[Horry MS.]

UXBRIDGE, August 20, 1782.

SIR:

I this day received your letter of the 19th inst., enclosing me a return of the state of Maham's corps, at which I am exceedingly chagrined indeed, for it appears there are no more than seventeen men whose time of service will not expire in a month or six weeks. This deficiency, together with that in the corps brought into the regiment by Conyers, makes the regiment at least but a skeleton, when I expected the State would have had the services of a very respectable corps; and, to add to the misfortune, I cannot command the means of making it better. I have, in two or three instances, involved myself in a vast deal of trouble, by making engagements which I thought I should have been able to comply with; but, on experience, have found myself deceived, and, in consequence of which, I have embarrassed myself exceedingly, and brought on myself much unmerited censure, for which reason I am determined never to pass my word for a guinea, without I have the means in my hands of fulfilling the contract the moment it becomes due; therefore, I have no present means in my hands, nor the least prospect of any before the meeting of the Legislature. It is utterly out of my power to furnish the money to re-engage Maham's men. I can only lament the injury the State must be subject to by this unlucky circumstance, for it is not in my power to remedy the evil. As a body of horse will be what we shall most want when Gen. Greene leaves us (which he will do immediately, as the town is evacuated) I think the best way of disposing of the regiment will be to select the best of the accoutrements and horses, and mount the whole of the men that are retained, and form them again into a regiment of cavalry, and let them remain thus until the meeting of the Legislature, which I shall call

14

together immediately on the evacuation of the town. As you are well acquainted with the state of the corps, I should be glad to have your sentiments on the matter. The enclosed is a copy of my letter to you by Col. Moultrie, who, being taken and carried into town, suppose the letter is lost.

I am, sir, your most obedient servant,
JNO. MATTHEWS.

ANDREW PICKENS TO CAPT. WILLIAM BUTLER.

[Original MS.]

LONG CANE, August 21, 1782.

SIR :

As the situation of this country makes it still necessary that a part of the people should constantly be on duty for the purpose of suppressing such parties of men, as lost to every sense of justice or principle of honesty or humanity, make it their sole study to ruin and distress by every means in their power, every man who shews the least attachment to honesty, regular order and civil government; and as this service will be better performed by men engaged for a certain determinate time, than by the militia called out from time to time as exigences may require, I desire that you will, with all possible expedition, engage and embody twenty-five good men for your own and Captain John Mitchel's companies, exclusive of one Lieutenant, one Quarter Master and two Sergeants, to serve for six months from the day the whole are engaged and reported to me.

They will serve on horse-back, each man furnishing his own horse, saddle, and other accoutrements if he can, but where that is not in his power, you will have horses, saddles, &c., provided for such as are in want by virtue of the warrant to impress such articles herewith given you ; you will be particularly careful to have an exact account kept by the Quarter Master of all such horses, saddles, &c., as may be impressed by you, specifying the person's name for whom they are got, the time when, and the sums to which they are appraised ; all which as well as the people's own horses, you will have the greatest care taken of, that you may always be in a condition fit for service, and that there may be no unnecessary waste of property, you will also take care to make the Quarter-Master give receipts for all provision and forage you receive, and keep a book in which he is to rate regularly all articles, either horses, saddles, provisions, or forage, the two last articles need not be appraised, but the quantity and quality exactly ascertained that the Legislature may with the more ease fix the prices.

You will be particularly careful not to distress any of the good citizens of this State under any pretence, as the interest of this company is to protect, not to injure; you will, therefore, effectually stop all plundering, of every kind, as no property is to be meddled with on any pretence whatever, unless such as may be taken in the field from men in arms against the State, which is to be the property of the captors, except what may be proved to belong to good citizens, doing or always ready to do their duty when called on, who are to have their property delivered to them when proved, without any reward or deduction.

All those who may claim property retaken from the enemy, and who have not themselves done their duty when called on, or who have refused or neglected the same, or moved into other States, will pay one-third part of the value of all such property, to be ascertained by three indifferent men, sworn to appraise the same.

Your company will be governed by the rules and articles for the Government of the troops of this State, and entitled to such pay as is allowed by the present militia law, and they will not be called out of this District, unless on some particular emergency, and by my particular order.

I am sir, your most obedient servant,

ANDREW PICKENS.

MAJOR BURNET TO GEN. MARION.

[Horry MS.]

HEAD QUARTERS, August 23, 1782.

MY DEAR SIR:

I have this moment received information that Major Brewerton was to leave Charlestown with a party yesterday, on an expedition to Santee or Georgetown. As the General will not be in camp till late in the evening, I have despatched an express to communicate the intelligence, that you may take the most effectual measures to counteract the designs of the enemy. Should there arrive any accounts more minute, I suppose Gen. Greene will transmit it as early as possible to you. It is probable the success of Major Doyle has induced them to make a second attempt to collect rice. Is the rice at Waccamaw much exposed?

I am, with great respect, dear sir, your most obdt. humble servant,

J. BURNET, Aide-de-Camp.

GEN. GREENE TO GEN. MARION.

[Horry MS.]

HEAD-QUARTERS, Ashley Hill, August 24, 1782.

DEAR SIR:

I have this moment received your letter of the 23d inst. Since the letter written by Major Burnet yesterday, I have been informed that a fleet, consisting of one sloop-of-war, three galleys, three armed brigs, with ten empty sloops and schooners, having 500 infantry under Major Brewerton and Doyle on board, passed the bar of Charlestown early yesterday morning, destined for Santee and Cambahce, to collect rice. It was supposed they would divide the force nearly equal. I have no doubt but you will take measures to make them pay dearly for the rice they may collect on Santee.—I am, dear sir, with esteem and regard,

Your most obedient humble servant,

NATHANIEL GREENE.

COL. DAVIS TO GEN. MARION.

[Horry MS.]

PRINCE WILLIAMS' PARISH, August 24, 1782.

SIR:

The foregoing regimental return is made according to your orders, and I hope it may prove satisfactory; but I am sorry to inform you that a great number are disobedient to the laws of their country. Your letter dated Murray's Ferry, July 8, 1782, I received the other day only, and in compliance therewith, I answer you per this opportunity. With respect to the names of those who refuse to do duty, their number is so large, that I have mentioned them collectively, which you will see by the annexed return; but could not go down, as I have received a letter from his Excellency the Governor, of a later date than yours, say 11th July, 1782, wherein he desires it to stand drafted as it is, with orders to march at a moment's warning, and let them remain where they are until further orders from him or you, and to give him the earliest notice of any movement of the Tories in my district, who are now quiet and peaceable, and are joining us very fast. I will keep the regiment embodied, and endeavor to enforce the law on the refractory, by going from district to district, till countermanded by your orders. But neighbors are not willing to take those measures which the law points out, with their neighbors, and a small party from your part of the country will do infinite service in making the laws to be observed. Wm. Robertson, Esq., of the Three Runs, is a principal adviser of the refractory. I have been also informed that Col. Thompson, formerly of my regiment, has advised the refractory to stand out a little longer, and they will gain their ends. Not willing to trespass further on your time, I conclude.

Yours, &c.,

WILLIAM DAVIS.

GOV. MATTHEWS TO GEN. MARION.

[Horry MS.]

UXBRIDGE, August 24, 1782.

SIR:

I have every reason to believe the information you enclosed me to be well founded. A note I got two days ago, from a person of good information, agrees substantially with yours. I think a fortnight more will decide the enemy's real intentions. By a woman from town last night, I am informed the enemy's plundering fleet sailed for Georgetown yesterday morning. I am in hopes they will not be so successful there as they were at Santee. I enclose you an order on Mr. Richardson for 200 stand of arms, as the presumption is they are arrived, as I have notice of their leaving Philadelphia the end of June. I have, also, enclosed in the order, a box of sugar for your use, which is now there at Richardson's. Enclosed is a brevet for Dr. Neufville. I find there is some uneasiness in Maham's corps about rank; I could wish you to order a board of officers to sit and determine in the dispute as soon as possible, or as circumstances will admit. As you agree with me that it is best to mount the whole corps to act as cavalry, it is more necessary to have all disputes about rank settled as soon as possible, as a new arrangement must necessarily take place; and I suppose the youngest officers must go out, as was the case in the late arrangement.

I am, sir, your most obedient servant,

JNO. MATTHEWS.

GOV. MATTHEWS TO GEN. MARION.

[Horry MS.]

UXBRIDGE, August 24, 1782.

SIR:

I enclose you a letter I have just received from Lieut.-Col. Benton, and wish you to take such orders therein as you shall think proper.

I am, sir, your most obedient humble servant,

JOHN MATTHEWS.

COL. BENTON TO GEN. MARION.

[Horry MS.]

ST. DAVID'S, August 29, 1782.

SIR :

Yours from Watbo of the 18th inst., I received, and in answer I assure you, that I have constantly been, since my arrival at home, and still am, using my utmost endeavors to send you the full one-third of my regiment. The twenty men with which I had your permission to guard the jail, have been constantly on hard duty, catching and bringing in the disobedient; so that, inclusive of what have been lately ordered, and the guard will bring you, in addition to Major Thomas's class, at least fifty men; and hope to have it in my power, about the 3d of next month, to send you some more, as I expect by that time to have another squad gathered. But, without this armed party to be constantly on duty, and monthly relieved, I cannot do anything, for the district is so extensive, the duty so hard, and the distance to your camp so far, that it can't be expected that the men who have just been discharged from your camp can perform that duty. This mode would have been better executed if the Commanding Officer of my regiment at home, when I was in the camp, had not have hindered every part of my orders (that was in his power) for that purpose. There are but fourteen of the twenty men mentioned that are at this time fit for duty, six of whom I send with the party, and the others will come with the next I have mentioned; though, I hope, you will send them back, as the law cannot be enforced without them. The people are, at this time, very sickly about home, as has appeared by the trials of a number of men by a regimental court I lately ordered, and held four days, when

I used every lawful and reasonable method in my power to turn out the men. There are several men, whom the guard will bring down, sentenced to some extraordinary duty, a list of whose names, and their term of service, I will send to Major Thomas.

I am, sir, with all due respect, your obdt. humble servant,

LAMB BENTON, *Colonel.*

N. B.—If you permit me to continue the guard at the jail, please to give some instructions about salt, &c., for them, as it is scarce here.

GOV. MATTHEWS TO GEN. MARION.

[Horry MS.]

UXBRIDGE, August 29, 1782.

SIR:

I received yours of the 27th the last evening. The information both Gen. Greene and myself had received, agree that there were two parties going out—one Northwardly, and the other Southwardly. However, I am very happy to find they have dropped the Northern expedition, which I am in great hopes will leave you at leisure to form some plan, if possible, to put a stop to this infamous traffic, that is carried on with the town through Goose Creek and down Cooper River. I cannot help thinking it reflects no great credit on our cavalry in this part, to lie still in their quarters and suffer about a dozen or twenty negroes to come out almost every night in the week, and carry off cattle, horses, and anything else they want, within twelve or fifteen miles of their camp; but I have spoke of it so often, that I am determined never to mention the matter again. I must entreat you, sir, to form some plan which will be most effectual to stop such a shameful commerce; it is no less villainous than true that the Charlestown markets are now daily supplied with the greatest plenty of everything they want. There is no political consideration whatever that can induce me to alter the substance of my proclamation. I must request you to have it carried into the most rigid execution. I am clearly convinced nothing will do with the Southern militia until you are at leisure to undertake the management of them. The news contained in the paper you sent me is very important indeed, and I trust will lead to happy consequences. I observe they are contending for a restoration of the confiscated estates. This, I knew, would be the case, and told the House of Assembly so when they were about passing the Confiscation Act; for it is a matter that must be finally settled by negociation. I enclose you a copy of a letter I have just received from Gen. Greene. Poor Laurens! I am very sorry for his fate. I also enclose you twenty blank commissions, which were omitted to be sent before.

I am, sir, your most obedient servant,

JOHN MATTHEWS.

COL. BENTON TO GEN. MARION.

[Horry MS.]

ST. DAVID'S, August 29, 1782.

SIR:

Yours from Watbo I answered, and expect it will be handed you with this, as also yours from Lind's Ferry, of the 26th, is just come to my hands. One-third of my regiment I have under orders to join you, and expect with this will come in about fifty men, in addition to Major Thomas' division, and those that may remain behind I will send with all possible expedition, so that if in my power the public service may not be hindered. As to the men's being relieved monthly, it is so late now that it will be impossible for me to get them in camp until near the middle of the ensuing month. I am very sensible that it will make a considerable confusion in the regiment, as the men do not look upon themselves liable to go to camp yet, and the law will not oblige them until each division does two months' duty agreeably to law; therefore, I must beg to be excused in that particular, and I will send relief early in October, when their tour will be out, according to law.

I remain, with all due regard, your most obedient servant,

LAMB BENTON, *Lieut.-Col. Commandant.*

N. B.—Excuse my paper, &c., which hindered me from writing more fully.   L. B.

GEN. GREENE TO GOV. MATTHEWS.

[Horry MS.]

August 29, 1782.

DEAR SIR:

I have just got letters from Gen. Gist, giving an account of a little action between Col. Laurens and the enemy, about twelve miles below the ferry on Combahee, where he had taken post, and thrown up a little work to fire on the enemy's shipping, as they passed down the river. The enemy landed in considerable force. The Colonel's party being small, was beat back, in which conflict the Colonel fell, and we had the mortification to lose a howitzer. Gen. Gist got up just time enough to save the party from suffering further injury. We had twenty-four killed, wounded and missing. After this action the enemy embarked, and went down the river to the mouth of it, where they lay when Gen. Gist's dispatches came away; it is said they are going to Port Royal. There is no mention made of the enemy's loss; but they must have suffered considerably, and I believe they have got little or no rice. This is the substance of the General's letter. I lament the unhappy fate of Col. Laurens.—I am, with great respect,

Your Excellency's most obedient humble servant,

NATHANIEL GREENE.

GEN. GREENE TO GEN. MARION.

[Horry MS.]

HEAD QUARTERS, Ashley Hill, August 31, 1782.

DEAR SIR:

I most sincerely congratulate you upon the very honorable check you gave the enemy, and I am happy to hear you give such ample testimony to the bravery and firmness of the militia. I wish in every part of the State they were equally deserving the same applause. From what has passed, you may see how little dependence is to be placed in the enemy's peaceable professions. It gives me the highest satisfaction to find that they are disappointed in their expectations of finding you off your guard, from the arts that had been practised to effect it. At the close of every month, you will give me a return of the Continental and State troops, and the militia serving under your command, specifying where they are employed, and for what purpose, as I want to give the minister of war as satisfactory an account as possible of the force of this country.

I am, dear sir, your most obedient humble servant,

NATHANIEL GREENE.

GOV. MATTHEWS TO GEN. MARION.

[Horry MS.]

UXBRIDGE, September 1, 1782.

SIR:

Your letter, received yesterday, relieved me from a great deal of uneasiness, as Mr. K. Simons came down two days before and informed me that he was apprehensive, from the accounts he had heard, that your brigade had been defeated, a total route ensued, and that they had suffered severely. Under these impressions, you may judge what must have been my feelings on receipt of your letter yesterday. I most sincerely congratulate you, sir, on your triumph over the deep laid scheme of our inveterate enemies. Their disappointment, in a plan they had depended so much upon, must chagrin them far more than their loss. Your account of the behavior of the militia reflects great honor on them, and exhibits an example worthy of imitation by the rest of their brethren. With respect to the prize you mention, I would have you by all means carry the proclamation into force against her in the most rigid manner—also, with regard to any others that might be taken; for, notwithstanding every exertion, the Charlestown markets are amply supplied with all kinds of provisions, by a parcel of mercenary, infamous wretches, who make lucre their only object, no matter how diabolical the means they pursue to obtain it, or how prejudicial it may be to the interest of their country.

I am, sir, your most obedient humble servant,

JOHN MATTHEWS.

GOV. RUTLEDGE TO CAPT. SIMONS.

[Horry MS.]

September 1, 1782.

SIR:

I have had the honor of receiving your letter of yesterday, requesting me to peruse a note from Capt. Giles, signifying to you that an officer of the Pennsylvania line had informed the officers of Col. Lee's legion, that you, at the Governor's table at dinner, had called them all a trifling set of fellows, and that they were all privates, sergeants or corporals in the army, and that Gen. Greene should not have restored them their commissions again, but have filled up their vacancies with gentlemen of merit resident in this State; and that the officers, having heard you make use of these illiberal expressions, or words to that effect, told you that the officers of Lee's corps were gentlemen, and that you were a rascal or scoundrel for saying what you did, of which abuse you took no notice. In compliance with your further request, that I would relate what I recollect of the conversation which passed at the Governor's quarters about that period, that some of the officers of Col. Lee's legion had resigned, I will state it as clearly and as fully as the length of time which has intervened will admit of. I do not now recollect, nor do I think, that we had any conversation at dinner relating to Lee's corps; but in the afternoon some of the company withdrew into the piazza, and others remained in the room in which we had dined. The officer of the guard, Capt. Blake, yourself, and, I think, Col. —— and Mr. Prioleau, were of the first party; I, and some other gentlemen, remained behind. Hearing some altercation between you and the officer of the guard relative to some order which had been issued, or letter written by Major Rudolph, I walked into the piazza, and after a time I asked what had given rise to the conversation which appeared to be rather warm, though by no means indecent. You answered it had been asserted, and to the best of my recollection you added, by the officer of the guard—but of this I cannot be positive—that Major Rudolph, when he resigned his command, assigned as a reason to the corps that he was tired of the service, and that you thought although an officer had a right to resign his commission if he considered himself ill used, yet he had no right to assign such a reason as might create disaffection in the corps; that you had served with the officers of the legion, you knew they were valuable, and loved some of them like brothers—still, if Major R. had issued the order which had been attributed to him, you should ever think he had acted improperly. The officers there endeavored to maintain the contrary. The conversation became general; it at last took a turn without your having reflected in the least in my hearing on the officers of the legion, and without any reflection whatever having been thrown out on you. The foregoing, sir, is, to the best of my remembrance, the substance of what passed at the Governor's quarters. I am truly sorry that any misunderstanding should have taken place on so very delicate a subject as the character of officers. As far as my memory can assist me, I have endeavored to do justice to all parties.

I am, sir, your most obedient servant,

EDWARD RUTLEDGE.

DEPUTY-ADJUTANT GENERAL STAPLETON TO GEN. MARION.

[Horry MS.]

CHARLESTOWN, September 3, 1782.

SIR:

I am directed by the honorable Lieut.-General Leslie to acquaint you, that in consequence of a requisition made by you some time ago, he gave permission for provisions and necessaries to be sent here for the prisoners captured at different times from the party under your command, and that such supplies might be forwarded under sanction of a flag of truce, whenever you should judge necessary to send them. But the Lieut.-General is sorry, sir, to find that such indulgence, instead of being confined to the humane uses intended—that of feeding and clothing your prisoners—is made to answer the most improper purposes; for the boat which last arrived here was loaded with stock and provisions for private families in town, and on its return some negroes were conveyed away from town in that very boat. This being the case, and in order to prevent such abuses in future, the General desires, sir, whenever any provisions, &c., are sent for your prisoners, the boat that brings them shall be with that sole intention; that a proper flag-master shall take charge of them, and deliver to our Commissary of prisoners an account of the quantity of every thing entrusted to his care, that no article of any sort shall be suffered to be put into the boat except provisions, clothing and necessaries for the prisoners, under pain of having the whole seized; and, finally, that no person, white or black, or any goods, merchandise, &c., &c., shall, on any pretence, be taken from hence, without express leave of the General.

I have the honor to be, sir, your most obdt. and most humble servant,

JOHN STAPLETON, *Dep.-Adj. General.*

COL. PICKENS TO CAPT. BUTLER.

[Original MS.]

LONG CANE, Sept. 6, 1782.

SIR:

Your favor, with the cattle by Mr. DeLoach came safe, for which I am much obliged to you. I am glad to hear you have got your company, and are quiet with respect to the out layers, though I would recommend to you to be on your guard, least they should return, at a time when you do not expect them, and come on you unawares. As it is determined to go against the Cherokees, I would be much obliged to you, if you can possibly do it, to collect on Edisto twenty-five or thirty good beeves and send them up so as to be at the Cherokee ford on Savannah River, on Monday, the sixteenth inst. I would not put you to this trouble, but expect beeves will be scarce. As I do not mean to take the men you have engaged to the nation, if any of them should come with the cattle, I will send them immediately back. I would recommend to you to send spies down Edisto, and if possible find out where Cunningham keeps, and what his intention is, and if possible drive him from those parts; though I would much rather you could destroy him and his party. I send you six swords which you will have care taken of, and when you have done with them, you will have them returned.

I have likewise sent you a few sheets of paper to make your returns. You have my best wishes, and am, sir,

Your most humble servant,
ANDREW PICKENS.

CHRISTOPHER GADSDEN TO MORTON WILKINSON, ESQ.

[Original MS.]

PHILADELPHIA, Sept. 7, 1782

To MORTON WILKINSON, Esq.

You have my ardent and sincere wishes for your safe and speedy junction with our common friends. Our cause is good; the cause of humanity itself, and as it would be blasphemy in the highest degree, to think a Good Being would create human nature to make it unhappy, and countenance its being deprived of those natural rights without which our existence would not be tolerable; our cause may, therefore, be justly called the cause of God also. These were my sentiments at the time of the Stamp Act, the beginning of our dispute, they have continued to be so ever since, and with the blessing of God, I am ready and willing to undergo any thing Heaven may still think proper to call me to suffer in support of it. We are tried, but I firmly trust not given over, and that God will once more restore us to our country and our rights, and that soon, when we shall have reason to look up to Him, and be convinced that his correction has been necessary, kind and proper, such as no father in our quandam circumstances could avoid giving to his 'children, unless he had totally delivered them up to their own wild and perverse imaginations, and abandoned us altogether. That we may pursue every prudent, reasonable, humble and truly political step, devoid of passion and vindictive resolutions is my warmest wish. Revenge is below a brave man; vengeance belongeth to the Almighty; He has claimed it expressly as His right, wisely foreseeing the shocking havoc man would make with such a weapon left to his discretion. However, a just retaliation, upon an abandoned and cruel enemy, may be sometimes absolutely necessary and unavoidable, but then that necessity should glaringly appear, be used sparingly and with propriety, that is, as near as possible on the offenders themselves. This even humanity may require; might show steadiness and firmness, and would meet the approbation of all the candid part of mankind. Instead of bayoneting poor soldiers for the cruelty of their officers, when we have them at our mercy—when the unexampled cruel treatment of our friends in their power absolutely required a return, and when they have unjustly tortured or taken away the lives of any of them, a retaliation in such cases, in my humble opinion, would be much better taken of the officers; I would save them in the field, and immediately hang a few of the heads of them on the lines, in presence of the soldiers taken with them declaring publicly the reasons why it was done, and afterwards if the enemy's lines were near, offer them the bodies of such officers to honor them with what funeral they thought proper. The higher the rank of the officer that fell into our hands, the nearer should we come to and punish the cause of the cruelties our friends had suffered, and in my opinion show the greater spirit and propriety in taking such a method, and the sooner prevent the repetition of their barbarities. Even Lord Cornwallis himself, if Fame says true, has been guilty of numberless cruelties, in cold blood, and if he fell into our hands, it would be the highest justice to make him suffer in an exemplary manner for them.

You will let our friends know our situation, and that though perhaps they cannot without great inconvenience detain all the prisoners they take, and are, perhaps, obliged, from peculiar circumstances, to parole must have been the case heretofore, yet such miscreants as have acted in high stations, have done us great mischief by the example of their defection, and otherwise are continually playing us tricks, and by no means are to be trusted, we hope they will for our sakes, keep such perfidous wretches at such a distance from Charlestown, and parolled if they think proper, at least, where they can do no more mischief. This, common fellow-feeling for our friends absolutely requires; indeed, a contrary conduct will encourage these worst of enemies, and make them contrive to throw themselves artfully in the way to be captured that they may carry on their cool, sly, detestable villainy with more security. I beg pardon, my dear friend, for troubling you with this long scrawl. My love to all our friends; tell them I hope to be with them soon, and to set out from hence as soon as possible after my family arrives—the beginning of next month at farthest; partienlarly make my compliments to Gen. Marion. I am much obliged to him for his friendship at my plantation on Black River; entreat he will continue it. If you cannot see him, contrive, if you can, to let him know it. If any thing from thence, by his means or through any of my other friends, can be transmitted to my family here, it would be of great service to them, and what they will stand in need of.

I am, dear sir, your most affectionate humble servant,

CHRISTOPHER GADSDEN.

P. S. Poor Knapp should not be forgot. His firmness and integrity under the severe trials we have been witness to, entitle him to particular attention.

COL. MOTTE TO CAPT. SIMONS.

[Horry MS.]

GOVERNOR'S QUARTERS, September 7, 1782.

DEAR SIR:

I received yours of this date, enclosing Capt. Giles' declaration. I remember perfectly well that you and an officer of the Pennsylvania line (his name I do not recollect) had a long and warm conversation respecting the resignation of the officers of Col. Lee's corps, at Mr. Thomas Waring's; but I do not recollect particulars. This much I can say, that I did not hear you make use of any expressions reflecting on those gentlemen for their conduct, than that you thought Major Rudolph was wrong, or to that effect, in giving as reasons for his resignation that he was tired of the service. On the contrary, that you knew them well, had served with them, and loved some of them as brothers; and I am sure, whilst I was present, the gentlemen of the Pennsylvania line did not make use of the words scoundrel or rascal to you—so far from it, that I never thought offence had been taken at anything that had passed that day.

I am, dear sir, your most obedient servant,

ISAAC MOTTE.

ROBERT BLAIR, ESQ., TO GEN. MARION.

[Horry MS.]

CHARLESTOWN, September 7, 1782.

SIR:

Although I have not the honor of being acquainted with you, I return you my most humble and hearty thanks for your favor and great humanity shown my wife, when in the greatest distress, and persecuted by some of her neighbors, and for the protection you afforded her, which must show your benevolence and goodness of heart. I would next beg leave to address you on my own account, as being unfortunate enough to be on the confiscation list. I must acknowledge my attachment to the British Government from principle; but surely, sir, you, yourself, who must have acted from principle, also, and from your steady and unwearied perseverance in that cause which you deemed to be the right one, will not condemn that in me which you have done with so much honor to yourself and country. I would further beg leave to acquaint you, that I have been very anxious to leave this town, which I would have done some time past, but for the reason above mentioned. Except my loyalty, I hope there is nothing else can be alleged against me. I have always been of a pacific disposition, and am entirely clear of the exceptions in your laws, such as murdering, plundering, house burning, &c. I reckon to prefer a petition to the Assembly, when they meet, setting forth my case; and, as I am informed some of the Acts will be repealed, I am not without hopes, especially if a gentleman of your character and influence would espouse my cause, and which, I hope, I shall not solicit in vain, from your innate goodness to assist the distressed. It does not suit me to follow the English any longer; it is said they are to evacuate this town next month. The nine sail of victuallers, and three of merchantmen, with goods, arrived two days ago. Be that as it will, I am heartily tired of this place, and have had time enough to repent of my folly. If I shall have the good fortune to be restored, I shall, undoubtedly, be a good subject to the State of South Carolina; if, unfortunately, it should be otherwise, I shall always regret having ruined my wife and children more than anything that can befall myself, though at this time in my fiftieth year. I hope your honor will excuse my detaining you so long upon a subject so interesting to myself. If you will, or can, grant me protection for myself, and what few negroes I have, I will go out the first opportunity. If I can not obtain that, should be glad to know if I can stay in town after the evacuation, otherwise, must go to Augustine, or some of the islands, till the Act is repealed in my favor, by the assistance of my friends. I hope I have several, never having injured any individual to my knowledge. I wish you health and happiness, and that you may live long to protect the distressed and unfortunate. With high esteem and due regard,

I am, sir, your most obedient humble servant,

ROBERT BLAIR.

GEN. LINCOLN TO CAPT. CARNES.

[Original MS.]

WAR-OFFICE, September 11, 1782.

SIR:

Congress have ordered that the Secretary of War forward to the Commander-in-Chief a copy of Gen. Greene's letter, on the subject of recruiting Lieut.-Col. Lee's partisan corps, and that he inform you that your further attendance on this business can be dispensed with.

I am, sir, your very obedient servant,

B. LINCOLN.

GOV. MATTHEWS TO GEN. MARION.

[Horry MS.]

UXBRIDGE, September 13, 1782.

SIR:

I have just received yours of the 12th inst. by Major Conyers. I certainly will not give Col. Maham leave to give up the horses you mention, and I think it extraordinary he should attempt to release them without my permission. I should imagine he would hardly presume to disobey your orders; but, if you apprehend any danger, I will immediately send you a press warrant, to prevent them from being taken away.

I am, sir, your most obedient servant,

JOHN MATTHEWS.

15

GOV. MATTHEWS TO GEN. MARION.

[Horry MS.]

UXBRIDGE, September 13, 1782.

SIR :

Yours of the 10th inst., came safe to hand yesterday. The mode I
have adopted in taking substitutes is to oblige all under fifty to furnish
two substitutes, and all above fifty one substitute, which is conforming
to the militia law as near as can be. All those who have surrendered
since the time limited by my invitation, I have parolled till the meeting
of the Legislature, to be dealt with as they think proper; a copy of the
parole I now enclose you. I am entirely of opinion with you, that a
body of good cavalry will be indispensably necessary to restore order
and good government in the different parts of the country, after the
enemy have quitted Charlestown; for there are a parcel of infamous
wretches whom the habit of plundering has taken such fast hold of,
that nothing but a military force will ever be able to subdue them, and
that force must be cavalry. But, unfortunately for this country, we
have not the means of procuring men to put such a corps on the respectable establishment, as it ought to be; however, as Maham's corps
at present stands, I flatter myself we shall be able to put it on a very
respectable footing as soon as we can get into the town. By the determination of the Council, the substitute money is all to be applied to
raise recruits for the Continental line of this State; therefore, any
application of it towards recruiting State troops would be improper.
You mention those who agree to find substitutes give twenty-five
guineas; they are to procure the substitutes, cost what they will; at the
same time great caution should be used that they do not go beyond
thirty guineas, otherwise, it would ruin our recruiting service. I, therefore, think the best way would be for them to pay the money into your
hands, and you to recruit the men, by which means you will be able to
prevent the service being injured by exorbitant bounties. I think the
State's share of seizures, that are made under my proclamation of the
14th of March last, cannot better be applied than to the purpose you
mention—that is, recruiting Maham's corps, and which I very much
approve of; but, I could wish you to reserve as much out of the first
sales as will pay Harris for the wagon you purchased of him, for I can
with truth assure you, that I have no present means, or a prospect of
any, until we get into Charlestown, of satisfying this or any other
demand against the State, as the Council have declined their assent to

selling any more negroes until the enemy quit the State. I am glad to find, by the surrender of the party you mention, that the Northern parts of the State are now clear of the disaffected. I don't apprehend any danger now from Fanning. Our printer has began to publish his paper again, and I enclose you one of them.

I am, sir, your obedient humble servant,

JOHN MATTHEWS.

GEN. GREENE TO GEN. MARION.

[Horry MS.]

ASHLEY HILL, September 15, 1782.

DEAR SIR:

I have received your letter by Mr. Pollock, with the returns enclosed. Intelligence from town induces me to believe the enemy are making preparations for another expedition after provision, and that the neighborhood of Georgetown will be their object, if there is a large quantity of provisions near that place. I beg that some steps may be taken for removing the rice, if possible, or for effectually covering the country from the ravages of the enemy. I am unable, at this distance, to determine with precision the position you ought to take, or the measures you have it in your power to pursue, to oppose their designs. You will, therefore, adopt the plan which you think most eligible.

I am, dear sir, your most obedient servant,

NATHANIEL GREENE.

MAJOR BURNET TO GEN. MARION.

[Horry MS.]

HEAD-QUARTERS, September 18, 1782.

DEAR SIR:

Gen. Greene has this moment received information that a detachment of the enemy are gone up Cooper River; their object is not ascertained. It is said to consist of more than 400 men, and that they left town yesterday noon. The General desires me to transmit you the information for your security.

I am, respectfully yours,

J. BURNET, *Aide-de-Camp.*

GOV. MATTHEWS TO GEN. MARION.

[Horry MS.]

UXBRIDGE, September 18, 1782.

SIR :

I have written to you by Major Conyers respecting Maham's corps; also, what must be done with those persons who come out of Charlestown.   Since the time specified in my invitation, the refugees have obtained permission to remain until the 26th inst.   I proposed a plan to Col. Lushington, some time ago, for manning the galley at Georgetown; I have not since heard from him on the subject.   If that plan does not take, I know of no other at present; for, as I have before observed to you, I have no money, nor have I the means of commanding any.   It would be a mere trifle for the merchants and inhabitants in and about that place, to advance as much money, or something else, as would fit out the vessel, and they are the most immediately interested in it.   A few years ago, the public spirit of our people would have stimulated them to do such a thing without being asked; but, alas! that seems now to be vanished.   Mrs. Matthews is now on her way from Philadelphia, and I expect she will be at the high hills of Santee about the 7th of next month; and, as the road from Laurens' Ferry to this place is very dangerous, I must desire an escort might be sent to meet her at the ferry, and conduct her down to my quarters.   Let the escort be at Laurens' by the 7th, and send on one of the men to Capt. Richardson's, to wait there until she arrives (if she should not be there before) that she might know the escort waits for her; otherwise, she may stay there a day or two, and I don't want the men to be absent longer than necessity requires.   You are a better judge than I am what number of horse will be sufficient to render her passage safe; therefore, I shall leave the appointment of the party to you.   I think it would be well to caution the person who is to command the party, not to say for what purpose they are ordered, lest some villains might be tempted to waylay the road before she gets to the ferry, for she has only one white man and two negro servants with her, and Capt. Richardson informs me there are some bad men in that neighborhood, who have lately plundered several people.   If it would not be fatiguing the horses too much, or attended with particular inconvenience, I would be glad they could be sent as far as Capt. Richardson's, to meet her.   However, I shall leave the matter to you, as I dare say you will be disposed to accommodate her as far as the service will admit.   Yours, &c.,

JOHN MATTHEWS.

COL. DAVIS TO GEN. MARION.

[Horry MS.]

PRINCE WILLIAMS', Salt Ketcher, September 20, 1782.

SIR :

Your letter of the 9th August I have received by Capt. Youngblood, wherein you desire to take all defaulters of my regiment who refuse to do duty agreeably to my orders, either to try them in my regiment, or to send them down to be tried in your brigade that is out; the latter you'll think best, and which I approve of, and will conform thereto. Capt. Youngblood has not attended according to appointment, which has delayed my carrying your orders into execution. I should be glad to know if you have given him orders to the contrary. I think it will be useless, without assistance, to endeavor to get them out, as I have many times endeavored to turn them out agreeably to your orders, without effect. They are of opinion that they will not be obliged to comply with the law, and think you will not send after them, as they are fed up, and have contrary opinions instilled into them. I will appoint officers to the three companies who are without, and order them out on duty; and, should they remain refractory, I must send them down to you, to be dealt with as you shall think proper, with some assistance, if agreeable to you.

I am, your most obedient humble servant,

WILLIAM DAVIS, *Lieut.-Colonel.*

P. S.—I do not know if you have received my last letter, with the returns annexed. It was the best I could make at that time; but, when I can turn out the regiment, and the men be more obedient to orders, I will send you a correct return. It is impossible to send you the names of the contumacious till the companies are officered and ordered out, and will comply.

CAPT. McGREGOR TO GEN. MARION.

[Horry MS.]

ECHAU, September 23, 1782.

DEAR GENERAL :

I received yours of the 23d inst., and am much surprised of your being informed of my supplying the British with cattle, and that one

Joulee was my driver; your informant was not just. Joulee did drive some cattle from the North side of Santee River to the South side; but the most of them were breeding cattle, which I did not think was against your orders to drive to this side. I could wish the whole of the Americans (though I say it) were like myself. I would freely give my all to serve my country, and, indeed, it has cost me nearly all, and still would give the remainder; if it were in my power the British should not eat or drink of what belong to the Americans. I always could give my friends a drink of grog or a cup of coffee until now, which plainly shows the dealing I have with the enemy; indeed, I have been plundered so often, that I have no clothes to wear on credit, nor as much hard money to purchase them. If I have traded, I must either have had money or clothes; but I can declare I have neither. I beg, General, you will satisfy me, in letting me know the informer. You know when I found what was carrying on, I begged of you to let me have a few men, and I could give you abundance of satisfaction in serving from Echau to the mouth of Santee; but you never were kind enough to do it. You say my conduct has deceived you; I am heartily sorry for it. I am in hopes you will yet have a better opinion of me than what you express at present. I am sorry I am obliged to write, as it is not in my power to come to you at present; but I shall wait on you as soon as I possibly can. I have always executed your orders as far as I have been able, and, indeed, have got a good deal of ill will for executing them; but, were it to do again, I should do it, or any orders you may give me, either on friend or foe. I have always made it my study to see that they were executed. My men should have been in camp before now, but the most of the relief are sick. Winningham and his sons, who say that you told them to collect the public cattle, do very little at it. I will be glad if you let me order them to camp, and with your orders will appoint some more qualified than them, and who are not of much other service. My lieutenant, who was to go with the men, has moved out of the parish. If nothing happens, in about a month I flatter myself I shall be able for business, and shall be able to give more satisfaction. About ten days ago I had some idea of some blacks collecting fifteen or twenty horses near me. I pursued, but missed them; they carried off their horses safe—and, for fear of my pursuing them, they pulled up Oindaw Bridge to cover their retreat, and went off clear. I shall be much obliged to you for a copy of the militia law. I have some men that deserve to be made Continentals; but think I had better send them to camp to be tried.

I am, dear General, your obedient servant,

ALEXANDER McGREGOR.

NO NAME (SUPPOSED TO BE GEN. MARION) TO GEN. GREENE.

[Horry MS.]

WATBO, September 24, 1782.

SIR:

Yesterday I received a letter from Major Call, at Smith's, in Goose Creek. By his account, he expected the enemy was out; but I have heard from Haddrell's and Daniel's Island late yesterday, and no troops are out. Marquis Rockingham's death has made a change of ministers, Lord Shelburn at the head, who is our most inveterate enemy, which I conceive will prolong the war; however, I have certain intelligence that steps are still taken to evacuate, and am very sanguine it will take place by the 15th of next month. If your cavalry will take post on Goose Creek, it would secure my right, and I would have a better opportunity to shut up my left; they being so near in your front, would prevent every necessary from being carried in town, and secure your position and mine; the communication would be so near each other, that a reciprocal support would be had in three hours. I must beg pardon for this hint; I wish not to exceed the station I am in, and pay every deference to your judgment. Should the enemy attempt me, I am determined not to quit this ground without I am forced. I have now thrice the number of men in the field that I had when Frazer made his appearance, and I trust I can make my men stand their ground. I could wish a more frequent intercourse of intelligence could be between us. At present I am acting without the materials from the Southward to form a judgment of my security.—I have the honor to be, with great respect and esteem,

Your obedient servant,

***

GEN. MARION TO GOV. MATTHEWS.

[Horry MS.]

WATBO, September 24, 1782.

SIR:

Enclosed is a copy of a letter wrote Gen. Greene. If you wish to stop all intercourse with the enemy, and prevent any supplies being carried into them, the position hinted for the General's cavalry is the

only means to effect it. The change of the ministry indicates a prolongation of the war. Our lenient countenance towards those people who
have surrendered to us, and are carrying a continual trade of provisions to the enemy, has obliged me to warn the people that they will be
taken into custody under the Sedition Act. So great a trade is carried
on along Wambo and Goose Creek, to supply the enemy, that all my
vigilance to stop it is fruitless; and I find, to stop the trade of feeding
the enemy, it must be effected by taking every person adjacent to town
and make them prisoners, or keep them a great distance from their
plantations, and remove all their possessions. Without such a mode, it
is impossible to prevent the infamous practice. I have already gone in
some respects in this measure, which I hope will meet with your and
the Council's approbation. What I have gone into in this respect, is
only threats, but wish to carry them into execution. My opinion on this
particular juncture is, that we should act with a determination against
every man whatever, who may be found playing a false game, without
which a small reinforcement will ruin everything in the former channel.
This obliges me to be more particular in having the State legion completed by every means that can be thought of, as Continental cavalry
cannot be commanded for that service, which I am certain you have
found by experience. Believe me, good sir, I wish to be clear of every
public employment; but, to retire when my country calls for my poor
abilities, I should call cowardice, and am determined, notwithstanding
my debilitated body, to do everything in my power to see this once
happy country enjoy its former liberty.

I am, with respect and esteem, your Excellency's obdt. servant,

FRANCIS MARION.

GOV. MATTHEWS TO GEN. MARION.

[Horry MS.]

UXBRIDGE, October 6, 1782.

SIR:

Your letter of yesterday's date is just come to hand. There is but
one way in which the negroes you mention are to be dealt with; that
is, as they were taken in arms, they must be tried by the negro law;
and, if found guilty, executed, unless there are any whose cases are
so far favorable as to induce the court to recommend them to mercy,
and the executive authority interpose and pardon them. Exemplary

punishments on such notorious offenders will have a very salutary effect, especially at this time. With regard to the subject of the trade carried on with the town, which you wrote to me about some days ago, I have not been able to collect a Council to advise with them on that subject, as they have almost all of them been so much indisposed, that they have not been able to attend to business; however, it would not be amiss still to hold up the threat of subjecting offenders to trial under the Sedition Act, and in the meantime to seize and condemn whatever is taken from them, in the utmost latitude of my proclamation. The enemy have lately sent some of their emissaries in the country, to persuade the people to carry all the provisions into them that they can collect, in consequence of which they are thronging to town in such droves, that the guard at Bacon's Bridge, detachments from the army, and even individuals, have made a great number of seizures, which have been condemned. This timely exertion has so far deterred them, that for several days past they seem to have given up their lucrative game, as no seizures have been made, so that their execrable policy has failed for once. The enemy has abandoned James' Island.

I am, sir, your most obedient servant,

JOHN MATTHEWS.

CAPT. CONYERS TO GEN. MARION.

[Horry MS.]

TRAVELLER'S REST, October 9, 1782.

DEAR GENERAL:

This will be handed you by Capt. Taylor, who comes to attend the sitting of the Board of Officers. Capt. Simons' resignation ends the dispute between him and Capt. Taylor. Capt. Martin claims the same as Capt. Simons; he was left out in the consolidating. How that matter is to be settled, you are the best judge. A few, and a very few of the junior officers, think Simons' resignation ought not to continue both Martin and Taylor, and that if Taylor is the youngest, he ought to be left out; but I hope he will not. I have enclosed the different claims, as I am confident I shall not be able to ride so far. I am now an object of pity, and the fever continues. Capt. Nelson informed me that you, as usual, have been helping us in clothing. It is to you, and from your favorable assistance only, that we can make that appearance, or be enabled to do that service to our country that is expected from us. The Governor is poor, and, I find, contracted in his opinion of matters in general; that he has no resource unless he has money, no stratagem, no policy; and, in short, he is poor.

My compliments to Simons, Muller, Edwards, Elliot and Neufville, and receive the best respects from, dear General,

Your most obedient and very humble servant,

JAMES CONYERS.

GOV. MATTHEWS TO GEN. MARION.

[Horry MS.]

UXBRIDGE, October 15, 1782.

SIR:

Those gentlemen who have for some time been so much indisposed, as to prevent their attendance in Council, having recovered their health, enabled me yesterday to convene a Council, when I laid before them your letter respecting the propriety of altering the mode of punishment for persons carrying on a clandestine trade with the enemy, from that pointed out by my proclamation of the 14th March last, to that pointed out under the Sedition Act; when, after mature deliberation, the Council were of opinion that an alteration in the mode of punishment would by no means be advisable at this juncture; but, at the same time, earnestly recommended that the proclamation before mentioned should be carried vigorously into execution, which, in their opinion, was very well calculated to put a stop to that iniquitous commerce.

I am, sir, your obedient servant,

JOHN MATTHEWS.

NO NAME (SUPPOSED TO BE GEN. GADSDEN) TO GOV MATTHEWS.

[Horry MS.]

October 16, 1782.

MAY IT PLEASE YOUR EXCELLENCY:

As your Excellency has taken the whole matter of the late agreement with the British on yourself, and that by the executive authority, and executive, &c., mentioned in the fourth article, your Excellency is to be understood. I was in doubt with myself (and took a day or two to consider further of it) whether there would be occasion to trouble your Excellency with the little mentioned; but, as I still unhappily differ from your Excellency in opinion, and am persuaded, if from nothing else, from the want of precision, at least, in the expression of that article, the State at large will be led to think the Privy Council are made a party thereto, and, of course, myself, a member thereof. As I dislike the agreement, very cogent reasons oblige me to send your Excellency my formal disapprobation thereof, nearly in the words. I drew immediately a rough sketch on seeing it, which I then showed to those gentlemen of the Council I mentioned to your Excellency, and should have sent it to your Excellency had not the Council been summoned so soon. The doctrine broached at the last Council, which I never heard or suspected before, that the Privy Council is in no case part of the executive, is, in my opinion, very alarming; it tends to make them insignificant, and the next step is, when an opportunity offers, to expunge that body altogether from the Constitution, and prepare the way to reduce this Government to a kind of Principality. I have frequently, in the Assembly, taken notice how great an eye-sore the Privy Council seemed to be to some gentlemen amongst us, and what indirect strokes were aimed at them. That the Governor is the sole ostensible executive of the State, is readily granted; further, that in all acts wherein he is not particularly retrained by law, he may be said to be absolutely so; but, in such laws wherein it is expressly directed that he shall not act but by the advice and consent of the Privy Council, there they are certainly part of the executive. For I have ever learned, that whatever is essentially necessary to a thing, that that thing cannot exist without it, most belong to it and participate of its nature—so in this last case, whenever the law requires that when a Governor is inclinable to a certain executive act, that executive act shall not be done but by the advice and consent of the Privy Council. If it be done without such advice and consent, it is illegal; therefore, they are certainly a *sine qua non* to make the Governor act legally in such instance, and, consequently, in such cases, are a necessary part of the executive, and the individual members thereof may be said to be parties thereof. What confusion this can occasion, or how by this omission there can be ten Governors in this State instead of one, notwithstanding what a learned, or any number of learned lawyers whatever may say, I cannot conceive. Besides, in case of the death of a Governor, during the recess of the Assembly, will not the Lieutenant-Governor immediately succeed, and, in case of his death, too, one of Privy Council? Does not this show they belong to the executive?

Their participation of the executive is but sometimes in particular cases, and that only internally or privately (as a Privy Council) without any external authority whatever; this belongs solely to the Governor or Commander-in-Chief. This, or something like it, I take to be the intention of the words in the eleventh article of the Constitution "in manner herein mentioned," placed immediately after to modify and restrain the words "that the executive authority be vested in the Governor and Commander-in-Chief;" otherwise, those words must be altogether nugatory, and put for no purpose whatever. I will now beg leave to trouble your Excellency with the letter already mentioned. "May it please your Excellency—I have seen the agreement with the British, dated the 10th, and find by its fourth clause that, as a particle of the executive, though unconsulted, I seem to be made a party therein to promote its acceptance with the public, which occasions my troubling your Excellency by letter, as my conscience and duty oblige me to declare that I disapproved almost every article. Indeed, I am not able to see any pressing occasion we had for any further meeting with the enemy's commissioners, after the last, convened at their request, broke up, which I was not sorry for, as we have so greatly the advantage of them, in point of British property, to lay our hands on when we please. This they well knowing, no doubt occasioned so much anxiety on their side for a further meeting. The agreement itself appears to me extremely injurious to the public, and fear it will involve us in endless ill consequences. With British lawsuits, no doubt, our courts will be filled; but these are trifles to what might be mentioned. The exception in the first article is not only, in my humble opinion, imprudent and impolitic with regard to ourselves; but, when taken with the second, has an unfriendly (if not inimical) aspect towards our sister States. Its eighth article is, in the last degree, humiliating. The greatest and tenderest care seem to be taken of the British interest, honor, and even delicacy, throughout the agreement, while our rights, and what is essential to our honor and interest, are totally omitted, or not mentioned with that unequivocal plainness and precision, and that decisive firmness we had room to expect. The whole agreement carries such manifest appearance of timid and over-cautious fear of offending the British, that instead of hastening, it has a natural tendency, when considered with the situation of the State for this last campaign, to retard their departure to the last moment they possibly can, in hopes that (as only interior disadvantages on their side oblige them to think of an evacuation) some external good luck may turn up in the interim, to bring about a recall of their orders. The plentiful markets, and great trade they have already had with our people during the whole summer, the prospect of still greater when the crops come in, together with no small advantages they may promise to themselves if they can but stay, to dabble through their emissaries at our ensuing election, must of themselves be strong allurements to a watchful enemy not to hurry away until it is absolutely unavoidable; and must not their inducements be still stronger when they consider what is too glaring to escape them, the lax situation of our Government for want of courts, notwithstanding the parade of an Assembly sitting at Jacksonborough. The preference too currently given them, of all kind of necessaries for their specie and goods, rather than to our own army, which has been more than once in want, even of our common staple, rice, and beef, for several days together (and I wish I may not soon experience more alarming wants than any they have hitherto felt, if something more vigorous than in terrorem threats are not speedily and resolutely fallen upon) is no small addition to their other advantages. Above all, are not the enemy sure that our army cannot compel them to go away, or restrain them from making incursions almost anywhere for many miles, but just about the spot they occupy? These must be great incitements for them to stay, if possible. The first article will be of more service than ever, as having experienced, they can put a confidence in them, and of the most dreadful consequences to us, by having such powerful arguments to induce others to join them, and exert themselves to the utmost to do us as much mischief as they possibly can, finding they will thereby recommend themselves the more to the British, and stand the better chance to insure them protection upon a pinch. In my humble opinion, better the whole value of these fellows should be lost altogether than that the public should countenance so dreadful a mischief.

"My duty to the State, and regard to my own reputation, (not desiring to be looked upon as a party to promote what I disapprove of,) has extorted this letter from me, which I hope will not give your Excellency any offence, which is far from my intention; for believe me, sir, no man more sincerely wishes that your administration, in these very difficult times, may prove not only serviceable to the public, but also honorable to yourself, and meet with general applause, than I do. I had some thoughts of reserving my opinion on this measure in my own breast till the Assembly sat; but, upon further consideration, it appeared uncandid to your Excellency, and looked too much like cunning, which I abhor.

"I am, with great respect, your Excellency's &c., &c.,

"C. G."

N. B.—The former part of this letter does not enter into the merits, whether the Governor had a right to exercise that particular act of agreement with the British solely of himself; but only takes up Mr. Rutledge's assertion in the Governor's favor, that the Privy Council were a part of the executive in no case whatever.

GEN. GADSDEN TO GEN. MARION.

[Horry MS.]

(NEAR THE GOVERNOR'S QUARTERS), October 21, 1782.

DEAR SIR:

Your favor of the 18th I received by Mr. Ferguson, on his return from Accabe, his commission about the negroes being at an end. The British, it seems, make a pretence that it was because Major Rudolph had taken a small party near their lines, and unless Gen. Greene returned them, they would not send a negro out; but this is a mere pretence, they had not the least right to make such a demand on the General. I should be extremely happy to have it in my power to oblige you, and serve Col. Horry, whose perseverance, firmness and merit, must be evident to everybody. Should the agreement be received, which I think there is little probability of, you may be assured that nothing in my power shall be wanting to serve him, Col. Horry; and, as Col. Moncrieff has the negroes, who is one of the principal opposers of the agreement being complied with, I will use my endeavors with the Governor, if he can do it with propriety, to make a particular demand for them. The measure was certainly amazingly to the advantage of the British nation; and, if their troops here had not as little spirit with regard to them as our people manifestly show with regard to this State (by that d——d communication with the town, which has now over-run all bounds) they would gladly have complied with the agreement to a title; but private interest on their side has overset it. Leslie has been very anxious about it for months past, and seen the advantages we had over him, and made several overtures before it was brought to a point. For my part, my friend, I was always for keeping coolly the ground the Assembly left us, pointing out to the enemy the glaring superiority we had, and, at the same time, hinting that, if they wantonly distressed us, the Assembly, however willing of themselves, would certainly make use of the means in their power to do the State justice. This, as often as I had opportunity in private conversation with the Governor, I constantly gave as my opinion; however, his Excellency thought otherwise, and, without consulting the Privy Council at all, made the agreement himself. As soon as I saw it, I was very sorry for it, looking upon it as weak in itself, unnecessary, impolitic, humiliating, and pregnant with bad consequence to the State. Finding by the penning of the fourth article that the Privy Council seemed to be made parties thereto, though never consulted upon that ground, I took the liberty to write to his Excellency, expressed my disapprobation of it in the warmest terms, and pointed out many of its defects. This I mention to you as a friend. We are all indebted to you my dear sir, and I shall always be happy to have it in my power to discharge part of my public debt to you, by rendering you any agreeable service. They still talk of the enemy's evacuating soon. I cannot but hear of the motions tending thereto as well as others; but seeing no reasons from within ourselves to oblige them to go away, but too many for their staying, I am still, and shall not think they intend absolutely to go until I hear they are over the bar. All their manoeuvring seems to be attended with a mixture of as much delay as possible, as if they still waited further orders, and were determined not to go a moment before they could possibly avoid.

Pray remember me to Col. Horry, and all enquiring friends with you.

I am, dear sir, your most obedient servant,

CHRISTOPHER GADSDEN.

LEWIS DeROSSET (COMMISSARY PRISONERS) TO GEN. MARION.

[Original MS.]

CHARLESTOWN, October 25, 1782.

SIR:

The Commissioners appointed by Gen. Leslie and Gen. Greene having settled the exchange of prisoners, the purport of Dr. Neufville's coming to town is by this means settled, and I have, in pursuance of that agreement, sent out all the prisoners I had in the prison ship, and those that were here on parole. You will be pleased on your part to send in here all the regulars and militia that may be with you.

I have the honor to be, sir, your most obdt. servant,

LEWIS DeROSSETT, C. G.

CAPT. MILLIGAN TO GEN. MARION.

[Horry MS.]

GEORGETOWN, October 27, 1782.

DEAR GENERAL:

After a small cruise of six days after two of the enemy's galleys, I arrived last evening quite late, and in the morning early my Lieutenant had intelligence of a sloop-of-war going loaded with rice and tobacco for Charlestown, without any flag, but a pass filled up in this place from the Governor, dated the 13th July last. I only want to know whether there is any later proclamation, or if this method of carrying on trade with the enemy is allowed by the Governor or not; for I like to have had my eyes pulled out by only putting an officer on board until I saw the passport, which was filled up. After I had done that matter, I then discharged him from on board. If such trafficking is allowed, I would be glad to be informed by a letter from your Excellency.

I am, sir, with respect, your most obdt. servant,

JACOB MILLIGAN.

CAPT. WARREN TO GEN. MARION.

[Horry MS.]

October 28, 1782.

SIR:

I am directed by Major-Gen. Greene to request you will have all the regular and militia prisoners, who are in Georgetown, immediately sent to Charlestown, under a guard. I shall be glad to know whether there are any sailors in Georgetown prisoners.

I am, sir, with esteem, your most obdt. humble servant,

SAMUEL WARREN.

GEN. GADSDEN TO GEN. MARION.

[Horry MS.]

(NEAR THE GOVERNOR'S QUARTERS), October 29, 1782.

DEAR SIR:

Hearing my friend Ferguson was unwell, I made an elopement to see him, and just returned last evening, a little before your express called on

me, much fatigued, which prevented your favor by him of the 24th.
I am obliged to you for the paper you sent, and think it would be of
general information to have it printed; but Dunlap is so unwell, that
he has left off printing, and, besides, his paper is so small, and types
so large, that I am persuaded one of his gazettes could not hold a
fourth part of it. This would make it far less useful and entertaining
than if it came out all together. Should any opportunity unexpectedly
offer of giving it to the public, I will not slip it. The more I consider
the late intended agreement, the more disgraceful (and that unnecessarily so altogether, in my opinion,) it appears to the State. On the
Privy Council not being consulted, and yet seeming to be made a party
thereto, I immediately wrote a letter to his Excellency, to disavow my
approbation of it; but previous to my sending it, receiving a summons
to Council, I kept it back till that should be over, expecting the matter
might be opened there; but finding we were called on a different business, and no probability of its being then touched upon, as I saw, I
took hold of something that seemed to tend that way, and purposely
brought it in indirectly in my argument on what was before us, pleading
as an excuse that as a particle of the executive, by the inaccurate word-
ing of the fourth article, I was brought in as a kind of party to an
agreement which I almost totally disliked; upon which Mr. E. R., to
my astonishment, said that the Privy Council was, *in no case whatever*,
any part of the executive, which he said was also the opinion of another
distinguished lawyer he named; and the Governor himself said, that
old Col. Pinckney, who is conveniently dead, had told him the same.
This, I think, as well as some other circumstances, leaves great room
to think, that though the natural Council, appointed by the State, was
not consulted on that most important occasion, yet that certain lawyers
at least, if not others, were. This novel and dangerous doctrine, so
contrary to the spirit of our Constitution and plain letter of many of
our laws, so roundly and positively asserted, and, although Lowndes'
lieutenant during his administration, and during the greater part of J.
Rutledge's, I had never heard a title of, or had the least suspicion that
any such tenet could be advanced, till this morning I heard it declared
in the strongest terms in Council, and a little before by that gentleman,
openly in the Governor's porch. This induced me, when I went home,
to add a note, by way of preface, to the letter I had prepared to send
to his Excellency, a copy of which I now enclose you; the proceeding
on the cause of it will serve by way of an explanation thereto. We
have been wanting, my dear sir, more troops for the General all this
campaign, but, in my opinion, we have wanted still more an efficacious

16

civil power; and, if the enemy leaves Charlestown, which still is a
doubt with me notwithstanding—I cannot help seeing appearances as
well as others, their advantages over the country, which at this instant
are so amazingly beyond any they ever had—I say, in case of an evacuation, and the sword has a little rest, we must lose no time to join
shoulder to shoulder to check the rapaciousness, tyranny and insolence
of too many of our lawyers, or this State will never be at peace, or in
a respectable situation again, or the citizens thereof upon an equal footing with regard to the possession of their property, which, in my
opinion, for many years past, the poor and middling people have only
held rather from courtesy than right, owing principally to that cause.
Nothing but the infinite number of our laws, and what is quoted as
authority in our courts (which, without exaggeration, a room of moderate size would not hold) together with the perplexity and confusion,
give these gentlemen their importance, or, indeed, any importance at
all.   These may be reduced, I am persuaded, to an octavo volume; at
most, very few of them will ever help, we may be sure.   But the
business is of such necessity, that it must be done, as soon as possible, or we shall, in all probability, be undone; for otherwise their
insolence as lawyers will be soon equal to what the famous Roman
Catholic Bishop Becket said to a gentleman he was not well pleased
with.   He told him very haughtily that he hoped to see the day when
no jack gentleman would dare to stand with his hat on before the lowest
priest.   Without great care this, or something like it, will be soon the
case with regard to the lawyers here.   I never thought there was much
riddle and finesse necessary in a good Goovernment—that honest men
of good plain common understanding, who would take pains to judge,
and always judge for themselves, not suffering their understanding to
be in any man's keeping, were fully equal to the task; but how is the
case?   The people may appoint whom they think proper (as in a Privy
Council), these may be consulted occasionally to pick the gilding off
of gingerbread, or some such trifling matter; but in an affair of the
utmost consequence to the safety, honor and interest of the State, it
cannot be expected they are fit judges (though, perhaps, a matter not
even depending on any difficult principle of law); no! without the
lawyers have the principal hand in it, or, indeed, the whole cooking of
it, all is undone.   I wish this may not have been nearly the case, my
friend, on a late occasion, which I think almost as disgraceful to the
State as was the agreement itself.   The public are extremely obliged
to you for your vigilance with regard to the gentlemen sending provisions to town.   I believe I cannot be reckoned a severe man in my

politics; but I assure you I have done all in my power, for many months, to no purpose, to get means used to have some of them tried by the sedition laws. If convicted, perhaps my bowels might yearn over a poor necessitous man, so as to endeavor to procure his pardon; but if a rich fellow, if I had ten thousand votes they should all go for a halter for him, and nothing else. Owing to the too great encouragement of these rascals, the army has given over, since the beginning of the campaign, to that villainous, destructive trade with the town; and to that impolitic infatuation, from Christmas last, of propagating the enemy's hums about an evacuation, we are brought to the present dilemma—which is, if the enemy actually goes, they even then leave us with the highest contempt, and may return; but, should any external advantage to them make Sir Guy revoke his orders, what becomes of us all then? In that shocking, corrupted state, the people are now in, 'tis heads or tails with us, and the stake, I am afraid, is no less than the whole State. Sir Guy is looked upon as an excellent officer, having the good of his nation disinterestedly at heart. No doubt so wary a commander must have men here on whom he can depend to give him information of our situation in all respects. Pardon me, my dear sir, for troubling you with so long a letter, when your time is so important to the public. Believe me to be, with sincere esteem,

Your obedient servant,
CHRISTOPHER GADSDEN.

P. S.—I send to the Governor's every day for my rations of beef; this moment my boy has returned without any, bringing a note that there is none, and that the army is dissatisfied about it. I wish these dissatisfactions may not increase daily more and more, and bring on some dangerous crisis. The whole proceeds from the d——d town trade, where they live in clover. The same note mentions that the Augustine fleet is arrived.

GEN. GREENE TO GEN. MARION.

[Horry MS.]

HEAD-QUARTERS, October 30, 1782.

SIR:

Your letter of the 28th inst. I have this moment received. Capt. Warren has written to you requesting the prisoners, mentioned in the list you enclosed, might be sent to Charlestown, except the dragoons, as they were exchanged by an agreement entered into the 23d instant, by which all citizens and militia of every rank and denomination, made prisoners of war previous to that date, southward of the Delaware River, with all the volunteers, and many Continental officers, a list of whose names will be immediately published by the Commissary of Prisoners. The safe-guard had certainly, by his conduct, forfeited his protection. I wish, however, you would send him to Gen. Leslie, with a remonstrance against the irregularities committed. Should there be an opportunity of injuring the enemy at the distillery, by a detachment from this army, I beg you will send me such intelligence as to enable me to give you the necessary aid.

I have the honor to be, sir, with much esteem, your obdt. servant,

NATHANIEL GREENE,

CAPT. MILLIGAN TO GEN. MARION.

[Horry MS.]

GEORGETOWN, October 31, 1782.

SIR:

I have this moment been honored with your Excellency's letter of 28th inst., in consequence of which have made a seizure of a schooner from Mr. Lockwood in Charlestown, deeply laden with tobacco, rice, &c., which was discharged from the sloop I mentioned to your Excellency I had seized before, and which I then cleared upon seeing a passport, signed by the Governor. I have put an officer on board of this vessel, and am determined to hold her until I hear further from you. Your Excellency may depend I shall strictly adhere to the instructions which your letter contains, and do all in my power to prevent the scandalous trade which is now carrying on with the enemy in Charlestown by numbers of people in this place, and its vicinity. On board of the schooner which I have now seized bound to Charlestown, are twenty-six hogsheads of tobacco and nine tierces of rice. The seizure of this vessel has already raised a clamour amongst those concerned, and am apprehensive it will be productive of more; therefore, shall wait your Excellency's further determination respecting this matter; but, at all events, am determined to keep possession of her until I hear further from you.—I am, with respect and esteem,

Your Excellency's obedient humble servant,

JACOB MILLIGAN.

COMMODORE LOCKWOOD TO GEN. MARION.

[Horry MS.]

CHARLESTOWN, October 31, 1782.

DEAR SIR:

As it is the Governor's desire, for the good of our country, I have made it my business to send out whatever I can send them, Dorchester way, without a pass, and one with the Governor's pass to Georgetown; but this day Daniel Shields applied to me for a recommendation to you, for a pass to go with his schooner to Mr. Swinton's, at Wappetaw. I know little of the said Shults, but am told he is a good coaster; therefore, must be of service to us, and doubt not but you will give him a pass to remain until further orders, as the Governor's passes run. Here is, also, a fine Virginia schooner, the Nancy, Capt. John Anderson, which wants a pass to Georgetown, and there to remain, which I shall be obliged to your Excellency for, by the bearer, as I have no opportunity at present to send to the Governor. The troops are to embark the 15th November, as Leslie says.

I am, with the greatest respect, sir, your most humble servant,

J. LOCKWOOD.

COL. LUSHINGTON TO GEN. MARION.

[Horry MS.]

GEORGETOWN, October 31, 1782.

SIR:

I received yours of the 28th inst., and note the contents. If I cannot act with honor to myself in the command of this garrison (for I am determined to support the character of an officer) must beg leave to decline the service. The order transmitted to Capt. Milligan, an officer subordinate to my command, is not only a reflection on me, but it carries with it a suspicion; and I defy any man in existence to say I received the value of one farthing in any vessel as a flag, or coaster, except some small present—say a cheese, and four chests medicine, belonging to the State. The military mode of transmitting orders goes to the commanding officer of armies, wings, divisions, brigades, regiments, &c., and not to an inferior officer, who is obliged to put them in execution, or abide the consequences. Hope you'll not say I have neglected yours, where it was possible to comply. It would not be likely Gen. Greene would transmit any orders to an inferior officer in your command; if he did, you would certainly think it hard. I could not but obey orders sent me by his Excellency the Governor, which I received at the time. Messrs. Heriot and Tucker received the pass-ports desiring I would aid and assist Mr. George Selby in his business, which was the transportation of the produce, arising from the sale of fifty negroes sold by Governor's orders. Six separate passports were sent, and I believe only four were made use off for want of vessels. The Governor has sent a flag by this schooner, and I must take the liberty of exculpating myself from any disobedience of orders. The other matters contained in the letter will be attended to, as all your orders. I have supplied this country with upwards of six thousand guineas' worth of property this year, for the use of the army, which comes not from the British, for which I have not yet received a single dollar, and I can say I never received a copper made from any person in the British service, by importing or smuggling goods, which I will attest any day. I am apprehensive you have received information from people on whom I have threatened formal practices. I have nothing further to add, only remaining

Your very humble servant,

R. LUSHINGTON.

N. B.—With this I transmit the returns. Prichard's vessel brought up prisoners, as you'll see by the list, and went from here empty.

HERIOT & TUCKER TO GEN. MARION.

[Horry MS.]

GEORGETOWN, October 31, 1782.

SIR:

We enclose you the Governor's passports, granted Mr. Selby for the purpose of carrying round to Charlestown the nett proceeds of fifty negroes.. The vessel loaded with a considerable part of this property (particulars of which is in the passport) with the Governor's flag be-sides, is seized by Capt. Milligan, and detained by him. We have wrote the Governor particularly on this business, and of a sloop-of-war stopped in the same manner, and prevented sailing. Col. Lushington has only delivered us Mordecai Myers' and Cohen's accounts, amounting to £20 1s. 4d. sterling, which we have assumed. Soon as we can have the others delivered, we will inform you what balance will be wanting. Capt. Roux shall have the articles you mention, and we shall strictly observe your orders.

With respect, we are, sir, your most obdt. servants,

HERIOT & TUCKER.

CAPT. JOHN COGDELL TO GEN. MARION.

[Horry MS.]

GEORGETOWN, Nov. 25, 1782.

SIR:

As I am in expectation of a vessel in a very short time, I will esteem it a favor if you will order the rice in payment for the powder supplied this garrison, as the account stands at foot; the other rice payable the 1st January next, I will give you timely notice when wanted, as it belongs to a person in Philadelphia, to whom I have wrote that the rice was to be received at that time, and I suppose a vessel will be sent for the purpose. I am sorry to acquaint you with the trade carried on to Charlestown from this place, by a set of people that I can't think friends to this State. I sometime ago wrote his Excellency, the Governor, respecting it in as full a manner as I could; he has taken no notice of it. Several are down now for that purpose to Daniel's Island, and may be expected back in a few days. I am told some are concerned that you could hardly suspect were those that commanded here. The Jews are all deeply concerned and do no duty, and are entirely excused. I could a few days ago have seized a cart load of goods going to Cohen's, but so many had already been cleared by applying to the Governor, I let them pass unnoticed. All our ready money is sent to Charles Town and the answer is, to supply the army. A few articles I wanted for my family use, such as blankets for my negroes, some cloth for my own wear, and a few things for my wife. I dare not send for them for fear they should be taken, and myself censured for a trade of the kind, though these things are laid by in town for me. I will thank you to advise me if this is allowed and how I am to act in such a situation.

I am with regard, sir, your most obedient servant,

JOHN COGDELL.

P. S.—State of South Carolina, Dr., for powder, £340 13s. 4d.

Cr.—Rec'd. from H. & Tucker £69 12s. 6d. Bal. due £271 0s. 10d.

REMINISCENCES OF DR. WILLIAM RÉAD, ARRANGED FROM HIS
NOTES AND PAPERS.

Dr. William Read was the second son of the Hon. James Read,
formerly one of his Majesty's Counsellors of Georgia. His mother,
was Rebecca, the daughter of Jacob Bond, Esq., of Christ's Church
Parish. Dr. Read was born on 12th April, 1754, at the seat of his
grandfather, Jacob Bond. He remained at his grandfather's until he
was about five years old, when he was carried to Georgia, where his
parents had settled. His early education was received at the boarding-
school kept alternately at Mr. Joseph and William Gibbons'. Here
he exhibited a bold, enterprising spirit, which accompanied him through
life, in resisting a tyrannical master; and, running home after that, he
was put to a school of select young gentlemen in Savannah, classical
masters being brought from Europe for the purpose. His aptness and
facility in acquiring the dead languages were remarkable. He being
intended by his father for the British navy, was particularly directed
to attend to mathematics; to this his mother was adverse, and he chose
physic as a profession. It suiting his father's purpose, he was taken
from school at fifteen years of age, and attached to the pharmacopolist
shop of some eminent practitioners, Messrs. Cuthbert & Brady, of
Savannah, (afterwards Brady & Irvine.) William Read was remarkable for a hardiness of constitution, undaunted by any difficulties; he
conducted himself so in this service, as to obtain the entire good will
and confidence of his masters. In the summer of 1774, he was sent
to Philadelphia, in further pursuit of a medical education. His father
perceiving a degree of roughness in his manner, contracted by the
laborious life he lead, and being addicted to personal conflicts (the
fashion of that day), introduced by certain English boys from Oxford
and Eton school—Harris, Jackson and Jenkins, &c.—placed him with
Dr. Benjamin Rush, of Philadelphia, remarkable for his mild, gentle-
manlike manners. W. Read was domesticated with Dr. Rush, who
was instructed to associate him much with him (Dr. Rush), and to permit his attending his clinical practice. Mr. Read, ever attentive to
his children's welfare, thought that sort of example better to mend
the manners of his son than any precept. Mr. W. Read lived as a
student with Dr. Rush in the utmost harmony, and was much esteemed
by him and his family. During his residence there, the contest between
Great Britain and her colonies commenced. Mr. Read, after the manner
and politics of his father, and the better sort of people of Georgia, was

a Monarchist in principle. He had read of the baneful effects of Democracy in the Grecian States, and dreaded its want of stability in Government. Dr. Rush used to hold friendly conversation with Mr. Read and his fellow students, James McHenry, (afterwards Secretary of War,) and with William Johnston, (afterwards a Captain in the British army.) Dr. Rush was mild and persuasive in argument, and soon convinced Mr. Read and McHenry that Kings were not omnipotent, or Parliament supreme; that the American community should govern themselves. In one of Mr. R.'s walks with Dr. Rush, they perceived a company of gentlemen, associated for the purpose of learning the military exercise, under difficulty for an instructor, when Mr. R. asked permission of Dr. Rush to give them a lesson, he having, during his education in Savannah, attended to the instructions of a Prussian officer. His service was well received, and Mr. R. was requested to attend them as often as he could. He did so, and completed them in the manual exercise, and certain useful evolutions. The said company being organized and officered, Mr. Read was offered a lieutenancy, and presented with a handsome sword; the late General Cadwallader was elected captain. Mr. R. was at pains to tutor the company in the art and exercise of long marching, equipment, encamping and swimming, and all the circumstances and etiquette of war; he exhibited a wonderful instance of his own skill, and continuance in the art of swimming, so useful to a soldier. Mr. R., at the especial instance of his father, refused the commission; but he had formed a resolution to enter the service afterwards, and had prepared to march, was to have joined and accompanied John McPherson in the Canada expedition, when he was influenced by Dr. Rush to relinquish the design, and return home, his father promising forgiveness for past errors, and to send him to Europe to complete a medical education. Mr. R. reluctantly gave up his adventurous scheme, distributed his articles of equipment among certain friends, and returned home. He carried with him an honor which he dared not avow—Georgia being still in allegiance to the Crown of Great Britain—viz., a handsome sword, presented him by a vote of said company for services. He, also, in these various occupations, was obliged to study hard, often burning the midnight lamp, and had obtained the medal annually competed for in the College in Chemistry, given by the Professor, Dr. Rush. He carried with him the affections of Dr. Rush and his amiable family; also, very particular letters to Drs. Huck and Fothergill, from Dr. Rush. It was not, however, Mr. Read's lot to prosecute this intention—the circumstances of the war came on, and put a stop to all intercourse with the mother country. Among Mr. Read's intimate acquaintances were James McHenry (afterwards Secretary of War), and James Wilkinson (late General), Horace Belt and Walter R. Cole, and William Johnston, of Georgia. On Mr. R.'s return to Savannah, he found things in great perturbation—the opposition to Governmental measures had commenced, was conducted by a small irregular band, headed by Joseph Habersham (late Col. Habersham), which gathered daily. Mr. R. found his father much agitated by reflections in Council, on "members of that Board, who had sons actually employed in training soldiers to oppose regal and legal authority," fostered by him. The fact being so, Mr. Read could only say that his son was of age, and now circumstanced as things were, beyond his control; that the principle had taken deep root, and he feared it had done so in thousands more than the Governor and Council were aware of; that they should rather rejoice provided the opposition was to go on, that some young men of honor and principle should join in it, and take a lead, rather than that the reins should get into the hands of a rabble, who would show no mercy. All this, however, was adverse to the opinion of Sir James Wright, and a majority of his Council; they were for crushing it in the germ, and for imprisoning every one who showed a disposition to rebellion. It was agitated in Council that Mr. Read should be sent to the British fleet for safety; his father opposed it, and called the measure insidious, treacherous. Warm arguments ensued, violence was threatened, and Mr. Read, with several members of the Board, rose, and stood with their hands on the hilt of their swords. A measure had been adopted in a secret meeting of the Board, which was to make head against the opposition by means of the British fleet, which lay below at Five-Fathom Hole. Troops were hourly expected, when Sir James intended to head the expedition, and oppose force to force. In the meantime, a popular meeting of the revolters had sent express to summon men from the distant Western parishes, and, also, resolved to make the Governor and Council prisoners. These separate things were known to Mr. W. Read, and to Thomas Lee, messenger of Council, whose heart being with the people, secretly communicated with Mr. Read, he being able to hear a part of the measures of the Board. About this time, Mr. W. Read heard his father summoned to a secret midnight meeting of the Council; he knew that things were nearly ripe for the above measure—rose hastily, armed himself, and followed his father without his knowledge. As he passed, several mobbish collections of people were on foot, and bonfires lit; they generally knew Mr. Read, and respected him, gave him the time of night as he passed, who civilly returned the compliment, saying: "Fellow subjects, had you not better be abed?" he little suspecting the state of things, that he was to be made prisoner, and never again to be out of bondage parole. Mr. Read went to the Government House, and, while sitting in Council, the Governor and his officers, and Board, were made prisoners, by a deputation from the meeting of the people, who had constituted themselves a Council of Safety. Joseph Habersham was chairman, and one of the committee; Mr. W. Read refused to act. He thought the task too indelicate—his father was implicated—his agitation now became extreme. He truly loved and honored his father, and deeply lamented the circumstance that had brought about the measure. Mr. W. Read remained on the ground all night. Two companies of riflemen had arrived, and were placed around Government House. Mr. R. spent many hours in conversing with these men, and inculcating on them the good of moderate measures, bringing to view the conduct of our Northern brethren on a similar occasion. On going home next morning, he found his mother in a state of distracting despondency. He informed her all he knew; she communicated it to Mr. Read in his confinement, on a slip of paper. On the second and third nights he still hovered about the Government House, and used dissuasives to any violent measures. At length the gentlemen of the Council were parolled to the Government House, and a guard set on them with drawn swords. The gentlemen were permitted to receive visits from their wives and families, and servants were permitted to go in with necessaries. On Mr. W. Reed visiting his parent, a tender scene ensued; he embraced him tenderly. The Governor accosted him with: "You see, young gentleman, what a state of things you have brought about." He replied, I have had nothing to do in this affair. I am reflected upon, and suspected, if I open my mouth in argument at any of the popular meetings. Sir James had treated Mr. Read roughly on his paying him the compliment of a visit on his first arrival from the North. Among other rough things, he said: "So you know, young sir, that you have a halter about your neck!" His reply was: Have I, sir; then it sits very easy? and if such is my condition, there are thousands, tens of thousands in the same predicament, and I should die in good company. Sir James was enraged, and expressed deep regret that he (Dr. Read) should have taken so ungracious a course. Mr. Alexander Wright sat in the audience room, and listened to all this conversation, on which Wm. Read observed civilly, that Sir James had the advantage of him, that he had an evidence; he (W. Read) had none, on which the Governor desired his son to leave the room. He then launched out in invectives against those who were driving the people to madness, naming especially Joseph Habersham, Francis Farris, Elbert, &c.   Mr. Read advised temperance and prudence, reminded Sir James of the scenes of the rebellion of '45, not very remote.   They parted on that occasion in good humor.   Sir James said jocularly, "is green and yellow the costume of medical students?"   Wm. Read said it was the best coat he had, and would certainly wait on the Governor in his best garb.   "Is it," said the Governor, "usual for students of physic to wear a sword." Wm. Read had, on that occasion, put on his sword, as he begun to feel confident from the gathering of the people in Councils of Safety. Read's reply was, that it was a drossy bauble, obtained for supposed services to a company of gentlemen in Philadelphia, in drilling and training them, and you, Sir James, know how I obtained the art, as you were privy to it, as he was one of a juvenile company who used to to muster in Sir James' presence.   Sir James gave Read a solemn warning, and Read returned the "take care," but they parted in good humor.   W. Read knew how far matters had advanced in the popular meetings.   Just ten days after this communication, the scene described above took place.   Dr. Read (we will in future call him so) watched over the prisoners incessantly, barely taking time to go home speedily, and take his meals.   The regiment of riflemen were encamped at the west end of the Government House, and the men would frequently fire their rifles at the house (a wooden house) notwitstanding his (Dr. Read's) remonstrances to the contrary, and the orders of Samuel Elbert, now nominated as General.   Dr. R. got one of his mother's servants to carry in a slip of paper, warning the inmates to lay down on the floor for safety against the rifle balls.   Sir James' two daughters, Sarah (afterwards wife of Sir James Wallis), and Bella (afterwards Mrs. Barry), were in the house, and all of his Majesty's members of Council.   At length these Western soldiers became tired of the service, and talked of breaking in and destroying the prisoners; Dr. Read's anxiety became extreme. ⋅ He saw that the parole was broken by the violence of these riflemen, as a parole implies safety and protection to the prisoners.   He advised Sir James to fly, and advised, by a slip of paper, the manner of getting clear, convinced that if he was out of the way the remaining prisoners would be more mercifully and leniently dealt with; and thus it happened, as the Council of Safety admitted the Counsellors to their parole on their plantations; Dr. Reed's father was confined to his plantation on Great Ogeechee.   Dr. Read was instructed to wait on his parent there, medically and filially.   Dr. Read repaired thither, and spent some time in dreary solitude, which to him who had been in very active habits, was intolerable; there he became better acquainted with his parent, and he with him.   Mr. Read was of lofty, austere manners, and rarely admitted of an opportunity of conversing.   On this occasion he relaxed and conversed freely with his young son, and made him narrate all the circumstances of his defence of his companion, William Allston, against assassination, from a sailor on the Chesapeake, in 1774, on which he said you are a brave boy, and I would trust you on any occasion.   Dr. Read narrated the cold and dubious reception given him by his brother-in-law, Lancelot Jacques, in Annapolis, on account of this fete, doubting his being a Georgia boy; on which he said that it was unkind in Jacques, and ill judged, and that his son was in the right to leave his house as he did, his uncle-in-law having expressed his belief doubtful of his identity, while his aunt acknowledged him with tenderness and confidence.   He had been at lodgings three or four days, when the coach of Benedict Calvert, Esq., of Mount Airy, came for him, and conveyed him to his aunt, Molly Read's, who, on hearing Mr. Jacques' doubt, called him an ignorant old man.   Here he received the kindest attention, and became current at the seat of Mr. Calvert, who lived in a style rarely to be met with; here he made himself useful in visiting and administering to the tenants and slaves of the family, inoculating two hundred young negroes; here, too, he improved in acquaintance with John Park Custis, Gen. Washington's son-in-law, which had commenced at the College of Philadelphia, and which subsequently grew into a firm friendship.   It is probable that the last letter written by that gentleman was to Dr. Read, just previous to the attack of Yorktown, where he died.   After this degression, the narrative goes on—William Read returned 1st September to his studies, and underwent the scenes glanced at in Philadelphia; and, on his return to Georgia, Dr. Read being almost solitary at his father's seat on the Great Ogechee, felt a longing desire to mix in the circumstances and turmoil of war, and offered himself to Gen. Robert Howe, who was organizing an expedition against Florida.   He was accepted, and desired to make a rendezvous at Ogechee Ferry, to receive and inoculate recruits.   It had been the policy of our enemy to turn loose prisoners having the small pox, to communicate it to our troops.   The business was done, and Dr. Read, not having full occupation, went into the practice of physic, and his success was wonderful all through the vicinity of Little and Great Ogechee.   In the meantime the war was carried on, armies raised, and the expedition against Florida failing, the army retreated, covered by the militia of St. John's Parish, Liberty county, where, on the last battle near the

Causeway, Gen. Scriven was killed, and Col. Maybank shot down with a fractured thigh-bone. About the close of the campaign, a party of militia were marching to Savannah, under the command of Col. William McIntosh; Dr. Read was crossing the ferry, when, observing two officers, prisoners of war, lying on the ground, tied in a cruel manner, he demanded, rather warmly, who these prisoners were, and why they were fettered, bound in that manner; he was informed that they were Capt. Bacop, of a British transport, and Lieut. Beacher, of the marines, that they had been taken with a marauding party of English on the St. James' River; that they had made sundry attempts to get away; that that young man Beacher ran like an Indian, and that he had nearly escaped, and they were obliged to pursue him on horseback, and knock him down. Beacher spoke and said, that he was taken out of his place; that he had only gone on shore to explore the country, with no evil intention, be discredited in the British army, and that he would as leave die as not. Dr. Read at once assumed the position of a friend to the distressed, and requested that the sentinel would slacken their ligatures. This he refused to do, urging that he (Beacher) would run off. It was in vain that Dr. Read plead that there were three rivers between these prisoners and their friends; the soldiers referred Dr. R. to their Colonel. Dr. Read rode up to the Colonel's quarters, and requested that act of humanity; but the Colonel would not deign to reply. Read became animated, and spoke rather unceremoniously to the Colonel, accusing him of want of proper feeling for a prisoner, &c., &c., and at length rode back to the prisoners, lit, and proceeded to slacken the ligatures, when the sentinel struck him on his head with the muzzle of a rifle, which cut to the bone. Dr. Reed rose, and was presently covered with blood. McIntosh saw it, and, it was said, regretted it. Dr. Read bound up his head, mounted his horse, and was proceeding homewards, when McIntosh sent his secretary after him to bring him back, but Read refused to obey; but sent him back with a pistol at his breast, with a bold and rough defiance to his Colonel. Notwithstanding this rebuff, Dr. Read rode next morning eight miles, in pursuit of the marching party, and carrying clothes and implements with him, he succeeded in having the prisoners loosened and shaved, and shifted, so as to be comfortable. The day after, his wound became painful, and was apt to bleed. On the fourth day a Capt. (Odingsell) was sent with a command to make Read prisoner, urging his conduct as aiding and abetting the enemy. Read submitted, and was conducted to Savannah, and, after some contention in the Council of Safety, he was committed to prison, in an apartment where he found Parson Zubly and William

Telfair, fellow prisoners; Zubly was in irons. Dr. Read lay all night without any bedding, laying on his breast, on account of the wound of his head, making of his arms a pillow. The prisoners reasoned and consoled each other, agreeing that it was chiefly from party rage that these irregularities took place. On the third day Dr. Read was released, leaving his fellow prisoners behind. He rode home, and met with his father's tender sympathy, and a regret in the old British officer that it was not in his power to redress his wrongs. Mr. Read now consented to his son going to the Northern army, enjoining him only to serve medically, by way of improving himself. Dr. Read then, as soon as his wound was healed, set himself about settling his affairs, and set out for the North. His employers generally approved of his purpose, and paid him in coin, Mr. William Elliott especially doubled his account, and presented him with the finest young horse in his stable. He took a solemn farewell of his father and mother, and young brother and sister, and set out about 31st May, 1778, with little hope of ever seeing them more. He made some improvements in his arms and travelling equipments, discharged a drunken servant and employed a steady, respectable Englishman. When he reached Georgetown, Winyaw, a letter overtook him, informing him of his father's death. Dr. Read returned express, and, after visiting his beloved father's grave, near Savannah, he rode to his late seat to offer consolation to his mother. In a few days he set out again on his expedition, and after some singular adventures, reached the field of battle at Monmouth; the battle was raging, Gen. Washington having rallied Gen. Lee's retreating columns, and ordered Lee into the rear. Dr. Read saw Gen. Lee standing at a tavern window with the landlady, and heard him call aloud to an officer riding by, and was told that the General asked, "What news?" The officer replied: "They are fighting on the plains of Monmouth, and the British grenadiers have given way;" when Gen. Lee replied, "That is a d——d lie, the British grenadiers never give way. Was an angel to come from Heaven and tell him so, he would say he was a liar." This was certainly said, as it came out in testimony on Lee's trial. Dr. Read, after a singular adventure, reached the battle-field. All appeared to him confusion and smoke; the weather was excessively hot. Dr. Read's enquiry was for the Pennsylvania line, and was told by a wounded soldier that Gen. Wayne had pushed it on to the field of battle; presently he saw an officer borne off by six soldiers, in a dying condition, and knew it to be that of Col. Bonner, the man he was on the enquiry for. He stayed by him a few minutes, when he rode into the thick of the battle, his servant all the time remonstrating with him to go no further, reminding him of a promise "not to carry him into battle." Dr. Read saw Gen. Washington riding to and fro along the line, sometimes at full speed, looking nobly, excited, and calling loudly to the troops by the appellation of brave boys. He saw Washington standing to the right of the line, with a number of officers near him, and saw a cannon ball strike a wet hole in the side of a hill, and the dirt fly on him. Two officers then rode up, and seemed to reason with him, and lay hold of the bridle of his horse. The General, coolly standing in his stirrups, was said to say to the officers who urged that that was no place for him, he being observed by the enemy, "that he was admiring the manner in which Proctor was handling their right." Dr. Read was near enough to hear the word Proctor, and was told what the General said. He then moved off at full speed, all the throng following, and Read among the rest. It was Col. Laurens and Huntingdon, he thinks, who prevailed on the General to change his position. The dust and smoke would sometimes so shut out the view, that one could form no idea of what was going on—the roar of cannon, the crackling of musketry, men's voices, making horrible confusion; then the groans and cries of the wounded. Dr. Read watched for an opportunity to speak to Gen. Washington, from old acquaintance, but it was not obtained, or of Col. Laurens. The evening at length came on, and the battle ceased, except some skirmishing at a distance, and some struggles to the left in arranging off prisoners.

The battle ceased with the approach of night, both armies exhausted by fatigue and the heat of the day—a deep morass lying between them. They lay down, man and horse, just where they halted; Washington and suit lay upon the field. It was generally understood the battle was to be renewed at the dawn of day. Dr. Reed, with his servant, rode on to the left of the line, seeing, in a few instances, regimental surgeons officiating, and administering to some wounded soldiers, and hearing the groans and cries of some men who had crawled, or been brought off into the rear. They reached a wagon which stood in an inclined situation, having the fore-wheels shot away; this position afforded a comfortable shelter to the two adventurers; their horses being tied to the wagon, lay down likewise. They had been rode seventy or eighty miles that day; but, being the finest horses in the army, they bore it well, and were not in the end hurt. At the dawn of day they heard the shout of victory—"the British are gone!" Dr. Read mounted, and rode down the hill which bounded the morass, and, observing several men entering the low ground to cross over, he did so also. The bog was very deep, and required the utmost effort of his and his servant's horse also, to get through it. As objects became visible, he saw several dead soldiers in the bog, mired to the waist, and probably shot. On the opposite side he saw an officer lying a few yards from the morass, nearly cut in two by a cannon shot; he was alive, and spoke, implored Dr. Read to lift him to a tree which stood near, alleging that he had been all night trying to do so, "that he might die easy." The clotted blood was piled up several inches on his front, and it had ceased to flow. Dr. Read, with the assistance of his servant, essayed to lift him tenderly, and, stepping backwards, they placed him against the tree. The blood now began to flow perceptibly, and in all probability terminated his life; they heard him utter a few words of thankfulness, and proceeded on. At the summit of the hill, dismal, indeed, was the scene; there lay fifty or sixty British grenadiers—some dead, some alive, calling for "help!" "water!" uttering the most dreadful and severe imprecations on "the rebels." Dr. Read and his servant ran down the hill, and found plenty of water; with his servant's hat he administered many draughts of water to these poor, famished soldiers; it was busy occupation for an hour. Dr. Read now found himself embarked in the business in a most remarkable manner; he proceeded to dress wounds and apply bandages. Tearing off shirts from the dead, he made bandages, and applied them, to the best of his skill, for remedying hemorrhage. Some country people and negroes coming to the field of carnage, Dr. Read enlisted their feelings, and hired them to assist in lifting and turning these wounded men, and, at length, in procuring wagons and straw to remove them to the court-house. In all this arduous undertaking, and work of humanity, he was greatly assisted by his servant, Peter Houston, who, until his death, must have felt it the sweetest solace of his life. They succeeded in moving twenty-one grenadiers, all with broken legs, or muscles so lacerated as to render them helpless. Dr. Read, seeing no medical aid come to him, proceeded to amputate wherever the patient would consent to the operation. In these operations he was aided by lint and bandages being sent, he knew not from whence, and every article of nourishment. Dr. Read continued to dwell in the court-house, sleeping, when he was enabled to sleep, in the Judge's bench. There he was observed by sundry groups of officers, who came riding around on a tour of observation, and his name enquired into. His servant sometimes entered into full explanations whence he was, and his motives, &c., and all he would say was, "at his own expense." This explanation must have had an effect, as on the third day he received from the Secretary a special commission, which gave him rank in the medical department, and extra rations and

17

forage. This circumstance fixed Dr. Read in the medical department, whereas, he had left Georgia with an intention of obtaining a company of horse, or foot, and serve in the line. No crusader ever set out for Palestine against the crescent with more sincerity than did he in devotion to the cause of freedom; but the above circumstance changed his purpose, and gave a more settled turn to his mind. On the fourth day of his care of the wounded grenadiers, two medical men came out of New York, and relieved him from the arduous duty. He explained to these gentlemen the nature and circumstances of the several cases, his amputations, &c.; to which they coolly observed, that he "had only given so many subjects to the Chelsea Hospital." Dr. Read then repaired to a house where lay a British officer, severely wounded through the groins, and in a dying condition. He barely spoke, and pointed to his wound. Dr. R. witnessed, on this occasion, the appalling circumstance of this gentleman's servants, a male and female, reasoning on the sharing of his silver, camp equipage and watch, which he evidently understood. While Dr. Read stood listening to this scene, he was accosted by an officer of rank, who, after enquiring if "he was Dr. Read?" desired that he would go immediately to Englishtown, and take charge of Col. Wessen, who lay there in a wounded condition. He did so, and found that gentlemen in a most deplorable state. He had received a wound from a cannon ball, which, striking his neck, he being in a stooping position, raked along the spine, tearing away clothing, skin and integuments, and muscles, to its extremity. He lay all night on the field of battle, supposed to be dead; but, being alive next morning, he was carried to Englishtown, about three miles distant. There Dr. Read found him attended by three of his artillery men, in a very sunken situation, while they appeared only to wait for his death. Dr. Read, with care and exertion, immediately undertook the case; by examining the wound, declared it not mortal, but capable of remedy. By his manner and cheering language, he raised the drooping spirits of the wounded man and his attendants, cleansed and dressed his wounds in such a manner as to revive hope, and afford ease and comfort. The patient was a large, heavy man, and difficult to manage; the suppuration of his wound was prodigious, and required four dressings in the day and night. In all this Dr. Read found his servant eminently useful; lint and dressings were sent in by some persons in the country in abundance, and many articles of nourishment. On the fourth day, Gen. Washington, with a number of officers, rode up to this nursery scene; Gen. W. alighted, and, enquiring for Dr. Read, was informed of the condition of the wounded Colonel. The General accosted him tenderly, and prevailed on him to take a tonic dose prepared for him, ending with telling him to obey the orders of his surgeon, and get well, " I cannot spare such officers as you are." Col. Wessen evidently improved after that day, and was more tractable. Dr. Read had the satisfaction of seeing his patient recover in twenty-three days, so far as to be conveyed away on a litter on men's shoulders. It is a remarkable circumstance, that thirty years after this scene, Dr. Read being in the town of Ipswich, in Massachusetts, met a gentlemen who knew Col. Wessen, and who had heard him speak of "a young surgeon from the far South, who attended him, and saved his life." The Colonel had died an old man a few months previously. Some interesting circumstances took place during this attendance, one of which we will relate. In walking out to enjoy a little fresh air, he met a chaise driving towards him, when suddenly he saw it guided out of the road, and turn over with a crash. He ran up, and saw two ladies on the ground; they appeared much disordered and disconcerted, the horse struggling with the entangled harness. He first lifted the old lady, the daughter had got up, and appeared in great confusion; he then seized the horse, disentangled the harness, and righted the chaise. Some civilities passed, some thanks were made; but with coldness and ceremony. It, however, became necessary for him to assist the ladies into the vehicle, and lead the horse around to the road. The ladies then seemed to rally their good feelings, and invited him to their house, which appeared in view. The mother and daughter, Mrs. and Miss English, became talkative and civil; Mrs. E. said she had an aversion to the American rebel officers, and did not wish to meet one, which was the reason of her turning out of the road in which she met with the disaster. Many gallant and reconciling things were exchanged, and the parties became acquainted. The old lady inquired of Dr. Read in what manner, with most security, she could put away her plate and wine. He advised her; but said, of the wine, madam, I should be apt to be a plunderer myself, as I have a patient in town whose life might be saved by a few bottles. Dr. Read took leave of the ladies, and that evening a dozen of old Madeira was sent, of which Col. Wessen benefited, and it was greatly instrumental in restoring him. Dr. Read now received orders to repair to Princeton, where the general hospital was fixed. There he found a dismal scene; a typhus fever prevailed to a fatal degree. Out of twelve medical men, five or six had died, others retired, and the department left to a German surgeon. Dr. Read took charge of the hospital, and endeavored to remedy the disorder, but in vain; five or six patients died daily. The attendants refused to do the duties assigned them; an awful scene of superstition prevailed. The duties all devolved on Dr. Read and the German, aided by a Scotch lady, the matron, with a few women, not one of whom would go into the hospital after night. At length Dr. Read was attacked with the fever, and underwent a severe illness; his first and second attendant died, and he was left to an Indian woman In a state of delirium he ordered the sick all to be carried out of town, and deposited in the farmers' barns. Although illegal and nuwarranted, it was done, and it pleased God that the measure succeeded, as no new case ensued, and no death happened after. Dr. Read's case terminated in an abscess of his arm, and resulted favorably. On his recovery, he was surprised at being told of his orders respecting the sick, being unconscious of it; but rejoiced at the happy consequences. At Princeton it was Dr. Read's good fortune to obtain of Mrs. Livingston a chamber, and a closet as an office, which gave him an opportunity of accommodating the young soldier, Marquis Lafayette, on a very cold night, when not a bed or blanket elsewhere could be had; and, on another occasion, of lodging Col. Tatnall, of Georgia, and his lady and daughter, who were passing through, prisoners of war on parole, on their way to embark for England. Washington lay at winter quarters at Morristown, and a general hospital was ordered at Brunswick. Dr. Read, dismissing the hospital at Princeton, went on to Brunswick to seek employment. Dr. Scott was the principal, and he being ordered to appoint an assistant, was on the look-out for some surgeon who might suit his purpose, and act in concert. Many were the offers made him by medical men of high standing, who were driven from various cities by the British army, some leaving their stations from principle. Dr. Read arrived at the time of this contest for preference, and saw little or no prospect of employment for him—young and a stranger, far from home and friends and resources; but, being one evening in company, in a large mess, accounts were brought of a battle at Spotswood, and that a wounded soldier lay in a dangerous situation, and wanted surgical aid. No one offered to go; the distance was twelve miles from Brunswick, the weather extremely cold. Dr. Read enquired: "Will none of you senior surgeons go?" Nobody consented. At length he said, with an asseveration, "that if he could get a guide he would go." It was reasoned against by several, both medical and officers of the line, and Dr. Read was told that the thing was impossible, and counselled him not to attempt it; he, however, persevered—a hardy earman, who knew the way, was obtained, who undertook the business for a promised reward. The whole country being covered with snow, no road could be discovered. The guide was excessively clad, and rode a fine horse of his own; Dr. Read was comfortably clad, and made no addition to his clothing, except a linen shirt over his body linen (at the suggestion of his landlady). Several gentlemen, learning the chivalric undertaking of a young Southerner, came to advise and take leave of him; they advised him to keep speaking to the guide—he did so, frequently enquiring if "he was sure of the way," as nothing was to be seen except the white expanse of snow for miles. At length, having accomplished about eight miles of the way, the man ceased to reply; on riding up to him, he was still—senseless—dead. Dr. R. led the horse to a house now in view, when the inhabitants pronounced that he was cold-struck, and that all was over. Dr. Read obtained another guide, and made the ride, found the wounded man bleeding, a ball having passed deep into the muscles of his thigh, and taken a direction around the bone, and which he extracted. The thigh bone was broke; he set it with great difficulty, having very little assistance. Dr. R. then became so exhausted as to be nearly insensible, when he was beckoned by a little girl to follow her, she taking up his saddle and bridle; he followed her into a room, where he found a gentleman and lady, and child, in a warm chamber, the only room in the house which had window shutters, or a door. The gentleman said something civil to him, and pointed to the floor, before the fire-place; Dr. Read sat down, and was helped to a bowl of chocolate, scarcely conscious of anything he did, or what was said to him—fell backwards, was covered by the humane inhabitant of the chamber, and fell asleep. The good man felt his pulse, and was satisfied that he was alive, and let him lay undisturbed until he awoke in the morning, quite refreshed. Dr. Read found that his horse was safe, being taken away and cared for by some fellow-soldier of the wounded man, who likewise moved him from the cold and dreary house where he lay; he saw the man some months afterwards, a tolerable cure. A day or two after this occurred, Dr. Scott appointed the several applicants for office to meet him. Dr. Read had travelled back to Brunswick, on the track he went as his guide; he repaired to the meeting, when Dr. Scott, hearing the several merits and pretensions, which were of the first character, said: "Where is the young Southern man who went to the wounded soldier lately?" Dr. Read replied, "I am he." "Then you are my man, I like such hardy enterprise and zeal for the service."

Dr. Read went on acting with Dr. Scott in the utmost harmony, in fixing and organizing this new establishment, and in receiving patients and prescribing. Their practice was similar, Dr. Read's first medical preceptor, David Brady, of Savannah, being coeval with Dr. Scott in

Edinburgh. There is a fashion in medicine as well as in other science. Dr. Read established a practice of an afternoon visit to the hospital, a thing never done by any other hospital surgeon; but, on a very stout horse, with corked heels, he used every day twice to ascend the frozen hill to the barracks. This was pleasing to the Doctor, whose corpulency and senior time of life rendered it irksome to him. It has been remarked above that the weather in 1775–'79, was extremely cold. This close attention to business was noticed by the Superintending Officer, Col. Carvel Hale, and by several other officers residing in the town, which attached them to the young, stranger Doctor. The army was at this time very full of women and children, and in its destitute situation they partook especially of its discomforts; widows, deserted wives and girls were many. Often they were seen walking down to Brunswick bare-footed, carrying an infant in their arms, with one or two little ones holding on to their skirts, through the snow; their resort was to the doctor's, and to the quarters of the officers. A camp woman was generally considered of loose character; but it was not strictly so in our army—many were innocent and correct, whose real history would be affectingly interesting. Dr. Read has at times, during a snow-storm, had three of these poor sufferers, with several children, sheltered in his chamber, whose protection from the weather, and a good fire, were their chief object; this was the case likewise with the other officers in the town. Charity, and its means and forbearance, being nearly exhausted, Dr. Read, with Col. Carvel Hale, Col. Abraham Beauford and Major Graham, met and devised a plan of aiding, clothing and supporting these wretched beings. They resolved to erect a theatre, and play, to raise funds for the purpose; a spacious room, called Whitehall, was gratuitously furnished by Mrs. Voorhees. The party contributed, and furnished materials, and fitted up a pit and scenes, and all the necessary appendages of a play-house, and commenced acting. The ladies of Brunswick, and the vicinity, took much interest in the plan, and did much for them; young college boys took the parts of women, and their sisters furnished dresses. It was the custom in those days to act in the costumes of the nation they represented. They played from Shakespeare and Addison; the dresses were made of camblet, which was got out of New York by strategem, and it was made up and fashioned by the ladies according to the cuts in the volumes they played from. They formed companies of working parties, and worked industriously to meet the occasions, while they retired to study their parts, and sometimes met in joint board to communicate with each other, and give the cue to the young scholars who acted the female parts. Dr. Read has often valued himself and his associates on their moral good habits and good conduct. A Mr. Harley, who had been a manager of a theatre in England, offered himself as director and prompter. Each of the gentlemen had seen some stage playing; Dr. Read, especially, had made it a scholastic exercise in Savannah, and was pronounced by Stanley master of the business. They played to full audiences, frequently twenty tickets were purchased, and only one or two were used. The intention was understood, and greatly applauded. Major Graham was the treasurer; the money was economically and judiciously laid out; many suits of warm clothing, and shoes and stockings, were got out of New York by industry and private correspondence. At length, all communication ceasing by flags of truce, an adventurous man was procured who would go in at night a slender frame, and come out next night a Falstaff in form, with goods of various sorts, which bestowed comfort on numerous needy women and children. It is highly satisfactory to reflect on the satisfaction felt on the grateful acknowledgment of the receivers; it was like bestowing life. There may be some actors in this drama still in being, and it would be a pleasant reflection to think on their associates; life, however, is fugitive and unstable. In 1809, thirty years after these scenes, Dr. R., on a visit, found no one scarcely that he knew; Dr. Scott was living, but very infirm, and it was with difficulty that he could make him recollect him, and not until Dr. R. Read pointed out a deep scar on his forehead, given him by a Commissary, in which Dr. R. attended him, and resented the outrage, that Dr. Scott could fully recollect him; on which, he embraced him tenderly, shed tears, and made many enquiries. The scenes at Brunswick having ceased, Dr. Read broke up the establishment, and moved the invalids to White's house, over the Raritan, where, covered by a detachment under Baron DeKalb and Major Hamilton, of the Pennsylvanians, they were supposed to be secure, and the battle of Springfield was fought. The department being moved back to Brunswick, was conducted by Dr. VanBuren. Dr. Read, ever on the alert for service and distinction, joined Col. Posey, of the Virginians, on an expedition up the East River. On the second night of their being on the river, Dr. R. being sentinel, discovered, by his peculiar long sightedness, an embarkation of horse and foot, on which it became necessary for the Colonel to retreat, having no horse with him. On the retreat, Dr. Read was taken suddenly ill, and obliged to go into a farm-house, uncertain of the principles of the landlord; he interested a young woman servant to give him early secret notice of the approach of the enemy, he having laid down with warm applications to a painful face.

The British arrived, faithful notice was given, when Dr. Read was obliged to leap out of a lofty window, and run. On passing through a gate, he saw his servant riding off, leading his horse. He was afraid to call to him, lest he should be heard, and pursued; but ran after him until he was exhausted, then turning from the river on his left, he entered a swamp, came across a saw-pit, found some boards so placed as to afford shelter. The weather was cold, and he had no cloak; however, he contrived to get some sleep in tolerable comfort—the pain of his face had vanished. At daylight he set out across the swamp, directed by the barking of dogs; he reached the high grounds at sunrise. His servant, an Irish lad, had reached the place before him, and on another hill, which was a camp, had been made prisoner, and severely questioned; Dr. Read coming up, likewise a prisoner, it assured his servant, and made him answer to questions without equivocation, in which he had deviated, replying to suit a purpose, admitting that the army might be on the British side of the question. The story of his having come over a bridge was discredited as an impossible thing, as the party had burnt it a few days previous, leaving only the sleepers. This mystery continued unexplained, and they were disposed to consider both Dr. Read and his servant as spies. Dr. Read demanded to be carried to the Commanding Officer, a Col. Van ——. He put a bold face on the affair, demanded to be released, and to be escorted to the camp of Gen. Clinton, whether he supposed Col. Posey had retreated; "that he was assured that Col. Posey would be here presently in search of him." This assurance, and Dr. Read's manner, having an effect on Col. Van ——, he hesitated. Dr. R. demanded pen, ink and paper, and sitting down, wrote a letter to Col. Laurens, at head-quarters, explaining his situation. On enquiring the Colonel's name, "say commanding a regiment of militia." Dr. Read finished and read the letter, and required that it should be sent to the care of Gen. Clinton. A militia man came up and complained that Dr. Read had ordered him off the river, threatening to make him prisoner, or shoot him, the day before; this, although urged in complaint against him, had the happiest effect; it confirmed his story, and that the equivocation had only been from his affrighted servant. Dr. Read insisted on the restoration of several articles which had been taken from his servant. He then proceeded on with four horsemen as escort or guides, to Gen. Clinton's camp. Col. Posey had not been there; the letter to Col. Laurens had been suppressed. Gen. Clinton heard Dr. Read's story with great interest, and said, "that man shall explain what he is about in four hours." Dr. Read heard no more of the affair, except that there was some hanging of that party. Dr. Read reached Round Brook next day, and laid down much fatigued and hungry, man and horse. He never met Col. Posey after this, to enquire and explain matters. He now resorted to head-quarters, and presently had a business assigned him; it was to ride to ———, a village in the south-west of New Jersey, and dismiss an hospital, with a surgeon, a physician, a nurse, and an orderly man, and only one patient, an invalid. He performed the duty, and the affair was attended with a circumstance of such peculiar pre-science, as would tell like romance; but, being attended to, saved him from capture, or being killed, and all the persons above mentioned. Dr. Read, and the officers of the hospital, had been gone about four hours, when a British party, headed by Col. Simkoe, rode into the village, and cut down all before them, set fire to the court-house, which had been an hospital, demanded and drank wine at the house of Mr. Clopper, the principal of the village, rode down the road to Brunswick. The Colonel had his horse shot under him, and was made prisoner, the militia having taken the alarm from what Dr. Read said on his ride to Brunswick, merely from the suggestions of a young lady. Dr. Reed rode all night, and probably was no more than four hours ahead of this party of horse when he reached Brunswick. The cavaliers did not stop to rescue their Colonel, but rapidly charged on, leaving the bar-racks, near the town, to their left, rode on to Amboy, where they em-barked by pre-concert, and got safely off; there were some shot down. On their passing the barracks, they encountered a Capt. Voorhuse, who was coming from the country, who imprudently but gallantly defended himself with his small sword, and was cut to pieces; he was brought into Brunswick in a dying condition, and Simkoe, at the same time, in a stunned condition. The British Colonel would have been made a sacrifice of by the populace, but for the humane interference of Levinus Clarkson and Dr. Read, who brought to view the circumstance of the Colonel being prisoner before the massacre of Capt. Voorhuse, which pacified the enraged people. The gallant Colonel had come out of New York with a corps disguised like Baylor's horse, drew rations and forage as such at one of our posts; and, charging rapidly over the Raritan, set fire to Washington's boats, in the act of being built on the Milstone, and made their retreat as above. Dr. Read repaired to head-quarters, and had to report this expedition. Hearing that Gen. Wool-ford had gone to his quarters a sick man just returned from Georgia, from Gen. Robert Howe's campaign against Florida, he rode to Bruns-wick, and took care of the General. After recruiting, he proposed a ride to confirm his recovery. They rode to Elizabethtown, and hearing that the Marquis Lafayette had given a ball, with general invitations to all officers, Dr. Read went to it, leaving the General to go to bed. At about 1 o'clock, P. M., the alarm was given—"the enemy in town!" Col. Sterling had crossed over, and was in hopes of surprising our General, Maxwell, and of catching the Marquis, but they escaped. The British set fire to the armory, and some other buildings, and pushed on after Maxwell. Dr. Read ran to his quarters, got Woolford on horseback, and mounted his horse; they rode off at speed towards the town gate, leaving his servant to follow with his pormanteau, which contained all his clothing, and every article he possessed—the hilt of the sword he had received from the silk stocking company (so called) of Philadelphia; his gold medal obtained from the clinical class of Dr. Rush, in 1775; his letters and memorandums. A party threw themselves immediately between his retreating servant, a soldier on a public horse and the gate, and made him prisoner. This he considered a great misfortune, as he had not the means or opportunity of supplying himself. He was, however, amply supplied by the man who had been his tailor when a student in Philadelphia, who subsequently would receive no payment, although pressed upon them. It being understood that large inforcements to the British army were expected, General Washington hesitated at sending troops to the South. Prejudices were great against the climate, and the safety of the soldiery; a wish was uttered at headquarters that some active, intelligent man would ride into Carolina, and ascertain the facts with regard to the real state of things. Several weeks had elapsed since there was any information carried to headquarters from South Carolina, and all was anxiety and uncertainty. Dr. Read at once offered himself as that man. He received his orders, went through the line to tell of his mission, and·enquire for commands, rode down to Brunswick, disposed of his servant and spare horse, mounted his hardiest nag, and set out. He went by way of Baltimore, Annapolis, Norfolk, Newbern, Wilmington and Long Bay, and Georgetown; his ride averaged fifty miles per day, on one and the same horse; he bore his own expenses on this march; they were not heavy, as he was temperate; his payments for horse, and his own feed and lodging, was often refused; there was no instance in which a woman would take money. Some remarkable incidents took place on this march, but would be too long in narrative for a memoir like this. Dr. Read reached the house of Mr. Jacob Ion, in Christ Church Parish, his horse completely worn down, and having lost his hair. His friend lent him a horse, on which he rode to Charlestown; next day to Stono, it being a few days after the battle of Stono. He found the sick and wounded well accommodated and cared for by the neighboring planters, especially at the house of Mr. Humphry Summers. In Charlestown he found a well-regulated hospital, under the direction of Dr. Tucker Harris and Dr. Earnest Poy, as an assistant. Dr. Read then crossed over the river to report himself to Gen. Moultrie. While there, Major Thomas Shubrick having organized an expedition at midnight to John's Island, Dr. Read joined in the adventure; there were twelve men chosen by Major Shubrick, among a number who offered. They embarked on board a canoe, with muffled oars, in solemn silence; this was an age of chivalry and enterprise. After many hours the party landed on John's Island, marched up a causeway, seized a sentinel who leaned against a coach-house door at Mr. Gibbes', gagged him, took from the stables two fine horses, Flimnap and Abdalla; these they sent off by Stono Ferry, by preconcert, dragged along the prisoner to the boat, and made their retreat good. The party had barely embarked, when Col. Thomson's corps was seen riding down the causeway, trumpets sounding; but they had got out of reach, and there was no boat, in which they could have pursued. They returned safe to James' Island. Gen. Moultrie spoke in warm terms against such "expeditions." Dr. Read rested himself one day, took from his father's gang of negroes, which had retreated to Carolina, a boy, whom he mounted and carried on to the North with him, who proved a faithful servant throughout the subsequent service. Billy was well known through the army, making himself useful in shaving, and dressing the hair of many officers. Kosciusko makes kind mention of Billy in a letter to Dr. Read. On returning to head-quarters, and making his report, he had the personal thanks of Gen. Washington. The reinforcements under Gen. Gates marched to the South. Dr. Read was then ordered to open an hospital at Trenton, for inoculating recruits, both soldiers and seamen, in course of which he treated 300 with success. In this service he met with some singular adventures, interesting at the time, but fitter for oral narration than for a written memoir; in one of which he met with unkindness and opposition from the magistrates of Trentown, and especially from Governor Livingston; but which he repelled with firmness, and came off triumphantly, supporting the dignity of the medical department, concluding the dispute by making a good use of a timely letter received from President Laurens on public affairs, from the South. Dr. Read's resistance to the Governor and the Magistrates was all got over, and salved over on its being made manifest that he was a friend and correspondent of Henry Laurens, President of Congress. This business being over, and the hospital dismissed, Dr. Read was ordered to Fort Pitt, on the Ohio, to fix on a site for an hospital, in case of the retreat of our army. He rode hastily to Baltimore, was politely received by Messrs. Buchanan & Smith. With one soldier as a guide, he travelled to the Chesnut Hills, and over the Monongahela, and to Fort Pitt. He could get little or no information, the popular man, Mr. Harris, being absent. He saw nothing except Indians, who daily crossed over the River Ohio, and annoyed him very much; at length, understanding that they had taken a fancy to the fine horse Dr. Read rode, and would buy or steal him, Dr. Read (being advised by a half-breed man to do so) started at midnight, and made his retreat good across the Monongahela. He reported the abortive mission, having only designated the spot for a site, probably on the place where Harrisburg now stands, or Pittsburg. Dr. Read now solicited an order to proceed to the South, Gen. Gates being on his march to South Carolina. He received his orders, and set out for Philadelphia, where he was to receive money as pay; and for the hospital department none was to be had. He applied in vain to President Laurens; but was told that a board was sitting, to pay officers who were on their march for the Southern service. It was composed of Colonel Grayson, Richard Peters (since Judge Peters), and Mr. Pleasants. There were many applicants, and the board received and settled their demands in rotation; such were the number of applicants, that it appeared improbable that Dr. Read could be heard for ten days. He was at private lodging, at a dear rate, and paying with his own hard money; this he spoke of and complained. Col. Benjamin Harrison was a fellow lodger, and took an interest in the young stranger, learning some interesting things in his being the drill and training master to the first company raised in Pennsylvania for the protection of the first Revolutionary Congress, and some other chivalrous things, felt embarked in his behalf; and, together with Col. Grayson, devised a scheme to get his pay. He was instructed to go to the board next day, and to force his way into the chamber through the crowd of applicants, and to demand his pay, urging the necessity of his going to join Gen. Gates in South Carolina. "Be as importunate and boisterous as you please, the thing will be understood and arranged." Dr. Read did so, and was presented with a quire of Continental bills, with, "let us get rid of this importunate young man, his case is a peculiar one." Dr. Read marched off with his money, and set out on the same day for Annapolis, where he had left a carriage and a portfolio, the carriage to be sold. He found his neat, elegant carriage in an outer livery stable-yard, almost gone to ruin, and his portfolio missing; there had, in the meantime, been a change of landlords, and no accountability. The carriage sold for $50, which barely paid him for his delay at Annapolis. Dr. Read now hurried on for the Southern compaign on horseback, with his faithful servant Billy, on two fine horses. On this march he avoided his old acquaintances of Marlborough and Mount Airy, leaving them to his left. He now travelled in the capacity of a poor soldier, with only a commission; formerly he associated with the distinguished inhabitants of that region, and of Mount Airy and Mount Vernon, and Arlington, especially, as a young gentleman. The case was altered, and he changed with the times. He met with some singular adventures on this march, which would tell too much like romance for a plain matter-of-fact memoir like this. Mr. John Park Custis, hearing that his old acquaintance, Dr. Read, had passed through the country with a portion of the marching army, made a prodigious ride to overtake him, and persuade him to return to his old acquaintance, if only for a day or two. He drove a set of fine horses in a phæton, and offered to carry Dr. Read back to Mount Airy, and to forward him on his march of duty; but, at the same time informed him of the death of his aunt, Molly Read, and of the engagement of Miss Elizabeth Calvert, being engaged to a Mr. Steward, and the wedding only postponed on account of the death of his aunt. All these things were interesting to him, but nothing could divert the purpose of Dr. Read from proceeding on to the army. Mr. Custis, then, with sorrow and chagrin, informed Dr. Read that there had been private information received the night before by a Tory neighbor, that Gen. Gates was defeated, and totally routed, and that his reinforcement under Col. Beauford had been surprised by the gallant Tarleton, and cut to pieces at Waxsaws. It is worthy of remark, with what industry the King's adherents kept up their information on all our movements and transactions. Their struggle was a hard one, to keep hold of the country; and much money and pains were expended in spies, express riders, and secret information.

Mr. Custis' hard ride after Dr. Read was to give him the above information, and to divert his attention from the disastrous circumstance of a defeated army; but it only served to stimulate his intention to proceed, and throw himself into the breach. At Fredericktown, where Dr. Read was to rendezvous, there was no information of the defeat in all the next day; but, fearing that the bad news was too true, he took a farewell—an eternal farewell—of his friend Custis, and proceeded on, leaving the rendezvous to Dr. Prescot. His ride was rapid, and the full account of Gates' disaster never reached him until he arrived at Petersburg, in Virginia. There he heard the sad detail, and the narrow escape of his old acquaintance, Col. Abraham Beauford. Dr.

Read never met Beauford afterwards; he fell in Gen. Sinclair's defeat. Custis died at the siege of Yorktown; he wrote Dr. Read tenderly the day before his attack. Dr. Read then proceeded on, and having joined Major Kendall, after some singular adventures they reached Hillsborough. There he met Gen. Gates, with the remainder of his defeated army; they were in a state of the utmost destitution; bereaved of their baggage, they were badly clad, many unable to leave their huts and tents for want of necessary clothing. Provisions, likewise, were very scarce and very coarse. A few officers who had money would send into the country and get some comfortable things; but in general the bread of the army was made from corn grated down on old canteens, with holes punched through them. The mills being generally burnt, or mill dams cut, no meal could be got. Gen. Gates' mess and family fared in the same manner, until an unexpected supply of butter and flour was sent to Dr. Read by the wife of Col. Elliott. It was a delicate acknowledgment of tender and polite treatment in his call at the Colonel's house. This supply was most welcome, and Dr. Read made a generous, liberal use of it. It restored the General to better health and good humor, which were sadly impaired; on several sick and wounded officers it had a salutary effect. Never was a barrel of flour, and a keg of butter more usefully expended, or so gratefully received. Gen. Gates was sadly low spirited at the time Dr. Read joined him, and made every one unhappy that had to communicate with him; he was uneasy at the state in which he stood with Congress, and with his Commander-in-Chief, after his defeat. He was under the impression of Dr. Read's knowing something about it, and he became short and unpleasant to him, notwithstanding, from dates, that he knew that Dr. Read had heard nothing of his battle until he reached the interior of Maryland; and that when Dr. Read left Philadelphia, all appeared prosperous in the Southern army, and that it was marching on confident of success. But, Dr. Read being a correspondent of Mr. John Park Custis (son-in-law to Gen. Washington), Gates was impressed with the idea of his having some information of the impression his defeat made at head-quarters, and with Congress; but Dr. Read had not heard from Custis since the disaster. Other surmises and injurious impressions against Dr. Read, were dwelling in his breast—one was, that he was an Englishman (which he concealed), another, that he was a Romanist. Dr. Read, abhorring anything like equivocation, had to bring Major Pierce Butler to head-quarters, and put such questions to him in the presence of the General, that convinced him that Dr. Read's birthplace was Carolina, and that he grew up in Georgia, and was educated in the end in Philadelphia. His suspicion of Romanism arose from Dr. R.'s proposing to make an hospital of a Protestant Church; it was a remedy against the sad prevalence of typhus fever among the soldiers. Gen. Gates enquiring of Dr. Read the cause of the fever, was told that it arose from exhaustion, fatigue and chagrin at defeat. The General fretted and said: "Then, I am to be blamed for an act of God!" Dr. Read replied that he had answered him candidly. Gen. Gates at length was attacked with a painful complaint, which Dr. Read remedied successfully, and the General became more pleasant with him. Shortly after this time the Southern affairs took a happy turn; the Georgians and Carolinians, South and North, mustered to stop the career of the British under Col. Ferguson. He was carrying terror and devastation through the Western country, when the combination of field-officers, with their men, overtook the bold, enterprising Commander, and brought him to battle at King's Mountain. The account of it belongs to history. He was killed.

This news elated Gen. Gates exceedingly, and cheered us all. The General did not possess the *equa mente*. He soon prepared to advance into South Carolina. The night before he marched, some thief got into the public stable and stole a fine horse of Dr. Read's from among fifty others; he was the horse on which Dr. Read made the ride into South Carolina from Brunswick, in 1779. Major Depeyster, second in command, being paroled, came to Gates' quarters, and there, at dinner, said that Col. Jacob Read would be executed, in retaliation for Major Andre. A dead silence ensued for some minutes, when, all eyes being on Dr. Read and Depeyster, Dr. Read rose and said: "How can you say so; was Major Read taken as a spy? Major Read is a militia officer, belonging to South Carolina, and not to the Continental army." Gen. Gates interposed, and said that Major Depiester did not know that Major Read had a brother at the table. The Major said he did not, and the matter was quieted. Several officers spoke, and said: "My brave fellow, if that is to be the policy of your army, a scene of carnage will ensue which will make you all rue it." Gates marched, and in a few days nine of the prisoners came to Hillsborough, directed to Dr. Read's quarters. He received them politely, and had to regret that his flour and butter was nearly exhausted; but some farmers, near the town, soon found them out, and supplied them plentifully; they would visit them, and cherish them. Dr. Read was struck with this instance of the attachments of these men to the British interests, and had to reprove it, reminding these men of their treasonable disposition, and he had to check their language to these officers, and to strictly caution them that their tongues were paroled as well as their swords; soon, however, they were forwarded to a Commissary of prisoners, and heard no more of. Gen. Nathaniel Greene now arrived, and took command of the Southern army; a long and interesting conversation took place between Dr. Read and the General. Gates had advanced as far South as Charlotte, in North Carolina. Greene found the remaining troops, such as wounded and invalids, well furnished with wholesome provisions, especially bread, which was contrary to his information. Gen. Gates had, a few weeks previous to his march, contracted with a Mr. Hog, by a secret understanding, to furnish our army with provisions, and corn meal especially. Protection and neutrality was afforded him by Gates, and he was permitted to bring corn and beeves from the south, where Col. Fanning commanded. Mr. Hog established within his enclosure, and worked, a number of mills; the enclosure was permitted to be neutral ground. Dr. Read has seen a hundred mules and horses, loaded with corn, ascending the rocky heights near Hillsborough, and he understood that they were in motion all night. It was a mutual accommodation between enemy Commanders, and, Dr. Read believes, brought about by Mr. Millet, an excellent Republican citizen of North Carolina, who attached himself to Gen. Gates, and was very serviceable to him after his disaster. Gen. Greene heard this arrangement with delight. It is probable that the British armament moved from their position when the defeat of Ferguson took place, and Gates moved South, as the supply from below immediately ceased. A good store, however, remained, and served Dr. Read's department during his delay, and on his march, until he reached the plentiful country about Salisbury. Gen. Greene proceeded on and superseded Gates, who soon returned to Hillsborough. Dr. Read made a point of waiting on his fallen General in sympathy; he saw him receive a dispatch from the North, and, on reading a letter, he saw a good deal of feeling expressed; the General put the letter to his lips, and uttered some words. Dr. Read waited a while, and then approached his old enemy in tender sympathy; the General received him gratefully and graciously, and, pointing to the letter, said, "Washington sympathises with me in the loss of my son, and commands me to the right wing of the army." There were several officers of distinction, invalids and wounded, who did not visit the General on this occasion. Dr. Read's instructions were to follow Gen. Greene's march as speedily as possible, and to fix his department at Salisbury until further orders. Gates called at Dr. Read's quarters, and bid him farewell, seeming to have forgotten their former hostility. Dr. Read moved on with his department in a few

days; on his march he met with a singular adventure. Feeling sore at
the loss of a fine horse, as related above, he wished to recover him,
and, as a mere possibility to obtain that end, he determined to make an
effort. He struck into a road which deviated to the left of the main
road, and rode rapidly on, in hopes to be able to regain the road on
which his department marched, and, struck with a track of a single
horse on said road, which resembled that of his stolen horse, he pursued the track for many miles, at a round gallop, not conscious how far
he was deviating from his direct road. At length the track ceased, by
the grass on a neglected road, and he saw a building; it proved a lofty
mill, now in disuse. On approaching the scene, he perceived two men
running; they ran towards a dwelling-house, whither he pursued them,
in order to speak to them. He was accosted by a respectable-looking
man with, "Who art thou?" and "What dost thou want?" He told
his errand without dismounting, and asked for some refreshment. Dr.
Read was invited in, where he saw another very respectable-looking
man, a senior. They called in a negro man, and set before him beef,
bread and eggs, and ordered his horse fed. One of his servants came
in and said, in an under voice, "he never saw such a horse before."
He rode his fine Irish grey. He felt uneasy, and wished for the time
that he had rode some less attractive horse; but his meal being finished,
he requested to be instructed how to fall in with the main road to Salisbury, and then informed them who he was, and his march towards
that town. These people had only a vague report of the battle of
King's Mountain, and the death of Col. Ferguson. This was a place
of mills; a vast quantity of lumber lay about. Dr. Read was now told
that, if he wanted to depart by any other way than that he came on, he
must be blindfolded, and obey instructions; he consented, and had
his handkerchief placed over his eyes. He and his horse were lead
over heaps of boards, and carried to a river, embarked in a flat, and
poled along by the white man and negro; no word was uttered except
"stoop," "stoop low." The boat appeared to enter a creek, and to be
poled along many miles. At length he was landed, and, being released
by his conductors, got directions to ride forward in a precise direction,
to ride hard, until he struck a deep swamp, and to course along about
ten miles, and he would strike the main road. He did so; probably
galloped twenty miles before he struck the swamp, and ten along that
course. About half-way along, he came to a settlement of new huts;
asked for some water; was known to the negroes; called young master,
and was told that they had belonged to his uncle Rose, and that they
had seen him at Oakhampton; said they belonged to the public. Dr,

18

Read, on reaching the main road, and perceiving no fresh track of his department, road down the road in hopes of meeting his party. In an hour's ride, now at night, he met some of his officers, who had been uneasy at his rash resolve to leave his party in the vain search of a lost horse, they being in an enemy's country. He moved on as speedily as the insufficient equipment of his department would admit; numbers of wounded and invalids insisted on going on in hopes of recovery, and being able to take the field again. Never was there an instance of such zeal, such enthusiasm, displayed in common soldiers, as was exhibited here on Gen. Greene taking the command. He reached Salisbury, and not being preceded by a Quarter-Master, had to ride through the town, and to put under requisition such buildings as he required for an hospital, and such apartments as he stood in need of for himself and officers. He did so as best suited the purpose, but it occasioned much discontent between the Republican and Royalist owners, and some warm conversations with him. Dr. Read's policy was to conciliate good will, and to make friends to the cause wherever he served, and he succeeded in many instances. At Salisbury he was well established, himself and the young gentlemen of his department, and some prisoners. Col. Rugely was a sick man, a prisoner on parole. They thought themselves well off for some weeks; and, had Gen. Greene been able to fight and repel Cornwallis, he might have remained stationary. When, behold, one night his landlord came to his bed-side, saying, " Dr. Read, I have bad news for you !" A marauding party has been to my wash-house, and plundered my washer-woman of all my clothes, and of yours, and of these gentlemen, meaning Col. Rugely, and of Capt. Churchill Jones (a sick officer, who was at my quarters). " Another piece of bad news is, that Gen. Greene is on the retreat, and there is an express now in town enquiring for you." They all dressed in a hurry. The express did come, and communicate the orders : " that Dr. Read must retreat immediately." Capt. Jones was not in a condition to ride; but, getting a litter made, he was laid on it, and they were all on the retreat towards the River Yadkin before daylight. Drs. Brownfield and Gillet were eminently useful in packing up their stores and medicines, and in getting off the patients. They crossed the Yadkin. Dr. Read, confident of his horse, remained in town until he saw Greene's retreating army march through. Greene followed, and was actually alone, the most fatigued man he ever saw. Read was seated giving paroles to certain prisoners of war. Some of this assumed service was attended with such circumstances of romance, as would not bear a narrative here, although strictly true. A scene transacted here is given in Garden's anecdotes. Dr. Read, having Gen. Greene's sanction and approbation, finished the business, and rode with the General to the Yadkin, and they crossed the river together at the Island Ford. Dr. Read continued with the General, no aid-de-camp or other officer being with him; his aides and secretary were all absent—gone, as he said, to meet Gen. Huger, and to hasten his march. Gen. Isaac Huger commanded such of Gates' defeated troops, and such volunteers as he could collect North of the Cape Fair, and to him all eyes were turned for the reinforcement to enable Greene to meet the foe. Huger's name was uttered a thousand times by the soldiery, as a desirable arrival. He at length reached the River Dan, and crossed. Gen. Greene requested an interview with Dr. Read the morning after their crossing the Yadkin; and, giving him his orders, said—"Your department would embarrass my march; you must march to the left, and reach Virginia as soon as you can. You are to take the prisoners (the Queen's Rangers) with you, about 150. You march through an hostile country, and these men may be rescued by the disaffected inhabitants; each man is worth the release of an American soldier, a prisoner, therefore be careful of them." Dr. Read said, "Gen. Greene, this is more than my duty." The General contemplated Dr. R. for some time and said: "Dr. Read, we must all do more than our duty, or we never shall succeed; this is not the first time that extra duty has been required of you. I rely much on you. I will give you thirty stand of arms, and you must organize a guard of volunteers from among the invalids, and be upon your guard." Dr. R. knew that Cols. Scophol and Cunningham were in the field, no great way from his march, as a short time previous to this he (Dr. Read) was sent by the General, express to Col. Lock, to order a thousand men raised, to cover Major Hyrne's retreat with the captive regiment, the British 71st, taken at the battle of the Cowpens, as Scophol and Cunningham were in the hostile position a little to the west. The service was promptly performed. The transaction was attended with a laughable circumstance, which was given to Major Garden as an anecdote. Dr. Read's march was made with all possible dispatch, lame and insufficient as his transportation was. On the first night, being on the way in rainy weather, Dr. Read riding in the van, was hailed—"Who comes there?" to which he responded, drawing out and cocking his pistol. Again they hailed, when Dr. Read, telling his name, was answered with the reply—"You are the man I am looking for, having come across the country with great perseverance." It proved to be Major Call, with a dispatch. Dr. Read went under a wagon, struck a light, and read the dispatch. The service was done to Gen. Greene's satisfaction. It was most important, and is told in Garden's anecdotes. The cartridges obtained by Dr. Read's vigilance, and his influence with Tranqut Buggie (the principal of the Moravians), were dispatched to the army on the Dan, and were probably the missiles at the battle of Guildford. Buggie would take no payment for the fare of the officers, and took certificates only for the rations furnished the troops. The march was continued, attended with many interesting circumstances, one of which may be told. Dr. Read, in riding forward in the van, reached a dairy, which in a manner overhung the road. He looked in, and observing a fine dairy, endeavored to buy all the milk, &c., in it, for his poor, sick and wounded soldiers. A bargain was struck for all in the dairy except the butter. The woman of the dairy went into the dwelling-house to ascertain the worth of her milk, &c., and stayed a long time. In the meantime his wagon and marching parties moved on, were ordered to halt, and the people to return with their canteens and cups; they did so, and carried off all the milky fluid. Payment was now offered; the price fixed was four-and-a-half crowns. Dr. Read held the silver in his hand; the woman did not take it, but opened a gate, and motioned Dr. Read to ride in; he said "no! that he was in a hurry," and again handed the money. The woman refused to extend her hand, but urged him to ride in. He thought that he saw something designing in her manners, and much trepidation, when, looking towards the house, he saw two men riding hard towards him; one of them was one of the Queen's Rangers, in green and crimson, a man that he had missed all the day previous. Dr. Read took the hint, and rode off towards his party. His soldiers were indignant at this treacherous affair, and were with difficulty prevented from returning and wreaking vengeance on the house; but policy, as well as humanity, restrained him. He was in hourly expectation of being pursued by Tarleton, or a detachment of his corps, as he knew they were to cross the Yadkin at the Shallow Ford, and would march through Salem, and there get an account of Dr. Read's marching party, which might be an object; he, therefore, proceeded in all meekness and benevolence towards the inhabitants. The two men were seen late on that day riding on the side of a mountain parallel with the marching party, out of reach of musket shot. Dr. Read was delicate in making requisitions on the inhabitants, except for provisions, and a few blankets for the needy. The scarcity of that article was severely felt in many instances. After the defeat of Gates, scarce one man in five had a blanket. · Dr. Read was at quarters out of Hillsborough, together with Gen. Isaac Huger and Col. Kosciusko, without a blanket, for more than six weeks, their only bedding being the General's cloak, under which they occasionally slept; they constantly hoped for a supply. The weather was in the meantime very cold, but they bore it without a murmur. The sick soldiers, women and children, benefited by the milk, and the treacherous woman lost her money. Returning this way some months after, nobody was at this house; all was ruin and desolation. On reaching Salem on a mission to obtain scalpels and lancets, he learned that the British army did march through Salem, and the respectable old Principal observed to Dr. Read that "he took all their milk," but said he, "the British took off all our milch cows." The instruments were obtained, and were probably used on the field of battle at Guildford Court House.

Dr. Read here retrogades to relate a story in the operations of this campaign, highly to the credit of Gen. Morgan, which should not be lost. Dr. Read, after parting with Gen. Greene on the evening of their crossing the Yadkin, walked into camp, and on enquiring for Gen. Morgan, whom he was desirous of seeing, he found him in a tent laying on leaves, under a blanket. On enquiry, the General said he was very sick, rheumatic from head to feet. The Doctor gave him advice to leave camp, and retire to some place of safety, and warm quarters. The General said, "I do not know where that is to be found until I reach Virginia." Dr. Read left him and walked down to the river, where were a number of officers observing the arrival of the enemy on the rising grounds over the river, column after column, which he and they contemplated as long as the light served them. Presently he saw Morgan come down to the river. Several officers approached him on seeing anxiety in his manner, and enquired what was the matter. The General's reply was short and evasive. At length Dr. Read made up to him, to reproach him for not following his advice, which was to seek an opportunity of perspiration as remedy against his painful rheumatic affection. The General said: "to you, Dr. Read, I will be explicit, as it may give you some business. I have laid an ambuscade of 120 Virginia men for the British; we hope to do them some harm." Dr. Read's reply was: "good God, is it possible!" He did not think they had a hostile man over the river, and expressed his wonder how they could escape. The General observed that this was one of the stratagems of war that must be resorted to, and as to the hazard, brave men were always prepared for it. At this moment a firing was heard; the General appeared in ecstacy. "There are my rifles, there the British pistol;" now a barking and howling of dogs were heard, then all was still, and a solemn silence ensued. Dr. Read stood looking over the dark expanse, reflecting on the horrors of war, when he saw an object which appeared like a vision. It was the discharge of a gun; a man on horseback falling backwards, then all was obscurity. He spoke of it; it was treated like a thing of imagination, and Dr. Read, mistrusting his own vision, insisted no more on it. Gen. Morgan was gone, and soon after Dr. Read retired to his camp. The next morning the General and a number of officers were at the river, to know the fate of the ambuscade. Presently was seen a company of men marching in loose order up the banks of the river—wet, and apparently much fatigued. Numbers made enquiry, and conversed on the subject. Dr. Read related what he had seen the night before, and pointed to the spot, where there appeared to lay an object like a dead man; when a young man stepped up and said: "It is true, sir, I am the man. I was pursued by a dragoon when running across that field; he overtook me, and I wheeled about and shot him; I think he fell. At the moment he gave my rifle a heavy cut;" and, showing his rifle, the sabre cut was evident. The horse ran off, and the rifleman made good his retreat. Dr. Read now accosted the bystanders with a hope that they were no longer incredulous. Dr. Read spoke encouragingly to the young soldier, whose name was Campbell, and advised him to keep that rifle as a sacred deposit. After this battle, some anxiety was expressed to know its fate, when two young men, Steel and Gillespie, volunteered to go over the river and see. They mounted fine horses, and rode down a hill, which seemed vastly precipitous, and riding to the western end of the rocky island that gives the name of Island Ford to the crossing place, they crossed the river, and saw numbers of soldiers burying the dead in large pits. Some of Morgan's ambuscade were missing, but Dr. Read never heard of their fate. He marched next morning on his important command, and never returned to this part of the country, and he never met Morgan again to enquire the history of this expedition. An army is a little world, composed chiefly of men; the members of it form an acquaintance which is speedily to be estranged—they contract friendships which are soon to be ended by arbitrary severation, never to meet again. A surgeon parts with his amiable young friend, and sees him on the same day brought in a corpse—he parts with an old college acquaintance to join him in serving, while in the midst of battle he sees him brought off the field a dying man. In another instance a wounded officer is brought many miles, a valued intimate acquaintance, to have a wounded arm amputated. Alas! poor Col. Ford! He had seen Dr. Reed amputate at Monmouth, and insisted on being brought to him for that friendly office; when, behold, the postponement became fatally destructive—he spasmed and died, and severed two manly hearts long attached to each other. Col. Ford departed with extraordinary fortitude, being sensible of his approaching death. He had been bred to physic; all matters for his funeral were appointed by himself. The music was instructed to practice at his quarters, and the tune prescribed. Some romantic circumstances ensued in consequence of this death. Ford was under the impression that the departed could communicate with the living, and he promised to appear to Dr. Read on the night of his death. Dr. Read, considering the possibility of the thing, sat up alone, anxiously waiting the event, but no ghost appeared. He waited until twelve o'clock, when ghosts are said to retire; then, putting on his night-gown, he walked out to Gen. Polk's burial-ground, where the mortal remains of his friend were deposited, and invoking him, remained there an hour. This proceeding was useless, no ghost was seen, no voice heard. It was imprudent, as his (Dr. Read's) appearance, in a white gown, gave an alarm which was attended with serious consequences; not, however, worth relating here. Dr. Read continued to exercise his professional avocations in Charlotte, receiving the sick and wounded from all the outposts, and the operations of Colonels Marion, Sumter, Hampton and Maham, likewise of the gallant Harry Lee, of the Legion; aided and assisted by Drs. Gillet, senior and junior, and by Dr. Robert Brownfield, he did a great deal of good to the service. The several gentlemen, aides-de-camp of Gen. Greene's army, came to Dr. Read in bad health, in succession, from their arduous duties in the low country—Colonels Lewis, Morris, Shubrick, Pierce, Pendleton, Major Burnet, Col. Kosciusko, Carrington and Gunby—the latter to decide an affair of honor. Gunby lost his right thumb. Dr. Read received them all in comfort, being enabled to do so by the zealous assistance of his Commissary, Matthew McClure, from his popularity with the people of the country, and mainly by the services of a soldier, who, possessing the art of slight of hand, would go through the country and exercise his art, to the diversion of the people, and profit of the mess, in poultry, pigs, eggs, and small meats. Elliot had been dismissed the Maryland line for diminutiveness, which he thought very hard, as he had marched and fought alongside of many a tall fellow, through a severe campaign; he was, however, eminently useful to Dr. Read's mess, enabling him to keep a table like any general officer. He was enabled to receive in comfort many of the exchanged prisoners who wended their way south after their exchange on the coast of Virginia; among them was Henry Middleton, John Middleton, Henry Peronneau, John Badly, &c., &c., and Dr. Read's young brother, George P. Read. About this time Dr. Read was informed by some of Gen. Polk's scouts that a British officer lay near the Catawba, in a lone woman's house, badly wounded. Dr. Read, ever ready in any work of humanity, feeling excited, determined to see and relieve the wounded officer, required of Gen. Polk a guide and two mounted men, set out, and after riding hard for two hours, reached the house. There lay a fine-looking officer, leaning on an old woman's bosom, while a negro man stood preparing to dress his wounded side. He appeared alarmed at his arrival until Read informed him his errand; he thanked him kindly. The old lady remarked that he could not have said so much three or four days ago; she then proceeded to relate the circumstance. "That about two weeks ago an officer of dragoons of Greene's army came there with this wounded man behind his servant, and left him with her, saying, that he could not wait, requesting me to take care of him. He stopped, however, a few minutes, and loosened his valise, and took from it a bundle, saying: ' on leaving home my mother gave me this bundle, saying, if you should be wounded, or any friends of yours, open this bundle.' He loosened the bundle saying, ' I consider this suffering fellow creature entitled to my kindness, although an enemy.' It contained lint and bandages, and a box of pills; he shared the lint and bandages, and divided the pills, and gave directions; they were as remedy in case of spasm. The good creature, God bless him, then rode off." The wounded man now spoke, saying, " I was sensible of all that passed, although I could not speak. I had lost a fore tooth, which happily made an aperture, through which I took water through the spout of a tea-pot, and by the same opening I took the pills. In about twelve or sixteen hours I could open my mouth, which was completely locked; I had taken four pills. On examining the mass, Dr. Read thought they were of opium, camphor and musk. Dr. Read had carried with him a bottle of wine; he made the wounded man take a glass of it, and proceeded to examine and dress his wounds. A musket ball had struck a rib, and glanced out, ripping the skin and muscle four inches long; a sabre or hatchet cut over the ear was to the bone. He had not been conscious of the wound of the head. He had belonged, or commanded a flanking advance of their army, which pursued Greene after the retreat from Ninety-Six, and was shot down and abandoned by his men. The officer who took him up was one of Greene's rear, and finding him on the ground alive, placed him behind his mounted servant, and brought him to this house as related.

The good lady's remark was, " that he was a fine young man, and that she dare say that his mother was a religious woman, and that her son was well brought up." Dr. Read made him repeat the glass of wine, and saw him in good spirits. The good woman was struck with his change of manner. He was jocular, and said to Dr. Read, "you have a fine fellow in your service, Abraham Beauford." Dr. Read replied, "yes, I know him well, and we think him a fine fellow." "But," said he, "after the surprise at Waxsaws, he sent in a flag to enquire for and ransom a pair of mares, instead of enquiring after his wounded and prisoners." Here Dr. R. counteracted his opinion, and said, "that Beauford would not discredit the humanity of your army so far as to suppose the wounded would not be taken care of." He smiled and said, "there you pose me." Dr. Read then took leave of this gentleman, giving the old lady directions in case of pain or future spasms, and rode off. Not long after this hazardous transaction, for he rode through a hostile country, at least infested with hostile marauders, by some of which, a little while ago, some miles to the west of this region, he had been chased to within five miles of Charlotte, when he went out to remedy the wounds of Gen. Sumter. The fleetness of his horse, with the General's instructions, saved his life or freedom. At about this time he says he was called upon to exercise his zeal and activity in carrying dispatches to Gen. Greene; a rider came into Charlotte very sick, with despatches, on a tired horse. They were from Yorktown, Virginia, from Washington to Greene, and thought to relate the capture of Lord Cornwallis. Dr. Read was on marching orders. On Gen. Greene encamping about the high hills of Santee, he directed Dr. Read to follow him as speedily as he could with his department, and fix a flying hospital in the rear of his camp. Dr. Read volunteered to carry these dispatches. Transcending his orders as above, he left his department under the guidance of Dr. Elisha Gillet, and set out; he rode his own horse. There was not at this time a man or horse at the command of Gen. Polk; his son Charles had lately been furnished with every disposable man and horse to scour the country around, and to protect Charlotte against the Tories, who were in the field in force. Dr. Read rode eighty miles in ten hours, lay down at Camden four hours, and then proceeded on at the rate of nine miles an hour on the same horse to Gen. Greene, at Gabriel Guignard's house. A council was immediately held of his aides-de-camp, and of Major Edmund Hyrne, who was at head-quarters. It would appear extraordinary that Dr. Read would condescend to be an express rider, but it will be acknowledged that the occasion was extraordinary. He saw, with somewhat of a soldier's eye, that it was all important that Greene should know the fate of Cornwallis's army before the British army, under Lord Rawdon, should hear it. Greene immediately moved down

and fought the battle of Eutaw, before he had time to retreat to Charlestown, where he gave our red coat enemy a severe dressing, with the
loss, however, of many men and officers. Out of six Colonels who
commanded regiments, all were killed or wounded, except Wade Hampton, and he made a good retreat and rally. John Eager Howard was
shot down with a broken collar bone. Lieut. Dobson and Woolford
were killed near him in the heat of the battle. Howard and Henderson were carried to the house of Thomas Jones. Dr. Read was sent to
Col. Henderson especially, and he found him in a deplorable condition,
with a shattered *tebia*. His pain was excruciating, and there was every
indication about him of approaching tetanus, of which Dr. Read had
seen too many cases, to be easy about this distinguished officer. He
immediately undertook the case, enquired what was his attitude, declared his attitude as to the position of his wounded leg to be most
unfortunate. Two surgeons stood by; he changed the position, and in
a moment made a dilatation through the obtuse bullet wound—a thing
all surgeons should do as soon as possible; this had been omitted more
than two days. Dr. Read introduced his fingers, and extracted several
pieces of bone, some of which lay transversely, of course irritating the
wound every moment. The surgeons stood by, and one said to the
other, "this is the effects of a fresh hand to the pump." Dr. Read
observed that he could easily conceive their fatigue with the wounded
to be very great. Col. Henderson expressed immediate ease. Dr.
Read ordered bitter fomentations, administered laudanum, and left the
Colonel to get the rest he had not enjoyed since he received the wound.
A wounded officer spoke, and enquired "if Dr. Read would dress him?"
He said "yes, certainly;" and on enquiry who he was, he told him he
was Col. Howard, commanding a Maryland regiment. Dr. Read well
knew his celebrity. He went up to him and said: "Yes, Colonel, I
would assist Beelzebub in the character of a wounded man." In stooping
over the Colonel to loosen his bandages, he gave him the information,
as above, of Woolford and Dobson being killed near him. Dr. Read's
observation was, that as they were doomed to die, he was glad that they
died so gloriously. It must be told that those gentlemen had been
injurious informers to their Colonel against Dr. Read, as principal in
the hospital at Charlotte, of his *hauteur*, his partiality to the Southern soldier, and his lending a Maryland soldier to a French officer.
The first charges were untrue; the story of lending a soldier as a waiter
to a French officer, was as follows:—Major Mt. Florence having recovered from severe illness, expressed a wish to ride into the country for
change of air, and to carry with him a convalescent, whom it might

benefit. He selected a young recruit that had been wounded through the arm, and the wound not yet healed, he was unable to carry a musket. Dr. Read, concluding that the ride and a fortnight's time might heal the wound, granted the request. The consequence was as he expected, the officer and soldier marched in that time. Dr. Read was, therefore, justified, and would have been acquitted by his commanding officer. A court-martial was threatened, but never attempted. Some severe letters passed between Dr. Read and Col. Howard, on the occasion, from the testimony of those two officers. Many years after the war, Dr. Read received a civil message from Col. Howard saying, that they had quarrelled severely in the war, but that he was wrong, and Dr. Read right. Dr. Read was told that the surgeons he so decidedly censured as relating to Col. Howard's wounded leg, were offended, and by one of them, a professed combatant, he would be called out; but he heard no further indications of hostility. Read continued steadily to do his duty to the end of the war.

There are digressions and little concomitant incidents, which may have been left out of this grave narrative of facts; but, to return to the thread of the story. Dr. Read continued his march, industriously laboring to reach Virginia. His orders were to watch over the prisoners, and to deliver them to Major Hyrne, on meeting him. Several prisoners made their escape, aided by the country people, who were generally disaffected to the Republican cause. Among the prisoners taken in Georgia, Dr. Read distinguished a very tall, sickly youth, and felt peculiar interest in him. He would often converse with him, and give him extra diet from his mess. The lad was intelligent, and gave a sad account of Gen. Howe's campaign against Florida.

This prisoner was in the habit of marching along, and keeping pace with Dr. Read in the van, and the soldiers would jocularly call him the Doctor's aide-de-camp. This sly fellow never once indicated that he was a man of this country, and that he was approaching his home; but one day, coming to a fork of roads, he advised Dr. Read to take a right hand road; when he said no! that he was advised to avoid all right hand roads. The lad appeared confused; it was his father's plantation he was approaching. He stepped along, as he had done some times before, and reached the house, and there he, no doubt, made himself known, and settled a plan of operations. Dr. R.'s party arrived, and were most graciously received, by a lady and two daughters. They got a comfortable meal, and seemed very obliging. Dr. Read was instructed always to put under confinement every individual of any family he spent the night with, for fear of information to our enemy, and treacherous combinations against his party. These women were given to understand this, likewise they were informed that the house must be searched for incendiary papers. At this they were much shocked; however, search was made, and a pile of addresses to the people were found, well calculated to rouse the energies of the country people to "turn out in the cause of their country, and second the efforts of their friends to subdue the rebels, and serve their righteous King, the Lord's annointed," &c., &c. These the gentlemen of the party amused themselves with reading, and committing to the flames. The women said that a man had been there, and left the papers. These women were put into a chamber, and some women in a loom-house put under guard. The Doctor's party lay down in the hall. In the morning a march was ordered, and the department moved off; enquiry was made for the young man prisoner, but nobody had seen him. He was in the practice of walking off before the party, and Dr. Read, concluding that he had done so at this time, was easy at his absence; but, on proceeding further, and not seeing him, he became apprehensive, and, on reaching a ten mile rivulet, where they were to breakfast, and not finding the tall boy (as the soldiers called him), he became suspicious of his having made his escape; and some symptoms appearing, he concluded that he had been seduced away by the family which he had just left. Dr. Read now resolved to ride back in pursuit of him, called for two volunteers to join him, and take the runaway prisoner. McGuire, an Irish soldier, first offered his services, Carr, a Scotchman, next. Several American soldiers then came forward, and begged to be employed, but Dr. R. preferred the first offers. They were ordered to chose the best horses, arm themselves, and come on. Many gentlemen of North Carolina were in camp a short distance off, and, on hearing of the expedition, came to Read's camp and remonstrated against it, called it rash and useless, held up the prospect of meeting Col. Tarleton, or some of his detachments; spoke especially against the jeopardizing the two soldiers for vainglory. On Dr. Read's persisting in his intention, and being about to march, a Mr. Shelton offered to lend two fine horses to the soldiers. Dr. Read was mounted on his horse, the Irish grey. The soldiers armed to their liking, they both proved skilful horsemen. The party rode off, and in less than an hour reached the plantation of —— Davis. Mr. Shelton informed Dr. Read that it was a family of notorious Royalists, that the pamphlets he found in the house were such as they were in the habit of receiving and distributing for their cause; that their eldest son was a notorious malefactor, a felon and convict, that he had been proclaimed an outlaw by the Government; that he had fled to Florida, but may have returned with the advance of British arms; that he was of gigantic size. He cautioned Dr. Read against such a man. On approaching Davis' house, the party distinctly saw the tall boy running towards a swamp. McGuire spurred on at full speed, and Dr. R. and Carr leaped a set of bars and rode up to the house. Carr stopped a minute at the bars to see if there was any one approaching. On Dr. Read's riding up to the door, with pistol in hand, he was met by the sally out of a gigantic man, brown as a mulatto, with a long bushy beard, his features, in fact, obliterated by the excessive growth of hair, black and shaggy, with a rifle to his shoulder. Now commenced a scene too terrific for narration. Dr. Read's horse, with more than common instinct, appeared to see his danger, reared and neighed, and pawed towards the assailant. Dr. Read pointed the pistol; but, from the flowing main of his horse, and the unsteady seat he had from the upright position of his horse, he could not take aim and fire. His situation was terrible, but he was nothing dismayed. At the moment he perceived Carr at his right hand, on foot, with his musket at a charge. Dr. Read said, "Carr, do your duty." In a moment he plunged the bayonet into the body of the assailant. It was driven through him, entering to the right of the umbelicus, and formed a blue spot on the left side of the back-bone, on examination. The monster fell, with dreadful screams and lamentations; endeavored to scramble off, but fell, beat his legs and arms about for fifteen minutes, and expired. Thus he was made the executioner of the outlaw. The mother and two sisters now came out, and criminated him, saying, that "he had brought ruin on the family." Several women came out of a loom-house, and made a talk against the deceased, enumerating his crimes committed on both sexes, and children, and of house burning. McGuire having pursued the fugitive prisoner as far as his horse could go, in vain, returned. The women had rallied in a most extraordinary manner, and became abusive, and lamenting the death, and threatening. McGuire drew his sword, and laid on them with its flat side, and drove them into the house. Dr. Read followed, lest he should be provoked to give the edge. On entering an inner room, he saw a pair of feet under a cupboard, and found an old man in great trepidation; he dragged him forth and criminated him. In the meantime Carr had turned over the dead man, and showed the effects of his bayonet. On measuring him with his musket and bayonet, he seemed above six feet five inches, and prodigiously brawny withal. Carr cut off his beard, and carried it away with him. Dr. Read's party now retreated, carrying the old man with them, whom he told the women that he should detain as prisoner until

her young son should deliver himself.   On reaching camp the old man
was known to the party of gentlemen, and they claimed him as a victim
of crime, he being accused of acting the incendiary and spy ever since
the war.   Dr. Read, however, plead his being *his* prisoner, and inter-
ceded for his life, and after some hours carried the unfortunate parent
back a mile or two, and turned him loose; the runaway prisoner never
appeared.   Carr was entitled to a reward, which Dr. Read certified, and
hopes that he got.   McGuire, he thinks, fell in the bloody battle of
Guilford.   The hospital department now proceeded on slowly, from
insufficient teams and broken wagons; they halted at the plantation of
a Mr. Spencer, a good Republican, who was then in arms in the field.
Dr. Read, with his officers, and others who accompanied him, consisting
of the medical gentlemen, Baron Glanbeck, Capt. Saunders, a wounded
man, &c., which made a considerable cavalcade, some of which (soldier
attendants) were in scarlet coats, taken off of the dead at the Cowpens,
spent the night in the house of said Spencer.   Not doubting the patriotism and good feelings of this family towards him, Dr. Read omitted to
keep under durance the family.   The gentlemen of the department,
for pass time, used to call Dr. Read Lord Cornwallis, and Baron Glanbeck   , which Dr. Read rebuked with severity, reminding
the young gentlemen of the impropriety of any equivocation, situated
as we were; still, the joke was sometimes sported, and it was nearly
attended by a fatal scene.   Dr. Read was in the habit of leaving off his
officers in the rear to watch over and bring up stragglers.   The prisoners
(the Queen's rangers), shewed a strong inclination to desert and join
the country people.   On this occasion it was his good fortune to leave
Dr. Brownfield in that situation.   Dr. B. halted at one Frey's, five miles
short of Dr. Read's camping ground; and, hearing a rumor that Lord
Cornwallis and suite were in advance, a party of Republicans assembled
at Frey's, and were organized to go forth and attack the party.   Dr.
Brownfield, convinced that it was the hospital department, and not Lord
Cornwallis, prevailed on this armed party to desist from an attack, and
to accompany him to the camp at daylight, when they were convinced
of the real state of the matter.   When Dr. Read took possession of the
quarters, there sat an old man in the chimney corner, who seemed
superannuated; but behold, he had enough of Republican ardor in him
to rouse his energies.   He, on hearing the appellation, Lord Cornwallis
and Baron, supposing that it was really the British party, stole off,
mounted, and rode through the country and raised the above force,.and
nothing but the prudence and circumspection of Dr. Brownfield prevented a murderous scene.   The purpose of the party was to attack the

harmless men while they slept on the floor of the house, by firing through the logs, and then rushing in with tomahawk and hatchet. This anecdote is in Garden's compilation. The department now proceeded on. They came to a settlement of superior size and accommodation, gave notice to the owner that they should want about six hundred rations, and some assistance in tools, and stuff to repair wagons. Dr. Read was called to the road by thirty or forty gentlemen, on their retreat, who told him that he had halted at the house of a determined Royalist, and to beware of him. Dr. Read thought there was a supercilious air about this man, that was uncommon with people of his condition. It seems that he counted on their being intercepted by Col. Fletchall, who was in the field with a strong Tory party, in consequence of which he became bold and confident. He had, on the approach of the hospital department, driven off his flocks and herds; and when Dr. Read demanded of him 600 rations, he replied, "you do?" He soon found that he had a determined character to deal with. Three young men arrived at this man's house after mid-day, much splashed and fatigued, man and horse. When Dr. Read demanded of them where they had been, they equivocated; he dragged them out one by one, and severely questioned them. The master of the house was in the meantime made prisoner. At length, pointing to a rope, and the limb of a tree, he drew from these lads that they had been to drive off the cattle, sheep and hogs. The purpose was easily seen through, and soon promulgated, and now commenced a scene of depredation that beggars all description. The soldiers running down poultry, picking or singeing off the feathers, and laying them on the fire; hunger was the plea, and revenge the cause of action. The gentlemen complained, but Dr. Read remarked that hunger could not be restrained, and made the man remark that the most active of the marauders were the lads in green and crimson, the Queen's rangers. Not a feathered thing was alive that night. Mr. Frey contrived to get a beef by next morning, but it was too late to save his poultry, and he became a loser, as Dr. Read on marching next day gave him a certificate only for 600 lbs. of beef. The party marched on without molestation. The next day, on enquiry for distances, and means of support, and reception as to accommodations for the sick and wounded, he was told of one commodious place a little short of Henry Court House, the owner and inhabitant of which, Capt. Howard, a sworn Royalist, had vowed that he would shoot the first Rebel officer that came to his house. Dr. Read treated it with levity, and continued to march on. Some North Carolina gentlemen joined in the march, and spoke of this terrible old gentleman; that he had killed an antagonist at a blow, &c., &c.; but Read, intent only on the good of his department, which had been so solemnly committed to his care by his commanding officer, and being informed that Howard's place afforded the best barracks, and means of support, determined to brave the danger.   On the day following he was met by a respectable man, who told him that Howard continued in the same resolution, and entreated Dr. Read to march on and avoid Howard's house; but, with the convictions above named, of accommodations, &c., he determined to reform and conquer his opponent, and rode steadily on.   He looked well to his pistols; wearing a hussar cloak, they were concealed.   On entering the yard alone, he perceived a very big man standing in his door, which he filled up, a gun in his hand, with the butt floored.   Dr. Read, in a moment, calculated to shoot as soon as this terrible bravo should lift the gun from the floor.   On nearing his antagonist, and perceiving his enormous size, he smiled at the idea of a sure shot, when Howard reached his arm out to the right, uttering: "By God, I cannot shoot a man that smiles in my face"   He then asked him if he had intended to shoot him.   He affirmed his intention; and Dr. Read, showing him his pistol, told him the manner in which he should have treated him.   Howard then yielded the contest, invited the Doctor in, and they soon became reconciled.   Dr. Read's officers arriving, he, at Howard's request, sent them over the river to Henry Court House with the prisoners, as being more removed from the probability of an attack and rescue from the Tory Colonel.   Dr. Read was well accommodated, and his guard, and certain patients put into negro houses as barracks. Dr. Read soon discovered that Howard's house was frequented by a set of gamblers, among them two certain Colonels, who were Howard's ill advisers.   They would argue on politics, and reason on the iniquity of rebellion, and the ingratitude of the Provinces, &c., &c., all calculated to keep up resistance.   At length Howard, listening to Dr. Read, became convicted and convinced, and after some time authorized Dr. Read to clear his house of these sophists in politics.   He did so, and thereby did what Mrs. Howard and daughter desired above all things, got rid of a set of gamblers.   At length a scene commenced, and soon terminated appalling, indeed, and almost too much like romance for narration.   Dr. Read's guard of thirty men continued to do their duty throughout the march; they were frequently drilled, and behaved like soldiers.   A wagoner, with a team of very worn-out horses, joined the cavalcade at the Yadkin, and continued along, but was not recognised for rations and forage.   He alleged that he had been employed by Gen. Robert Howe, on the Florida expedition, and had worn out his team, demanded Dr. Read's certificate to that effect; but he, knowing nothing of it, refused a certificate; and, as the wagoner was addicted to liquor, and made much noise, he ordered him away; he did not go, but rather rudely demanded a paper, and remained in camp. He was not idle, but persuaded the men of the guard to desert, go over the mountain, and there be free; no magistrate, no law, but land enough, plenty of girls and provisions. These things appeared delightful to the soldiers. All but three fell into it, and had made up their mind to do so—to plunder the hospital store, to carry off Mrs. Howard and daughter, a lovely young woman, who had lately come home from school. They were to rob Howard's stables, with Dr. Read's fine horses, and to kill any one who made opposition to them. These things were known to three men, who continued true to their colors, and to Dr. Read's interest—Carr (his old friend), Brown and Jamieson (Englishmen), and they informed Dr. Read of it, but he could not believe it. At length, one night, a tap at his window roused him, and he was told that they had begun, and Miss Howard said they were breaking open the storehouse, and showed Dr. Read what ten or fifteen of them (armed) were actually at. He saw them handing canteens to each other filled with the plundered rum. Howard and wife, Dr. Read and Miss Howard, met in the front room, and sat in sadness. Several guns were now fired at a house where Carr lay, whose wife was in childbed, and just now an uproar was heard at the stable; blows were heard, and bitter oaths, and then they ceased. It seems that two men had engaged to bring off the horses, and in accomplishing it they had to unloose a chain and bolt, in attempting which the two men who continued true, and Dr. Read's faithful man, Billy, having armed themselves with clubs, would stoop out of the hay-loft door and strike their hands. The swearing was from their pain and discomfiture. Not succeeding in getting the horses, they halted a while, and placed the wagoner in an advanced situation, as a sentinel. Dr. Read proposed to go out and quell this riot. The Howards opposed it, and would dissuade the Doctor from going out; but he determined to do so, and taking up a club, which was of mulberry root, worked partly into a bow, he walked towards the barracks deliberately, and coming to this sentinel, he enquired calmly why this riot, and suddenly struck the tall, stout fellow on the side of the head, and he fell helpless. Dr. Read followed up the blow by three others, and laid him quiet. He then called out, "I thought it was no other than that drunken rascal the wagoner." He then called for a torch. One was speedily brought, and walking leisurely towards the barrack, he heard a clattering of cartouch boxes, and, on going into the

19

barrack, he saw all the men under blankets on their bed of ware. He
then repeated, " I am glad my lads that it was nobody but that rascal
the wagoner," and he retired; but things had gone too far to be winked
at, and passed over.   He sent a son of Howard's to Gen. Greene with
a letter, describing the state of things.   The distance was forty miles,
and the young man, on a very fine horse, probably made the ride in
three hours, for by nine next morning Dr. Read saw a squad of horse
coming over the hills.   He immediately went to the barracks, and
called out to the company to turn out for drill.   They turned out with
alacrity, all except two, who, it was alleged, had sore hands—the broken
hands received at the stable-door.   It was, however, admitted, and the
rest were drilled, ordered to stack their arms and march.   At this
moment the dragoons rode up, and made the twenty-seven mutineers
prisoners; they were securely tied.   The soldiers took some refresh-
ments, mounted, a prisoner behind each dragoon, and conveyed them
away.   The battle of Guilfold was to be fought the day following.   Gen.
Greene, in order to strengthen his ranks, had proclaimed that all men
under arrest, or any way implicated, should be forgiven if they joined
in battle, and did their duty; these twenty-seven mutineers probably
took advantage of the amnesty, fought, and were killed, or deserted.
Dr. Read never met with one of them again.   The two young men
with broken hands probably made off, as they could not possibly bear
arms.   Dr. Read was next ordered to Perkins' Station, on the Dan,
the army advancing.   He next repaired to Guilford Court-house; and,
after organizing the hospital, and leaving the sick with Dr. Brownfield,
&c., and the good offices of the excellent Quaker inhabitaats of that
place, he, with a party of staff and medical officers, marched across a
trackless country towards Charlotte—Gen. Greene having marched to
Camden.   This journey was attended by some interesting circumstances,
in one of which Dr. Read's presence of mind saved his party from a
surprise and probable massacre.   In his march to Virginia, a circumstance took place of a thrilling nature, which he has felt loth to narrate,
as it was brought upon him by his imprudence.   On his crossing Smith's
River, which divides North Carolina from Virginia on that route, and
fixing on a spot for encampment, he returned wading and swimming.
Dr. Read being mounted on his fine horse, and bearing fatigue better
than any other man, concluded to recross and inspect the rear rather
than send one of the other gentlemen of his department.   On crossing
he saw two of his party, invalids, standing behind the rocks, waiting
for his coming.   On chiding them for loitering there, they appealed to
his benevolence, telling him that they were two young men who had

been recruited in that country for the Florida war; that they had grown up in the service, and now were near their parents and native home, from which they had not heard for four years, and they petitioned for a furlough. Their case was a singular and moving incident, and it induced Dr. R. to deviate from his rule not to give leave of absence, and he gave his consent for two weeks, when they were to meet him at Henry Court House. These men, observing Dr. Read wet and cold, and knowing that he had been comfortless, and on horseback all day, advised him to go to a house down the river, which they named, where he and his servant, a soldier boy, might get some refreshment. They went, found it a manufacturing place, having a loom. He was referred to the dwelling-house for fire and something to eat. On Dr. Read approaching the house, a lady came out and offered to hand him some victuals, but forbid his dismounting, telling him that there were bad people about there; he, however, regardless of that advice, persisted in alighting, and going in, asking for something to eat, and proceeding to take off his boots and stockings to dry them. His boy did the same. The woman seemed horror struck at this proceeding, and begged Dr. Read not to stay; he, however, did stay, and dried his clothes, and ate in comfort. This good woman, in the meantime, seemed unhappy; went listening at a back door. At length Dr. Read, having accomplished his purpose, offered the landlady payment, which she refused, but hurried him off, telling him that there was a good passing place lower down the river, where he would see lights, as there was a recruiting party there. Dr. Read was just in the act of going to the door to depart, when two men rushed in from the back door, and with a wild shout exclaimed, "here is one of them!" This was what the good woman was apprehensive of. Dr. Read, under great trepidation, concealed his feeling, and replied that he was a non-combatant, a surgeon, and he thought not liable to hostility. The most prominent of these men said, "yes, but I know who you are, I have been two nights in your camp." Some women came from the room and said, "that wretch is a spy." This exclamation he treated with severity and threats. He now attempted to be cheerful and sportive with Dr. Read in a back country slang, and was very provoking. The other man was the man of the house, and seemed to be very drunk. The British officer (as he proved to be), now signified that he would introduce Dr. Read to Lord Cornwallis that night; he should, by G—d, be his peace offering. On perceiving the landlord very much in liquor, Dr. Read, conscious of his own skill and strength, determined to resist. He was peculiarly situated with some of the gentlemen of his family, differing for argu-

ment's sake on the merits of our cause, and its ultimate result, and this
sudden absence might be construed or distorted into an act of deserting
his colors, and he was determined to resist to the death. Dr. Read
had no arms, and there was none perceptible on his antagonist; he wore
a split-shirt, which covered a much better dress. The conflict now
commenced, The soldier boy, approaching the scene, was laid hold of
by the landlord, thrown on the floor, and tied severely. On seeing this,
Dr. Read was convinced of the inefficiency of this drunken man to assist
his companion, and he saw his situation more deplorable; added to this,
they uttered some enquiries about an expected third person. Dr. Read
was then embarked in a deadly conflict. The purpose of the officer
was to get possession of Dr. Read's hand, which he resisted, with heavy
blows in his face. The contest went on, blows, argument, imploring,
wrestling and grappling, and continued two hours. The unfortunate
gentleman frequently said, "I will not hurt or disfigure you, but introduce you to Lord Cornwallis a decent prisoner." In the meantime the
old man would rise as though he would interfere, when his wife would
push him back and speak to him, and she frequently warded off blows
levelled against Dr. Read. His antagonist would say, "is this possible?"
on being floored by Read. The dress of split-shirt was now torn off,
and a scarlet coat displayed. The landlady took a decided part for Dr.
Read, and called in the women weavers to assist her in extricating him
from captivity; but the officer said, "I will put my dirk into any woman
that enters the house." Horrible was the scene, and Dr. R. expected
nothing less than death, and would have welcomed the catastrophe;
but it pleased God to decree it otherwise. Dr. Read, by a decided,
calculated blow between the eyes of the man, felled him, jumped on
him, and was searching for a side arm, which in their latter struggles
he had felt on his thigh, when the old man raised up from the bed, and
struck Dr. Read a blow under the short ribs that laid him senseless.
On his coming to, by chafing with vinegar by the good woman, he found
himself bound by ligatures, and seated on a bench. The boy pointed
out the instrument by which he was struck the fatal blow. Dr. Read's
horses were led around to a back door, and all things ready to carry
him to the British camp, which he said triumphantly was not more
than fifty miles off. His face was so battered as to be disfigured already.
Dr. Read begged for water, which delayed the march a minute, when
footsteps were heard, and in an instant two men burst into the front
door; they had halted at the loom, and were told by the weavers the
state of things, when they ran and burst in as described above. Horror and dismay struck the officer; he ran towards an end door, and

endeavored to draw his side arm, but one of these men seized hold of him, threw him on the ground, and disarmed him; he scarcely resisted. The other soldier laid hold of the old man, and loosening the ligatures on Dr. Read's arms, tied the landlord. The old scoundrel was in tears, supplicating for mercy, and quite submissive. All this was observable to Dr. Read, but he could not speak. He fainted, and when recovered found himself on the bed; the good woman chafing his temples with vinegar, and speaking kindly to him. He saw the old man on the floor tied, the soldier boy fixed in a position with a musket for shooting him, in case of an attempt to escape. The two soldiers had hold of the gentleman, dragging him to the back door. Dr. R. saw with deep concern the intention, and would, if he could, have spared him; but he could not speak. He saw the poor victim struggle hard; having his shoulder to the door post, he made resistance, and roared out for mercy. In about half-an-hour's time the two men returned, one of them having a large bundle on his bayonet. They now hurried Dr. Read on his horse, and mounted the boy, and placing the landlord behind him, proceeded on to the lower ford. Dr. Read was still unable to speak, and scarcely able to sit on his horse. On crossing the ford, he was surrounded by a number of men, recruits, lifted off his horse and laid down. The two friendly soldiers returned, after telling who he was, and the whole story, and they mentioned the kind behavior of the woman. After two hours' repose, Dr. Read awoke refreshed, and, although much in pain, called for his horses, and with a guide proceeded on to his department, reached it about two o'clock, P. M., and lay down in a wagon.

The scene was divulged by the boy, although he was cautioned to the contrary, when Dr. Read met with much sympathy.

[Here end Dr. Read's notes from which the foregoing has been prepared.]

CPSIA information can be obtained
at www.ICGtesting.com
Printed in the USA
LVOW07s0422050917
547553LV00021B/1161/P